Edmond de Pressensé, Louise Corkran

The religions before Christ: being an introduction to the history of the first three centuries of the church

Edmond de Pressensé, Louise Corkran

The religions before Christ: being an introduction to the history of the first three centuries of the church

ISBN/EAN: 9783337263249

Printed in Europe, USA, Canada, Australia, Japan

Cover: Foto ©Lupo / pixelio.de

More available books at **www.hansebooks.com**

THE

RELIGIONS BEFORE CHRIST:

BEING AN INTRODUCTION TO THE HISTORY

OF THE

FIRST THREE CENTURIES OF THE CHURCH.

BY

EDMOND DE PRESSENSE,

PASTOR OF THE FRENCH EVANGELICAL CHURCH, AND DOCTOR OF DIVINITY
OF THE UNIVERSITY OF BRESLAU.

TRANSLATED BY

L. CORKRAN.

WITH PREFACE BY THE AUTHOR.

EDINBURGH:
T. AND T. CLARK, 38, GEORGE STREET.
LONDON: HAMILTON, ADAMS, AND CO. DUBLIN: JOHN ROBERTSON.

MDCCCLXII.

PREFACE

TO THE

ENGLISH TRANSLATION OF THE INTRODUCTION.

The book I here present to the English public, through the medium of a careful translation made by a friend, forms part of an extensive work upon *The History of the First Three Centuries of the Church*, four volumes of which have already appeared.

Before entering upon the details of the struggle between the new religion and the religions of the past, I felt myself bound to draw up a fair statement, a balance-sheet, of their respective forces, and to show what were the resources, and what the obstacles, Christianity encountered in that old world which it was about to destroy and to replace. Although this Introduction forms a distinct part in itself, it is nevertheless closely connected with the main body of the work. My readers must also bear in mind that I do not pretend to give in this Introduction the religious history of humanity before Jesus Christ, but simply a sketch of it.

The presiding idea of this portion of my work, is that which animated Saint Paul in his discourse at Athens, when he found, even in that focus of Paganism, religious aspirations tending to Jesus Christ. I have endeavoured to show that the whole of the ancient world, notwithstanding its depravity and shortcomings, concluded by desiring and seeking "The Unknown God," by demanding Him from all forms of worship, from all schools of philosophy. The work of preparation in the pagan world consisted in the development of this immense, this painful desire,—too often, alas! sullied and alloyed; but it was a flame kindled by God Himself, and could not be extinguished. It is thus evident that I do not limit the work of preparation to Judaism, though it was only in this privileged land of Judea that this work was directly pursued. To the Hebrew people alone, were confided the sacred oracles; they alone had prophets; but nowhere was the human soul abandoned by its Author: He who was its source, never under any sky, ceased His action upon it. This fact I have endeavoured to prove by the history of the different religions.

I have raised no altar to human pride; for I believe no fact comes out more clearly from the study of the different civilisations, than man's utter powerlessness to save himself. While, on the other hand, I know nothing more calculated to rejoice the Christian's heart, than the firm persuasion that God has from the beginning included the whole race of Adam in His beneficent designs, and that, as Saint Paul says, 'He hath determined the times before appointed, and the bounds of their habitation.'

These ideas were dear to the Church of the first centuries, and were formalized in the boldest manner by Justin Martyr and Clement of Alexandria. It would be well if they could in our day be recovered from oblivion. Now, when modern science is resuscitating the religions of ancient Asia from the grave in which they seemed to be for ever sealed up, and throwing a new light upon the more virile religions of the West, it is of the last importance that it should be proved, by an exact, scrupulous study of facts, that Jesus Christ, the Christ of the Scriptures, the Eternal Son of God, the Redeemer, was truly, as the prophets expressed, 'The Desired of nations.' In proving this, we prove that He is essentially the desired of every soul of man, that there is a profound affinity between conscience and Him, and that Tertullian was not mistaken when he wrote the *Testimonium animæ Naturaliter Christianæ*.

It is in this direction, already opened up by so many noble minds belonging to our cotemporary Church, that I desire to see the defence of Christianity engaged, at a moment when faith in supernaturalism is so profoundly shaken throughout the world. We do not weaken in the smallest degree the supernatural element by seeking what are its points of contact with conscience, and by proving that man, who could not rise to revelation, was nevertheless made for it, and tended towards it, with all that subsisted in him, notwithstanding the degradation of his fall, of that original nature, which Saint Paul did not hesitate to proclaim divine.

'Whoever will do the will of God,' says the Master, 'will know that My doctrine is of God.' The moral road is then the royal road that leads to Christ: this is my profound conviction, and it breathes through every page of my Essay. If my work contribute in the smallest degree to the defence of the eternal Gospel, at a crisis of time whose gravity it would be madness to dissemble, and in this noble Protestant England, towards which the evangelical Christians of the whole world look as to the bulwark of the Reformation, it must be to me a profound source of happiness.

EDMOND DE PRESSENSÉ.

PARIS, *November* 1861.

THE ANCIENT WORLD AND CHRISTIANITY.

INTRODUCTION.

It is impossible to retrace the triumph of Christianity in the first ages of our history, without referring to that ancient world which it came to destroy. If it found that old world armed at all points for the combat, and ready to turn against it the vast resources of a refined civilisation, without neglecting the employment of material force—this last resort of waning faiths, it was not wanting in points of contact with the society of the time. The new religion did not break upon the earth as a sudden, abrupt event, unconnected with the past. It was, to a certain degree, the outcome of the whole religious history of humanity. Christianity was the answer of Heaven to the aspirations of earth. It brought to the wearied world the solution that the Zoroasters and Platos had sought after and caught glimpses of. It was at once divine and human—profoundly human, precisely because it was divine: that is to say, adapted by God Himself to man's real necessities. It will not, therefore, suffice to contemplate the heaven from which it came. We must also consider the earth on which it took footing. Without in the smallest degree sacrificing its divine origin, we may acknowledge the harmony existing between it and human nature. It was made for human nature, as human nature was made for it : so much so, that while rejecting it, and often cursing it, human nature proves, even by its agitation, that it cannot dispense with it. The history of the religions of human origin is the most striking proof of the agreement of revealed religion with the soul of man ; for, on the one side, each of these forms of worship is the expression of the wants of conscience, its eternal thirst after pardon and restoration—rather, let us say, its thirst after God. On the other hand, their succession proves their insufficiency, and the necessity of a higher religious form, which would supersede them, and in which humanity might find rest. To isolate it, then, completely from the past, would be to voluntarily refuse to comprehend the nature of Christianity, and the extent of its triumph. Although the Gospel is not, as has been affirmed, the produce of anterior civilisations—a mere compound of the Greek and Oriental elements,[1] it is not the less certain that it brings to the human mind the satisfaction vainly sought by it in the East as in the West. *Omnia subito* is not its device, but rather that of the gnostic heresy. Better to say, with Clement of Alexandria and Origen, that the night of Paganism had its stars to light it, and that they called to the morning star which stood over Bethlehem. These are the manifestations of the human conscience, which has always borne its testimony, and never been without its witness, even in times of thickest darkness. Far from despising them, let us piously gather them up. The worst sort of tactics would be to reject this noble ally given by God to the religion of Christ.

The study of the history of the ancient world is likewise important from another point of view. Christianity found in it not only vigorous foes or latent

---

[1] This thesis was ably advocated by M. Vacherot, in his work on the Alexandrian School.

sympathy, but, according to a strange law, by which the vanquished almost always end in exercising over the victors an influence, the greater because least suspected, we shall see the ancient world, at the moment that all things announced its defeat, morally regain the ground it had externally lost. Heresy was nothing but a hypocritical reaction of Paganism against Christianity. With what care the fathers of the second and third centuries strove to unmask it, that it might appear plain to all eyes that, under a Christian disguise, false doctors were endeavouring to bring into the Church a perfidious enemy, as one might introduce a traitor into a besieged town! 'Like those who repair old clothes,' says Saint Hippolyte, with familiar energy, 'the heretics are giving an air of novelty to what is most worn out in Paganism.'[1] The reaction of the ancient world did not stop there. It not only raised up different heresies, which were in turn crushed, but it in many respects succeeded in infiltering its spirit into the Church—altering its dogma, falsifying its morals, if not in an absolute manner, yet sufficient to remove it far from its primitive type. If, then, it is important, in order to understand the central place of Christianity in history, to know the circumstances that prepared its advent, it is not less so to know what was destined, at a later period, to modify it. Thus the task of this Introduction is twofold. We have to show, in the development of the religions of antiquity, the successive phases of preparation for Christianity; then to seek, under the different symbols which enveloped without ever concealing it, the first principle of Paganism, the old dualism, that eternal temptation of the human mind even in the Church. In fine, we shall have to characterize Judaism, the appointed precursor of Christianity, but which failed in its divine mission from the moment

[1] Οἱ αἱρεσιάρχαι δίκην παλαιορραφῶν.—*Philosoph.* 94.

it endeavoured to survive it, or to perpetuate itself under its shadow. It will then be easy for us to determine the real nature of definite religion. We shall know both the support and the obstacles it encountered in the old world, which it replaced, and which was not unfrequently restored by its unfaithful interpreters.

The most singular theories have been conceived of the religious development of humanity up to the time of Christianity. Some—the worthy successors of Evhemere—have seen in the religions of antiquity a symbolical reproduction of the great facts of history, or the phenomena of nature. Dupuis, the most celebrated and most learned of these writers on myths, saw a sort of elementary astronomy in the different religions; and Christianity itself was, in his eyes, but a more perfect theory of the movement of the stars.[1]

Others, availing themselves of the labours of modern criticism, and freed from the narrow prejudices of the eighteenth century, while at the same time possessing the æsthetic sense in the highest degree, declare that it is degrading these religions to make them simply the symbols of nature and history. To these writers they are the spontaneous creations of conscience, thus powerfully manifesting its want of an ideal. But, as they fail in showing clearly in what this ideal consists, as the divine and moral idea are lost in vagueness, we obtain no guiding thread to direct us through the rich confusion of ancient mythologies, and find it impossible to comprehend their origin. They are but the curious play—often an attractive one—of the imagination of man at its first awakening, the expression of his first enchantment in presence of the delicious spectacle of a world still young.[2] It is evident that this theory marks

---

[1] Dupuis, De l'Origine de tous les Cultes.
[2] Renan, Études d'Histoire Religieuse, Paris, 1857. Voir, l'Etude sur les Religions de l'Antiquité.

no notable progress in the philosophic appreciation of the various systems of religion. They succeed each other without any binding link between them; without possessing any internal reason for their development. Mythologies sprung up and disappeared like brilliant flowers, made for a season to shed their beauty and their perfume. Herder, in his famous work, translated by M. Quinet, endeavours to account for the difference in the various religions, by the difference in the circumstances in which they were produced. 'The history of all humanity,' he says, 'is but the natural history of a system of forces, of doctrines, of human dispositions in relation with time and place.'[1] Such a theory cannot satisfy us. It exaggerates the dependence of mind on matter, by chaining the conscience to the condition of time and space. Benjamin Constant—in this the pupil of Rousseau—entertains a higher idea of those religions. They give, according to him, a popular form to the eternal revelation of conscience. The symbols may vary, they may even at times be unworthy of the substance they should express; but this substance is ever identical. In reality, he says, there is but one single religion, the natural and universal, whose manifestations are modified according to outward circumstances, but whose essence is always the same. This theory is developed with equal art and eloquence by the illustrious writer.[2] But neither does this satisfy us; for it fails to explain the succession of creeds fundamentally different; and under pretext of distinguishing the essential from the accidental—the moral idea from the myths and forms that envelope it, suppresses the history, the original development of religion. The evolution of the human

[1] Herder, Ideés sur la Philosophie de l'Histoire de l'Humanité. Traduit par E. Quinet. 1824.
[2] Benjamin Constant, De la Religion considérée à sa Source, ses Formes, et son Developpement.

conscience is overlooked. The same omission we find in the vast Mythological Encyclopædia of Creuzer, which has been completed in so erudite a manner by M. Guigniaut,[1] and which has become a precious and indispensable resource for those who devote themselves to the study of the ancient systems of religion. 'The symbols that are at the basis of the different forms of religion,' we read in the Introduction, 'are the vague expression of the sentiment, that nature is essentially an animated being, and that natural phenomena are the signs by means of which nature speaks to man. Priests reduced and fixed this language in symbols.'[2] We do not think that in this direction we shall succeed in establishing a real gradation in the different religious systems. There is only the difference of symbols—the things signified are identical. This cannot supply us with a history of the mythologies.

Pantheistic philosophy pretends to furnish us with this history; but no fixed point is given us in this vortex of incessant change that whirls before our eyes. The Absolute, according to this system, one and identical with the world, is carried away by the torrent of active contingent life, which is its own life. The history of religion is not simply the history of man's conceptions of God: as, outside these conceptions, God would not exist, it is in reality the history of the determination of God. God, in appearing to the human conscience, appears to himself; that is to say, he has for the first time a consciousness of himself. The vigorous dialectic of a philosopher of genius cannot, however, prevail against the sovereign prescription of the moral conscience.[3] Religion disappears with the personal

[1] Religions de l'Antiquité considerées principalement dans leurs Formes Symboliques. Traduit de l'Allemand par J. B. Guigniaut. 1835, 1851.
[2] Tome i. 14.
[3] Religions Philosophic (W. W. xi. et xii.), 1832; 2d Edition, 1840. See the excellent analysis given of it by M. Erdmann, Geschichte der neueren

God. From the pantheist's point of view there can be no history of religion; and we might conclude, with Fuerbach, that the best of all is but a dream, the illusion of a man adoring himself while he believes he is prostrating himself before his Creator.

The advocates of Christianity place themselves at very different points of view in their appreciations of Paganism. We have already alluded to the large and profound ideas of the Alexandrian fathers on this subject. We shall have too frequently to recur to them in the course of this history, to enter now into details. They agreed with Justin Martyr, in admitting that a ray from the Divine Word shone in the human soul, and that it turned towards the light of God as a plant turns towards the sun.[1] These fathers carefully collected every portion of truth contained in the old religions and philosophies; and, while admitting a certain amount of Judaic influence upon Greece, they likewise believed that the human soul had a presentiment of the precious blessing that it was unable to procure for itself.

Theodoret, in his curious apologetic work, at a later period exposes the same point of view with equal grace and precision.[2] 'Obey,' he says, in addressing the Greeks,—'obey your own philosophers; let them be your initiators; for they announced beforehand our doctrines.'[3] It is true that Theodoret adds, that 'those philosophers are like birds, that hear human language without understanding its meaning.'

Philosophie, 3d vol., 2d part, p. 822. We find traces of these theories in M. Quinet's work upon *Le Génie des Religions*, of which a new edition has just been brought out. The recent publications of this learned writer incline us to believe that, were he now to write this book for the first time, the influence of German pantheism would not predominate to the same degree.

[1] Clement, Λογος προτεπτικος, ch. vi.
[2] Theodoret. Episcop. Cyri. Græcorum affectionum Curatio, tome iv. des Œuvres. Edit. Paris, MDCXVIII.
[3] Πείθητε τοίνυν τοῖς ὑμετέροις φιλοσόφοις προτελοῦσιν ὑμᾶς καὶ τὰ ἡμέτερα προδιδάσκουσιν.—P. 483.

Nevertheless, it is not that they are destitute of all divine light. In the depths of human nature, there are characters inscribed by the hand of God.[1] The Divine Creator did not suffer these to be totally effaced, but renewed them in some degree amongst the best of the pagans. If the race of Abraham received the divine law and the gift of prophecy, the God of the universe led other nations to piety by natural revelation and the spectacle of nature.[2] If the rain from heaven waters by preference cultivated fields, still God, in His abundant liberality, lets it fall also on solitary places and barren hills. And so it is with the gift of truth, bestowed first upon the chosen people, yet is scattered in a certain measure amongst all people, as the rain waters the desert places.

Most of the fathers of the Church professed, on the subject of Paganism, views very different from those of the schools of Alexandria and Antioch. They contented themselves with attributing to the demon the invention of these myths, which were the legitimate objects of their aversion, as well as the pretended miracles of the pagan divinities; or they adopted the explanations of Evhemere. Modern apologists are divided into two camps. The one side, in order to enhance the revelation given to the Jews, have so darkened the picture of ancient Paganism, that not one luminous point is visible: outside of Judea they allow no spark of divine life. The other, the traditional school, brilliantly represented under the Restoration by Bonald and Lamennais, believed that they discovered the primitive religion of humanity under the impure myths of Greece and of the East. This religion, communicated by revelation to man at his creation, was substantially preserved by all

---

[1] Ὁ τῆς δυσεβείας πλάνος τὰ θεοχάρακτα πάλαι διέφθειρε γράμματα.—P. 483.

[2] Ὡς τί ἰσήμους ὁ ὑετός.—P. 484.

people, and to tradition alone is to be attributed all the truth that has ever been in the world.[1]

Error is closely mixed up with truth in these two schools. It is an undoubted fact, that the Jews had the inestimable advantage over all other people, of being guided in their march towards the great future promised to humanity by a divine revelation. But it is not true that all other nations were abandoned to themselves. We find in their history, and especially in their religious history, the clear traces of this preparatory work accomplished by God. On the other hand, although it cannot be contested that, at the Dispersion, men carried with them a common fund of recollection, yet is it an outrage on human nature to reduce to the mere operation of memory all progress towards truth. Conscience is not a parchment, passively receiving what is inscribed upon it, but a living organ; and we entirely subscribe to Schelling's grand idea, that the formation of the successive religions reveal to us the great crises of the human conscience. If we cannot admit, with him, that the history of the mythologies is a sort of repetition of the history of creation in the mind of man, who by the fall became subject to nature, and only able by degrees to rise from the lowest to the highest scale, where he may again find the life of the spirit; if it appears to us that he justifies this daring theory by still more daring explanations of the different myths; yet his general view seems to us full of beauty. Yes, the different religions, which bear the impress of the fall, also mark the progress of the work of restoration; they are landmarks on the road humanity has followed in its return to God, who awaits it—rather, let us say, to the God who comes to meet it.

[1] A Protestant writer of learning and elevation, M. de Rougemont, has developed analogous theories in his work, entitled, ' Le Peuple Primitif,' 3d vol. Paris, Cherbuliez, 1855-57.

We do not mean to enter into all the ramifications of the great problem of the fall. To us, it is an established fact, broadly written in the world and in history. Finding it impossible, without doing violence to our conscience, to assimilate evil to a natural imperfection, which would be but a step in the scale of progress, we attribute its origin, not to the necessary conditions of a finite being, but to the evil determinations of man's will. He took part against God, at that mysterious epoch which precedes history, and which comprehends the solemn trial through which he, like every moral creature called to the serious exercise of liberty, must pass. If his fall was great, it was not absolute; not that man was not ruined by it, but he was not left destitute of all higher life. He retained some vestige of his primal nature. A sense of the divine, a religious aptitude, the longing to return to God,—these subsist in his heart. It is these that render his redemption possible; for the moral law, which had been vindicated by the terrible consequences of the fall, is maintained in all its integrity in the restoration of the fallen creature. A certain harmony was necessary between man and the God who desired to save him. Had his nature been thoroughly perverted, no contact could have been possible; he would not have had the capacity to receive the gift destined for him, which was nothing less than the gift of God Himself!—the only mode of repairing the fall of a being created in His image, and formed to possess Him. Thus, as soon as salvation was determined by the sovereign liberty of Him who is Sovereign Love, man was subjected to a gradual education in order to prepare him for the reception of this inestimable gift,—the first step of which was, that he should be led to desire it. The whole work of salvation consisted, then, in developing the *desire* of salvation, which is no other than the desire of again finding God.

But man's heart cannot be moulded as clay; liberty implies the possibility on his part to retard the divine plan. Accordingly, this preparation proceeds, not in an inflexibly straight line, but in an incessantly broken one; terrible falls mar it, and there are delays which involve centuries. Nevertheless the work goes on; for it is the work of Infinite Love, whose patience is unwearying because it is eternal. The whole history of humanity gravitates round this great thought of salvation, which is its pole, often hid, but ever present.

Humanity before Jesus Christ may be divided into two categories: one, a privileged minority, placed under the immediate direction of God. This was the Jewish theocracy. Later on, we shall show how this privilege was in reality in the interest of the whole race. The mass of mankind was only apparently abandoned by God. We should be on our guard against supposing that the historical revelation was God's sole mode of acting on the human soul: He exercises upon it a direct and invisible action, which is universal, and which pagan nations were partakers of. The Divine Spirit moved over these sullied waters, whence at a later period was to spring a new world, and in which it never ceased planting the seeds of a higher life. Preparation for salvation amongst these nations did not consist, as it did with Israel, in a succession of positive revelations; they were subjected to another education,—to that of experience under the superintendence and direction of God, albeit often compromised by the aberrations of liberty. By this means these nations likewise were led to the great aspiration, which was the one possible and useful result of the work of preparation.

In order that the desire of salvation should attain its full intensity, two things were necessary: first, that the object of this desire should be determined with an ever increasing definiteness; and, in the second place, that the impossibility of man's ever attaining it by his own unaided endeavours should be irresistibly evident. These two conditions were realized in the history of the pagan religions. The desire of redemption manifested itself at first in a confused, but powerful manner. Hardly is a people constituted, than we find among them a religion—a form of worship, altars, sacrifices; thus expressing man's inherent want, to restore the once subsisting union between himself and the Divinity. Pagan religions, gross though they may have been, were nevertheless religions, and as such were the endeavours of man to re-attach himself to a superior power, on whom he was dependent. He was unable to find satisfaction in yielding himself to the enjoyments of material life. Nor could he do so with security until he had deified it. This deification is no doubt abominable; but it proves how invincibly rooted in man is this want of a God, since, rather than make an abstraction of it, he transfers to matter the attributes of divinity. But he cannot rest there: his religious craving being unquenched, and growing keener after each deception, he goes through the series of the religions of nature without ever having reached the world of spirit. He at last rises one degree, and invents a religion whose divinities are in his own likeness. This deification of humanity leads him to the limits of a higher world. What he now adores, although not God, approximates him closer to Him than did nature. The moral idea takes possession of him; he has a glimpse of the true Divinity, and a presentiment of a holier union with Him. In tracing the evolution of the ancient creeds, we are tracing that side of the work of preparation which consisted in rendering more precise and definite the desire of salvation, in disengaging it from a voluptuous pantheism, and in penetrating it with the moral element. But this moral element is destructive of all that preceded it. As soon as it finds entrance into man's conscience, it renders Paganism impossible. Paganism, therefore, sinks under what appeared to form its triumph. Once having attained its highest form, it could exist no longer. The religious edifice of the ancient world was rent at the summit; however brilliant and dexterous were the attempts at reconstruction, its ruin was irremediable. Ancient Paganism took many centuries to die out completely. All its gods were for a moment collected in the Roman Pantheon, only that they might perish together amid the maledictions and mockery of humanity, tired and disgusted with its idols, while sending up to heaven, from amid its impure wrecks, a confused but passionate prayer of sorrow towards the unknown God. To paint the decline of Paganism, after having described its progress, is to represent the second side of the work of preparation,—that which was destined to bring home to man his religious impotency. This picture of the ancient world must necessarily be abridged, being confined to the limits of an introduction. We shall not forget that not alone in their religious creeds is this to be sought, but in the whole course and progress of their philosophic labours, in their works of art, and in the national life of the different people.

PREPARATION FOR CHRISTIANITY IN PAGANISM.

I. ORIENTAL PAGANISM.

IN breaking loose from the law of the moral world, man falls under the dominion of the lower world; his equilibrium is lost; that which should govern being enslaved, that which should be in subjection obtains dominion. The sensual life stifles the spiritual. The soul, separated from God, has lost its power over the body, and learns by its own degradation that its force lay in submission. This fatal disorder is not limited to the individual, but is realized on a large scale in all humanity, whose conscience is perverted, whose religious sense is falsified. Thus, when removed by successive migrations from his original birth-place, man retained but a confused recollection of his origin, while the creeds he invented bore the impress of gross materialism. Although feeling the deep instinct of his dependence upon a higher and mysterious power from which he could not escape, yet he failed to seek this power above Nature, stopping at its first manifestations therein; and before Nature he prostrated himself. After man's fall, Nature was the first object of his worship. The various forms of the worship of Nature exactly correspond with the perversion of his moral being, and distinctly mark the triumph of the senses over the soul. Sad signs of man's degradation! We might look upon them as the sure vengeance of an offended God, could God know any other vengeance than that of love which overcomes evil by good.

All those forms of worship rest upon the same basis. The moral world was to them a sealed book. Man is not brought face to face with the laws of conscience, but placed in contact with the forces of Nature, where a twofold power manifests itself,—at one moment overflowing with profuse life, the next, furiously destroying every germ. Here, a prodigal, laughing mother pouring out her treasures into the lap of all, making the radiant sun to shine, sending the flowers of spring, and the fruits of summer and autumn, communicating her fertility to all that moves on earth, and being herself the source of all felicity and enjoyment. Then again she appears as a malevolent, cruel power, blasting everything,—the power of death and destruction, seen in the blackness of night and the killing frost of winter.

The religions of Nature are thus hedged within the circle of an inflexible dualism. These contrary forces are necessary forces, eternally opposed, but never destined to yield one to the other. What remained, was to bow down and to adore them equally. Man was not yet prepared to honour the Divinity by the practice of justice. The best homage to the gods he had chosen for himself, was evidently to resemble them: thus we find him giving himself up without restraint to sensual enjoyments in order to glorify the beneficent power of Nature, or subjecting himself to voluntary sufferings and sanguinary rites in order to glorify or appease the malevolent power. The worship of the religions of Nature must always be a worship at once voluptuous and barbarous, in which infamous pleasures blend with infamous cruelty. The nearer we approach the origin of these religions, the more palpable becomes this double characteristic; we shall find them, later on, approximating the moral world, almost reaching it through a transparent symbolism; we shall see them elsewhere giving infinite proportions to this dualism, in assigning the whole of the visible world to the power of evil. Arrived at this point, the religions of Nature had run through their cycle, and nothing remained for them but to disappear before other creations of conscience; they had given the death-blow to their own principle, by laying down as their ultimate conclusion the destruction and annihilation of Nature. It is this cycle we now propose to rapidly survey, ever keeping in view the groundwork common to all these forms of worship, whilst carefully indicating their special peculiarities. These peculiarities did not solely depend on the evolution of the religious sentiment, but on external circumstances as well. If it is false and offensive to man to maintain that his creeds are invariably determined by his external surroundings,—that they are the result of the climate and soil he inhabits,—that, in short, his religious ideas are but a sort of symbolical geography; it is not the less true that the conditions in which Providence has placed him exercise a powerful influence upon him, once he has made himself the slave of Nature. It is not in an abstract manner that he contemplates the forces of Nature. These forces assume in each country a certain aspect; and it is this aspect he reproduces in his creeds, which in the last residuum are but the reflection of the grand scenes of which he is the daily spectator. But if it be so, it is that he willed it. Man himself forged the yoke he bears. If he is the slave of external circumstances, of the accidents and phenomena of Nature, it is because he refused that free obedience to God which would have secured to the world the dominion of mind and liberty. We are not therefore to be surprised if we find in each form of worship the peculiar features of the country which gave it birth.[1]

---

[1] We desire here to make two preliminary remarks. The first is, that we consider those religions alone which underwent a certain elaboration, leav-

THE RELIGIONS OF WESTERN ASIA.

Under the burning sky of Asia, in the midst of a splendid nature, where the powers of production manifest themselves by immense fertility, but where also the powers of destruction strike their incessant and fearful blows,—in this country of the sun and of the hurricane, where flourish the vine and the fig-tree, the cedar and sycamore, but which at the same time is devastated by appalling scourges from the simoom of the desert to plague and leprosy,—on this half-privileged, half-vexed land, from Babylon to Arabia and Syria, as in Palestine and Phrygia, the same religion prevailed, varying in some degree its symbolism in the different nations, but all carrying dualism to its extreme consequences. Here, however, there was no line of demarcation separating the two powers of Nature, and the same force is by turns benign and cruel. It is the same sun that leads on the spring, which burns in summer, which alternately revives and destroys vegetation, and which even strikes down man himself. Thus in those primitive religions the same divinities are at once beneficent and malevolent. The fundamental idea of the Asiatic form of worship is the adoration of the sun and moon, considered as the personification of the general forces of Nature. By an easily understood anthropomorphism, the astral divinities are classified into two series—the male and female divini-

ing aside that grosser fetichism which is the lowest stage of idolatry, and which corresponds with the purely savage state. Our second remark is, that we only speak of those nations which were brought directly or indirectly in contact with primitive Christianity, and who co-operated towards the formation of the religious and social conditions in the midst of which Christianity was produced. It is easy to mark the place of the different nationalities, which we pass over in silence, in the scale of ancient Paganism, such as we have traced it. As to Western Paganism, in Gaul and Germany, we shall have to speak of it in our account of the Christian missions of the first centuries.

ties. In all these religions, death and voluptuousness play an important part, and abominable symbols figure conspicuously in their rites. Having pointed out what they had in common, let us next endeavour to determine their points of difference.

At the two extremities of the zone wherein these primitive religions prevailed, we find forms of worship less sensual than in the intermediate space. In the vast plains spreading out at the foot of the Caucasus lived a warlike and half-savage race, whose cruel instincts were developed by their rude and nomadic existence. The young Scythian was bound to drink the blood of the first enemy whose life he had taken; and he who had not drunk of this horrible draught was condemned to sit apart in the great festivals presided over by the chiefs of the tribe. The principal divinities of this people were the god of heaven, or Papaios, and the divinity of earth, or Tabiti. According to the Oriental practice, they adored separately, under different names, the various attributes of their great divinities. Thus they had a goddess of love and a god of war, which personified in a definite form the two great forces of Nature. Their temperament and mode of life led them to cede the first place to the war-god, to whom they built no temples, but whom they worshipped under the image of a sword, and to whom they immolated by thousands the prisoners taken in war.

At the other extremity of the zone we find the nomadic tribes of Arabia. Intrepid, warlike, and inhabiting a more favoured country,—one producing myrrh and precious stones, and brought by commerce into contact with the people of Asia,—we do not find in them the cruel instincts of the Scythian, nor the unbridled sensuality of the Babylonians or Phrygians. They also adored a twofold divinity: a male divinity, the god of heaven, beneficent as light and terrible as the hurricane; and a female divinity, the symbol of fecundity, sometimes represented under the form of the earth and sometimes as the moon. The Arabs were the first to extend to the stars the worship offered to the sun and moon. The star-lit sky shines down upon the desert with incomparable splendour; a vivifying freshness breathes over the burning sand as soon as the stars kindle up the azure heavens; and it is they that guide the traveller in his nocturnal wanderings through those vast solitudes. To the Arab, the stars represented the beneficent side of Nature, and he attributed to them a powerful influence over man's fate. Upon the tops of hills he adored the god of heaven; while the goddess of fecundity, he believed, inhabited the green trees. He also attached particular value to certain stones. The god Baal, which the Midianites and Amalekites worshipped on high places, was the Arab's god of heaven.

The Babylonian form of worship resembled in many respects that of the Arabs of the desert, but modified by the sensual character of the people. The Chaldeans, who had come down from the mountains into the plains, and had been the civilisers of the country, formed the sacerdotal caste. Like the Arabs, living under the pure magnificence of a starry sky, and holding constant communication with these nomadic conquerors, they were penetrated with the thought that the affairs of earth were regulated by the movements of the heavenly bodies, and were thus led to astrology. They gave the name of Bel to their supreme god, which they represented under the form either of the sun or the planet Saturn; and the goddess of fecundity, we find represented sometimes as the moon and sometimes as the planet Venus, and worshipped by them under the name of Melitta. The beneficent and malevolent sides of nature were united in these two great divinities. The Babylonian religion attributed a sinister influence to two of the seven planets; two others they regarded as auspicious; whilst the three remaining exerted a mixed influence, sometimes good and sometimes bad. The sun's course was divided into twelve stations, each bearing the name of some animal, which also designated the month of the year. The days of the week were called by the names of the different planets. The rites performed in their acts of worship were of a most infamous character,—prostitution playing a conspicuous part; every woman being bound, once at least in her life, to yield herself to the embraces of a stranger in the Temple of Melitta.[1] Dwelling in a fertile soil, possessing a brilliant, even a refined civilisation, and enriched by vast conquests, the Babylonians developed the sensual side of the religion of Nature.

In Phœnicia and Syria, this primitive dualism reached its most finished form. These were the richest countries of Western Asia. Instead of the monotony of the immense plains of Mesopotamia, the land is intersected by hills and mountains; and being bounded by the sea, its inhabitants were enabled to carry on relations with other parts of the world. Accordingly, we find that civilisation there attained an extraordinary pitch: as inventors of the art of writing, and possessing a genius for commerce, we are all acquainted with the fact of the high culture of the ancient Phœnicians. Unlike the Babylonians and Arabs, they were not a contemplative people, and were less preoccupied by the heavens and the stars than by the earth and its contrasts. They endeavoured to paint the struggle between the opposite forces of Nature rather than seek to read man's fortune in the stars. The two fundamental divinities of all the Asiatic religions are

[1] Herodotus i. 189.

likewise at the basis of Phœnician worship. The god of heaven, the active, masculine principle, they designated by the name of Baal or Dagon; the goddess of earth they adored under the name of Baaltis. But their mythological system is much more highly elaborated. The various attributes of these vague and fluctuating divinities, which are elsewhere confounded in a sort of hermaphrodism, are here personified and individualized with great art. Baal is presented under two clearly defined aspects: the productive force, when he is Adonis; and the destructive, Moloch. Sometimes, by a subtler distinction, he appears as the *preserving* power; whence his name, Baal-*Chon*; but this aspect is involved in the first. Thus we see how clearly marked was Phœnician dualism.[1] The female divinity underwent similar transformations, under the names of Ashera or Astarte, according as she appeared under her voluptuous or her severe aspect. Baal, as Adonis, represents the beneficent rays of the sun in that delicious period when he diffuses fertility over the earth—the vernal spring. Baal-Moloch, on the contrary, personifies the devouring burning fire of the summer sun. The fable of Adonis' death, torn by the wild boar, is the symbol of the transition from spring to the burning sterile heats. The summer sun is the wild boar of Mars, which devours the beautiful youth,—the graceful emblem of Nature in her first freshness.

The funeral ceremonies, which lasted seven days, during which the women cut off their locks and wept for Adonis,[2] were intended to represent Nature's lament, as, later on, his resurrection was represented by joyful festivities. Moloch, the terrible god, exacted human victims. Young children were sacrificed to him, burned upon his altar. Thus voluptuousness and death were

---

[1] Movers's Die Phœnicer, i. 180, 181.
[2] See Ezek. viii. 14. The Thammuz wept for by the women is Adonis.

blended in these rites, to which the prophets so frequently referred.[1]

At Tyre, the two sides of Nature personified in Baal and Moloch were united in one single divinity. The Tyrian Hercules, or Melkarth, was both creator and destroyer, having the attributes of Baal and Moloch. He also is represented under the twofold aspect of the terrible and the voluptuous; and under the name of Hercules Sando, clad in female garments, incites to orgies over which he presides. If he destroys, he, like the sun, draws life out of destruction. He is a wandering god, made in the image of the wandering people that adored him. The female divinity, under her cruel aspect, and under the name of Astarte, also presides over war and destruction. She demands the sacrifice of young virgins, and imposes chastity on her priests, who were required to mutilate themselves in her honour. Under the name of Dido, she is the wife of the god Melkarth, who pursues her at a distance. In Asia Minor, we find her under the name of *Ma*, where the warlike virgins, the Amazons, are the favourite priestesses of this savage divinity. Stripped of her terrible aspect, she is the Venus of Cytherea. Later on, she was the famous Diana of Ephesus, the great mother, the Phrygian Cybele, in the celebration of whose wild festivals mutilation was practised. The festivals of Atys were in all points similar to those of Adonis. The female divinity, in which were concentrated all the contradictions of dualism, inspiring alternately voluptuousness and mutilation, became gradually the great symbol of Nature, and was exalted to the rank of principal divinity in Western Asia. Lucian, in his curious work on the Syrian goddess, describes in vivid colours this infamous worship. The temples were built on high places, and divided into two parts: the sanctuary, in

[1] Jer. vii. 31, xix. 6. Lucian, De dea Syria.

which was the typical column of Baal, and the impure symbol of the religions of Nature, was only open to the priests. These had a pontiff at their head, and under them a multitude of servants, attached to the temple, given by the neighbouring towns.

Some attended to the service of the temple, while the rest spread themselves over the country, begging alms in behalf of their god or goddess. These were the famous *Galli* whom Apuleius describes. They abandoned themselves to frantic transports, and joined to the most repulsive abominations the most sanguinary ascetism. While they mutilated themselves, the women dedicated to the service of the divinity prostituted themselves. Mutilation and licentiousness were the natural results of this unrestricted dualism. It was impossible that art could give a definite form to such incoherent religious conceptions, or represent with any approach to beauty, a divinity so confused and multifarious as one summing up in itself all the forces of Nature. Pillars of wood or iron, symbols of the god of hills; grotesque idols with faces of different animals; vast edifices ornamented with precious stones,—such were the productions of religious art, beyond which it could not rise. Thus, while civilisation was rising to a high standard in Tyre, and the dwellings of men were richly decorated, the temples of their gods were but a conglomeration of hideous forms. Nothing can more clearly demonstrate that man was better than the gods he had created.[1] Art seems to have attained a far higher degree of perfection in Babylon and Nineveh. Recent discoveries enable us to appreciate the high cultivation these great empires had reached. The excavations made by Botta and Layard show clearly a highly developed civilisation. The hanging gardens of Babylon, its immense walls and iron gates, its magnifi-

[1] Ottfried Muller, Archæologie der Kunst, p. 301.

cent royal palaces, its gigantic temple of Belus, were previously known. We now learn that Nineveh in no way yielded in splendour to her rival; the palaces discovered beneath the soil are as spacious and as richly decorated as those of Babylon. We see, by the sculptures that abound, what reverence was paid to kings in these ancient monarchies. The king was looked on as the vicegerent of the divinity, and is represented, bearing the sword in one hand and the sceptre in the other, seated on his throne, commanding the respect of his subjects. Scenes of war and chase, vividly depicted upon the walls of the palace, reveal an animated and brilliant existence.

The symbolical figures of their gods are stamped with imposing majesty; the artists having evidently aimed at reproducing the calm solemnity of Nature, in which they, for the most part, succeeded. They were likewise successful in giving life and movement to the human figure, and to the scenes they represented. There is nothing sacerdotal in Assyrian art, which succeeded in emancipating itself from all conventional stiffness of form, and moves with ease and liberty. This may be explained by the fact of its being more national than religious. Its superiority is precisely owing to this subordination of the religious idea. We cannot consequently attribute the merit of its production to those religions of Nature, which found their artistic expression rather in Phœnicia than in Babylon or Nineveh.

THE EGYPTIAN RELIGION.

If from Asia we pass into Egypt, we shall find the same religious groundwork, but bearing the impress of an entirely different nationality, which here leaves on dualism the mark of its own characteristic austerity. Egypt is the land of routine, of unvarying, monotonous life. Nature itself wears in Egypt this aspect. Subject to no violent alternatives of a burning sun and tropical rains; the sun never clouded; the fertility of the soil being secured by inundations of the Nile, which are determined with the same regularity as the courses of the stars,—agricultural labour in such a country has none of the emotions of a doubtful struggle, the people needing only to stand as spectators, and allow Nature to act. The sole precaution necessary, is against periodical inundations, to guard against which, solid constructions were built. The Egyptians are essentially a building and conservative race; duration, not extension, is their instinct. They love immobility as others do movement. The mummy, stretched for thousands of years in its solemn attitude, is the Egyptian ideal. Hence this something sad and mournful which is the indelible character of the nation. Egypt loves the past; her national monument is the pyramid,—that is to say, a gigantic tomb; and in this funereal labour whole generations were swallowed up. It is easy to conceive the influence the priest would exercise over such a people: he is made for them; rather, made by them. Egypt is pre-eminently a sacerdotal country, and is styled the sacred land; the king of which is but the chief of the priests, and is depicted on their monuments as the son and representative of the gods. The system of castes was invented by the Egyptians, though it never attained in Egypt the rigidity it did in India. The sons did what their fathers did; and nothing is left to chance, either in the employment of the day, or in that of life. The existence of an Egyptian, or that of the king, who was the type of the whole nation, was regulated with the most exact minuteness, of which the old Spanish etiquette gives but a feeble notion.

Their worship consisted in a ritual of endless details, than which a stronger chain was never devised by a priesthood to hold a people in subjection. Constant purifications, circumcision, no contact with foreigners: such were the principal ordinances of this ritual. As to the groundwork of their creed—the worship of Nature was, in Egypt as in Asia, connected with the stars and sun, the latter being held to be the symbol or organ of the power of Nature. Before the union of Egypt under a single sceptre, each district had its own gods: thus we find the same divinities under different names. Upper as well as Lower Egypt adored a god of light, whose attributes were personified in several secondary divinities; beside him was placed a female divinity, the principle of the receptive and passive power of Nature. In Lower Egypt, the god of the sun was called *Ra* or *Phra*; at Memphis, *Ptah*. In Upper Egypt, he is called Ammon; and beside him are Mentu and Atmu, symbolizing the rising and the setting sun. The female divinity was called in Lower Egypt, *Neith* or *Pacht*; and in Upper Egypt, *Mut*, or great mother. In this part of Egypt was also adored the god *Kneph* and the god *Chem*, both symbolizing the productive force of Nature; also the god *Chensu*, identical with the moon; and the god *Thot*, the celestial scribe. It is probable that *Isis*, *Osiris*, and *Typhon* were local divinities, like Ptah and Neith, before their admission into the grand cycle of the national mythology.

It has even been maintained, on the authority of some ancient inscriptions, that Typhon had been revered as a beneficent divinity, until, having been adopted by the Hycsos, he became an object of horror and fear.[1] The Egyptians endeavoured to represent the various forces of Nature by this multiplicity of gods, all of which can easily be reduced to the original duality of Oriental Paganism. Particular animals were consecrated to each divinity, whose living symbol they were believed to be.

[1] Bunsen, Ægypten, t. i., p. 513.

The gods were represented under the forms of these sacred animals. Thus the scarabœus represented Ptah; the goddess Pacht had the head of a lion or a cat; and Kneph the head of a ram. The bull belonged to Ptah and to Ra. A particular bull, possessing certain marks, was chosen, and the name of Apis given it. This bull was supposed to be the offspring of a cow and of a sunbeam. Fed in the temple, and worshipped above all other animals, his death was the occasion of universal lamentation.

After Egypt had become one vast monarchy, there was a fusion of all the local mythologies, although the nomenclature continued to vary from Thebes to Memphis. There were, first, seven principal gods, with their goddesses. All these divinities represent, by their various aspects, the male and female principles of Nature. Ptah, Ammon, Ra, Ma, Osiris, always represent the active, fertilizing principle; while Tefant, Nuptve, and Isis represent the passive, receptive principle. Typhon represents the sombre, sinister side of Nature. Inferior in rank to these great divinities were twelve minor ones; then thirty demi-gods or genii. At a later period philosophical ideas may have been attached to the names of these principal divinities, and an effort made to elaborate a metaphysical theogony; but it is not probable, as some writers have contended, that the religion of Egypt owes its origin to such profound views.[1] It was, like the religion of its neighbours, Nature-worship, and characterized by the same dualism. In the ancient worship of Memphis there are traces of the struggle between the good and bad principle; the latter being represented under the form of a serpent, the symbol of night, seeking to extinguish the sun.[2]

---

[1] See Bunsen's most interesting chapter on the religion of Egypt, Ægypten, t. i., p. 511.
[2] Dunker, t. i., p. 57.

But the struggle between the good and evil powers of Nature was represented in a very dramatic manner in the myth of Isis and Osiris, which Herodotus and Plutarch have handed down to us in such detail.[1] Osiris, the husband of Isis, and offspring, like her, of the gods, meets, in a journey through Egypt, the wicked Typhon, who, assisted by seventy-two companions of his crimes, kills Osiris, and places his body in a box, which he throws into the Nile. Isis, a prey to the deepest affliction, seeks everywhere the body of her husband; at last she finds it at Byblos. Osiris, resuscitated, is to reign over the kingdom of the dead; whilst Horus, his son, sacrifices Typhon to his just vengeance. This myth corresponds with those of Adonis and Atys. Isis is the earth; Osiris, the fertilizing principle of Egypt,—that is to say, the sacred and beneficent river. Typhon, who, with his seventy-two companions, kills him, is the burning sun, which during seventy-two days consumes the soil and strikes it with sterility. At the expiration of this time fertility reappears, and has for its symbol the young and brilliant Horus, son of Isis, and conqueror of Typhon. Each year a solemn festival, celebrated at Byblos, recalled the leading features of this myth: the lamentations of the Egyptian women over the murder of Osiris were like the echo of the lamentations of the women of Phœnicia over Adonis. On the return of vegetation, when the body of the god was found, joy succeeded to mourning, and solemn festivals to lugubrious ceremonies. But the myth of Isis and Osiris appears to us to possess something higher in it than the analogous myths just mentioned. Here, there is not merely a succession of opposite events—there is a struggle. Isis seeks the body of her husband. Horus fights Typhon. What is especially remarkable, and entirely new, is the glimpse

[1] Herodotus ii. 40.

opened to us into the dwelling of the dead. Osiris, the beneficent god, reigns there; the sombre way is illumined by a hope of immortality. We know how preoccupied the Egyptians were about the future life. Ideas of a metempsychosis have been wrongly imputed to them; but they were rather importations at a later period from other creeds. According to the Egyptians, Osiris judged the dead; and, having weighed their heart in the scales of justice, he sent the wicked to regions of darkness, while the just, having received the water of eternal life, which distilled like dew from the branches of the tree of life, were sent to dwell with the god of light. 'The latter, we read in an inscription, found favour before the great God; they dwell in glory, where they live a heavenly life; the bodies they have quitted will for ever repose in their tombs, whilst they rejoice in the life of the supreme God.'[1] We see by the last words that they attached great importance to the preservation of the body, believing it to be a condition of the immortality of the soul; they therefore thought themselves bound to embalm the body with the most religious care, and to build indestructible tombs.[2]

Lovers of tradition, destined to immobility, their one passion was to preserve the memory of the past. They wrote their history and that of their kings on those tombs by means of their symbolical and mysterious hieroglyphics, which have secured to their chronicles the stability and duration of stone. We there find the first elements of writing; not having yet attained to abridged signs, they sometimes painted their subjects, and sometimes represented them by conventional symbols. Nothing can more plainly prove the ponderous immobility of this people, than their tenacity in preserving for centuries these rudiments without further developing them. Egyptian art reproduced the national

[1] Dunker, t. i., p. 72.   [2] Herodotus ii. 86, 123.

character with singular fidelity. It was not fertility it wanted, for its works are innumerable. Pyramids and obelisks cover the soil. The Labyrinth, and its long lines of palaces; the palace of Thebes; the immense palace of Sesostris; the equally magnificent temples; the vast tombs hollowed out of the rock;—the air of grandeur and majesty about these constructions fill us with awe, and prove that the artistic faculty of the race was highly developed. But architecture completely crushed sculpture and painting; for these arts, in order to flourish, require a certain development of human individuality, whereas Egyptian art was essentially sacerdotal. Wanting liberty, spontaneous inspiration, sacred fire, it was the docile servant—rather, we should say, the slave—of tradition. Their temples and palaces do not form one harmonious whole, like the Greek temples, but are a series of porticoes with innumerable columns which might be indefinitely prolonged. Sculpture is tied down to consecrated types, the forms of which may be described as rather geometrical than organic. The human face is without beauty or individuality, but stamped with the same solemn immobility that characterizes the nation itself. The gods are represented by a grotesque assemblage of animals, amongst which the sphynx is the most prominent figure. Thus we see, as Ottfried Müller has well observed, that Egyptian art was never intended, like Greek art, 'to express really æsthetic ideas; its aim was to preserve the memory of the past—to relate facts. Far from being consecrated to the ideal, it was rather a kind of monumental writing—a development of the hieroglyphics, destined, like them, to perpetuate history, and to recall, for the requirements of religion, the acts of their gods.'[1] The artist, despised as a member of an inferior caste, had no independence, but was merely a skilled workman in the

[1] Ottfried Müller, Archæologie 257.

service of the priest.¹ The productions of his chisel necessarily bear the impress of his subjection,—rather, of the universal subjection. The most remarkable of them all, the sphynx, is the faithful personification of the sad, motionless, yet grand genius of Egypt. 'Such,' says Dunker,² ' is this marvellous country, this ancient Egypt, whose richly developed culture brings us to the threshold of historic times. Favoured by nature, placed on a fertile soil, the inhabitants carried into their national life and civilisation the splendour and the calm of their climate.'

Their conservative genius created an immutable organization, in which the sons lived the life their fathers had lived. The beneficent powers of Nature, the mystery of life, the regular course of the year, the incessant resurrection of the earth, its forces, its laws, were the objects of their worship, and they thought they saw in the regular life of animals the reflection of the immutable life of the gods. The life of the people themselves was regulated by priestly rules, in order that they might participate as much as possible in the immutability of the laws of Nature.

THE PERSIAN RELIGION.

Assuredly from Phœnicia to Egypt the religious idea has made notable progress. It is no longer the mere contrast between life and death, between blood and voluptuousness. Already the distinction is recognised between good and evil, and light cast on a future life by the dogma of the judgment of souls. Although still shut up within the circle of dualism, the human conscience has spoken. It speaks still louder in the religion of ancient Persia, without, however, getting beyond the bounds of the religion of Nature. Three great fami-

---
¹ Raoul Rochette, Leçon sur l'Archæologie ii.
² Dunker, t. i., p. 103.

lies of nations issued from that vast area which is bounded on the west by the Indus, on the east by the Euphrates, on the south by the ocean, and by the Caspian on the north. The Persians, Medes, and Bactrians, on the one side; the Greeks and the inhabitants of India, on the other, have all a common root, as is proved by the profound analogy of the languages they speak. We find this identity underlying, like a solid indestructible foundation, all the elaborations of their national genius. Hence we discover the same fund of religious ideas lying at the basis of their mythologies, although each nation developed them in very different directions.

If Western Asia is a land of contrasts, Iran is still more so.[1] 'Immense steppes border countries of luxuriant fertility; a fiery sun burns up the soil, while at the same moment, in neighbouring districts, the frosts of winter check all vegetation.' 'Winter,' says their sacred book, 'envelopes the flocks, to destroy them; it freezes the water, the trees, the fields, even the heart of earth.'[2] It is especially at Bactriana and Sogdiana, not far from the Caspian Sea, that these contrasts are most striking. In the mountain regions are fertile valleys, richly clad with luxuriant vegetation; while farther on stretches out a barren and boundless desert. In the clear atmosphere of Persia the stars shine pure and serene; while on the steppes the tempest thickens the fogs, and raises clouds of dust. The contrast between the inhabitants of the two countries is equal to that of their soil and climate. On one side, a peaceful industrious people, occupied in agricultural labour; on the other, nomadic tribes, leading a wild and warlike life, and ever ready for inroads, rushing down upon Iran with the impetuosity of the sand of the desert. The inhabitants of Bactriana were led by this state of

[1] Dunker, t. ii., pp. 335, 355.   [2] Vendid. iii. 69.

things to look upon the land of the North as cursed, and as belonging to evil spirits. The melancholy West, where the sun sets, they held also to be the dwelling of spirits of darkness. It is probable, when Zoroaster, six centuries before Christ, gave a religious code to his cotemporaries, that he was not an inventor of a religion, but that he merely reduced to order the confused myths already in existence.[1] These myths originated in a land of striking contrasts, and bore their impress, constantly recalling the struggle between the beneficent and destructive forces of Nature.

It is difficult to distinguish accurately what belongs to the ancient myths, and what specially to Zoroaster, whose personality is at once obscured and adorned by the halo of mythology. It is equally difficult to discover the first nucleus of the sacred books bearing his name, from amid the many additions made at the time of their collection under the Sassanides. Nevertheless, by laying aside all that bears the evident trace of metaphysical elaboration or foreign influence, we may, by availing ourselves of the labours of modern criticism, succeed, in a certain measure, in reconstructing the ancient Bactrian and Persian religion.[2]

It has been maintained, on the authority of certain disputed texts, that dualism was not the fundamental dogma of this religion, but that it admitted a first principle absolutely good, named Time without limits. But this subtle idea, which evidently belongs to an age

---

[1] The date of the Zendavesta may be nearly fixed. As it makes no mention of the great conquests of the Medes and Persians, it was probably written before this period, and at all events before Cyrus. The *Vendidad Sade* and the *Yacna*, books of liturgy, filled with forms of prayer, constitute the most ancient part of the Avesta. The *Bundchesch*, which has been added, is long subsequent, and bears the trace of a religious eclecticism.

[2] Besides the books already named, we must cite the translation of the Zendavesta by Anquetil Duperron; and above all, the commentary upon the *Yacna* by Eugene Bournouf, a masterpiece of philology and profound criticism.

of speculation, cannot be reconciled with the simplicity of the religious conception which we gather from the sacred books of Persia, or with the way in which they speak of Ormuz: of him they speak as the Being *par excellence*, the Creator, the beneficent Ordainer of the world. Ormuz is also the god of light,—the Baal of Phœnicia, the Ptah of Egypt,—but purified and transfigured. Light no longer simply representing the fertilizing power of Nature, but also all that is good, salutary, and upright; for the moral idea makes its first appearance in this mythology, though not yet disengaged from the trammels of Nature.

'I invoke,' says the Persian's prayer of prayers, 'and I worship the Creator, Ahava Mazda (Ormuz, the master who bestows wisdom),—luminous, resplendent, very great, very good, very perfect, very energetic, very intelligent, and very beautiful; eminent in purity, who possesses the good science, source of pleasure; him who created us, who formed us, who nourished us; him, the most perfect of intelligent beings.'[1] Opposed to Ormuz is Ahriman, or the evil genius, representing darkness and death. Like to an immense reptile, he envelopes the world in his coils, and infuses his poison into every creature. 'He said, I will spoil, by looking on them with an evil eye, the flocks and the sun. The pastures shall be without water. The old infernal serpent lays his touch on every creature.'[2] Ahriman created no evil beings, but he deposits a germ of evil in all the creatures made by Ormuz.

Under Ormuz and Ahriman are ranged a multitude of spirits, which carry on, in their name, the great struggle between light and darkness. The first in this category are the Amschaspands (the venerable). They personify the highest virtues and the best blessings. 'I invoke and worship benevolence, purity, a worthy life, that

[1] Bournouf, Yacna.   [2] Anquetil, pp. 172, 305.

which is holy and submissive, and that which produces all and gives life."¹ The six Amschaspands, with Ormuz, reign over the seven parts of the universe. Militant spirits follow, which take an active part in the struggle against Ahriman. Mithra is the chief of these —high, immortal, pure, god of the sun, rapid in action, eye of Ormuz. 'Mithra, the victorious, seats himself, after the dawn has risen, girt in pure light, upon the summit of the mountains.'² It is he that dissipates darkness and falsehood, and it is he that gives patience and health. Other luminous spirits—the stars; the moon, which contains the fertilizing power or the seed of the bull; above all, Behram, or the light-bringer of Ormuz—are objects of adoration. A divine hero, Serosch, the champion and servant of Ormuz, who strives against the spirits of darkness, is associated with them. In fact, the Persian adored all that exerted a beneficent, fertilizing influence, especially fire, the most rapid of the immortals; then the vivifying water, and the verdant trees. 'I invoke and worship,' we read in the Yacna, 'health and goodness. I invoke and worship the male and female of animals, houses—the storehouses where corn is kept—water, earth, trees, corn. I adore this earth and sky; the stars, the moon, the sun; light, which had no beginning and is increate; and all the works of the holy and celestial Being. I invoke and worship the mountains, depositories of the wisdom given by Ormuz, radiant with purity; and all mountains radiant in purity, perfectly radiant; and the splendour of kings given by Ormuz, and their unborrowed brightness. I invoke those who are holy and those who are pure.'³ Thus we find that the adoration of pure men was commanded: their spirits were worshipped under the name of *Ferouers*. 'I invoke and worship the

¹ Bournouf, Yacna, p. 174. ² Vendid. ix. 91.
³ Bournouf, Yacna, p. 559.

powerful ferouers of pure men, the ferouers of the men of the ancient law, the ferouers of living men, my parents, the ferouer of my soul."[1]

The ferouer or spirit of Zoroaster, the master of holiness, is the object of an altogether special worship. These quotations serve to show that the whole creation was considered as an emanation from Ormuz; and that all that is living, fertile, luminous, brilliant, from the sun to the king, is divine by virtue of the same.

The spirits that preside over the divisions of time— the Gahanders, or masters of the six divisions of the year, the spirits of the months and days—are likewise objects of worship. In this way the whole year is made divine; it is subdivided into six periods, corresponding to the six periods of the creation of Ormuz, and is terminated by a solemn festival, called the Festival of All Souls. It was believed that the souls of the dead then returned to visit their families, and that their prayers and expiations obtained forgiveness for the guilty.

In opposition to Ormuz and his luminous legions, Ahriman gathers together on the burial-places his sombre army of malevolent spirits, or *devas*. Amongst them is the spirit of winter, *Agis* the slayer, who seeks to extinguish the fire; the genius of heavy sleep and sloth; in fine, the genius of falsehood. Animals are divided between the two adversaries. Ahriman succeeded in perverting and appropriating to himself a great number of the creatures of Ormuz: amongst others, the serpent 'which is full of death.' All ferocious animals, such as 'are pernicious to the earth,' belong to him. On the contrary, the cock that announces the dawn, the dog that is the enemy of wild beasts, as well as all useful animals, are the servants of Ormuz. In such a religion there can be no tendency to asceticism. On the contrary, its injunctions are to develop life richly, and to

---

[1] Bournouf, Yacna 454, 571.

combat death in every shape. 'O man,' says the sacred book, 'give children to the woman who has borne none. Eat, as a wise man, the fat of animals.'[1] The first commandment of the Avesta is to plough the fields, to plant trees, and in this way to prepare food for man. 'With the fruits of the field increases the law of Ormuz, and with them it is multiplied a hundredfold. The earth rejoices when man builds on it his house; when his flocks abound; when, surrounded by wife and children, he makes the grass and the corn to grow, and plants fruit-trees abundantly.'[2]

We know that the Median and Persian people imbibed from their religion an energetic and conquering spirit. They founded great empires. Cyrus and Darius carried to the highest pitch the civilisation and glory of their race. With the Persian, the question is to live, and not to die; and the more intensity and splendour there is in his life, the more Ormuz is glorified, and Ahriman, the eternal hater of life, confounded. But it does not suffice to richly develop all the elements of life, to cultivate the earth and cover it with fertile harvests, to decorate the dwelling of man, and to shed a splendour over human life: the worship of Ormuz must also be celebrated. The Persian has no idols: such gross representations would be a profanation of his luminous god. But his religious duties are fulfilled by keeping alive the sacred fire—that sole image of his god and god himself—and when he has pronounced his invocations conformably to the ritual taught him. The sacred word plays an important part in the Persian religion. It is the sovereign means of expelling evil spirits and drawing down the favour of Ormuz; for it is an emanation from him, and is also divine. 'I invoke,' must the worshipper of the god of light say,—'I invoke the excellent efficacious word, given

[1] Vendid. i. 18.   [2] Vendid. iii. 85, 86; iii. 1, 20.

through the medium of Zoroaster, the long meditation, the good law of the adorers of Ormuz, against the devas.'[1] Surrounded by the influence of Ahriman, man endeavours to escape him; but, it being impossible for ever to ward off his poisonous breath, a system of purification was devised, against all possible pollutions. The chief contamination was contact with the dead. The house which death had visited was to be purified with excessive care, and the body to be deposited in a solitary place, to be devoured by wild beasts; for the sacred fire could not be profaned for such purposes. The Persians at a later period renounced this custom, Cyrus having had a magnificent tomb erected for himself. The cemeteries are the natural domain of the destructive genii, the devas.

Caste distinctions were by no means so strict in Persia as in Egypt and India,—the labouring caste being held in almost as much respect as the military. Neither was the distinction between things sacred and profane as rigid as in other religions; since a man by cultivating his field was performing a religious act to the glory of Ormuz, whose service consisted in the development of all life and activity. Priests had not the same influence amongst them as elsewhere. They presided at the ceremonies, but the performance of the rites was not left to them alone. Zoroaster's religion is imbued with a lay spirit not very favourable to the priesthood. The magi are called in the Avesta by the name of Athrava, which signifies guardians of the fire; and this, indeed, is their chief office, with that of regulating the sacred ceremonies. 'Do not style them priests,' says the Avesta, 'who wear the garb, but are not crowned with the divine law. Call him priest of Zoroaster who labours all night to acquire the knowledge of sacred things and the purification of sins.'[2] The high priest—rather, the representative of the divinity—is the

[1] Yacna, p. 314.   [2] Vendid. xviii. 1-17.

king. It is he who concentrates all the vital forces of the country, who diffuses them abroad and increases them by use. It is he who, by the splendour with which he is surrounded, by the impulse he gives the useful arts, and the glory he acquires,—it is he who best represents Ormuz, god of light and life. Thus Persian art is kingly rather than sacerdotal, and occupied itself more with the construction of palaces than of temples. Those palaces were built in terraces, with gigantic gates and avenues of columns. The king appears in all the pomp of costume, and the exercise of his royal functions: sometimes in the animation of the combat; sometimes exercising acts of clemency. The gods are represented by symbolical figures of animals. Their mythology is nothing — their history everything. Art is thus the symbol of an essentially human and laical religion, yet without any tendency to materialism; on the contrary, it is much more preoccupied about a future life than is the Egyptian religion. Whosoever has lived in purity, and has not suffered the devas to have any power over him, like to a free spirit, will pass after death into the realms of light. 'Souls, three days after death, as soon as Mithra, the victorious, seats himself with his celestial father on the mountains, pass the bridge *T'shinavat*, or of retribution. There the gods and devas fight their last fight for their possession. Ormuz examines them; and those who have practised holiness and purity of life pass the bridge, and are conducted into heaven. The pure soul mounts joyously to the golden throne of Ormuz. Impure souls are abandoned to the evil spirit, who carries them away into regions of darkness. According to the *Bundehesch* (a sacred book added to the Avesta since the Christian era, and which bears evident traces of the influence of Christianity), the whole world will end by receiving the law of Ormuz through the medium of Serosch, the divine hero, transformed into a kind of Messiah. But we have no right to attribute to the Persian religion, ideas which are evidently of foreign importation.

If we judge it as a whole, it appears far superior to all preceding forms of worship. It impelled to action, to energy, to progress; it looked on life as a combat and a field of ennobling labour; it sanctified the sweat of the labourer and the life of the family. The gods it adored were the beneficent gods, the champions of light and goodness. Still dualism prevails. The creation was held to be an emanation from Ormuz, and, by virtue of this, claims our worship. The moral world was not distinguished from the material. The pollution of the soul is identified with the pollution of the body; falsehood is ranked with the involuntary contact with a dead body; presumption is to be cured like a fever. Light is not merely a symbol of holiness, but an integral part, as much as chastity and integrity. The darkness of night and the cold of winter are as much manifestations of evil as are moral impurity or dishonesty. The religious law of the Persians is a mixture of material rules and moral ordinances. The ablution of the body is mixed up with the sanctification of the soul, and a fine field of wheat is as pleasing in the sight of Ormuz as is a purified heart. Conscience has not yet conquered its entire domain, but is advancing towards it; for, between the worship of Baal and the worship of Ormuz, the distance is great and the progress real.

THE INDIAN RELIGION.

To the east of the Euphrates and Tigris, and forming the southern declivity of the great central plateau of Asia, rises the lofty mountain range of the Himalaya. Beyond it lies India, that marvellous country which so filled the imagination of the ancient Greeks—the land where gold abounds, and where, under the shadow of gigantic trees, gigantic animals have their haunts. The Indus and Ganges, the largest rivers in Asia, take their rise in the eternally snow-crowned Himalaya. Certain tribes from the highlands of Iran, and of the same family as the Bactrians, Medes, and Persians, established themselves in the country watered by these rivers, driving towards the coast the native inhabitants, who are still recognisable by their long hair and bronzed features. This migration must have taken place before the year 1300.[1] The *Rig Veda*, a collection of sacred hymns with which the Vedas open, contains a brilliant description of the social and religious state of those Aryan tribes during the period preceding their invasion of the fertile valley of the Ganges.[2] In them we find the creed that is at the basis of the religion of Zoroaster. The god of light we find adored under the name of Indra. He it is 'that makes the lightning spring forth and launches the light.' Like Mithra, his symbol is the bull. 'He bears the victorious thunderbolts, and is true as a father is to his child. O god, may thy arm give us happiness.'[3] The malevolent divinities fight against Indra: they are the clouds that darken the sky, and that march under the guidance of Vritra (that which obscures). The swift winds that chase the clouds are the auxiliaries of Indra. The two first rays of the morning were adored under the name of Açvius, twin-brothers who traverse heaven seated on a rapid car, scattering along their passage fecundity and life. The Aryans of India, like those of Iran, adored all that tends to increase, animate, and embellish life. Their hymns breathe a simple, joyous pantheism. Fire,

---

[1] Dunker, t. ii., p. 17.
[2] Rig Veda, sec. vii. lect. 1, hymn 4 (we quote from M. Langlois' translation.) See also Lassen, t. i., pp. 755, 766.
[3] Rig Veda vii. 7, 15-18.

water, earth, heaven, the dawn, plants, rivers, holy libations,—all are deified and celebrated in poetry, at once monotonous and brilliant, but singularly expressive and fresh. Fire is adored under the name of Agni— 'this winged creature that shines upon our earth. Prayers caress this trembling nursling, this golden bird that rests on earth. Young Agni, in the different hearths in which he is born, springs up from the wood, in the midst of eternal libations. He is a sovereign whose standard is smoke; his dazzling flames spread; they burst with a sonorous noise; and with his sharp, long, radiant darts, that seem in their power to play, he mounts toward heaven.'[1]

Water is glorified with equal enthusiasm; but it is the Soma, the symbol of the liquid element, which is used in libations, that is sung in every tone. 'O Soma, pure and loved, to thee we owe our rich renown. Prayers and hymns celebrate the friend that circulates in our cups, and who has his place at our festivals—the immortal who, to win our praises, gives us the sweet dew. He follows by a thousand paths; he falls into our cups. He makes his voice heard, and he shines when the fertile dawn arises. The hymn and the song are the wheels of the sacred car of sacrifices.'[2] But this brilliant poetry cannot mark all that is elementary, and even gross, in the ideas of the early Indians relating to their gods. These divinities altogether belong to the domain of Nature. Offerings repair their strength, and libations quench their thirst. The gods are in a condition of dependence on the priests, who prepare these draughts, and are acted on magically by them. Nevertheless, even at that period, we can discern amongst the Aryans of the Indus eminent poetical faculties, and especially the gift of translating into symbol their primitive impressions. A profound transformation was

[1] Rig Veda vii. 7, 15, 18.   [2] Rig Veda viii. 6, 9.

soon after effected in the religious ideas and the social life of the Aryans.

As long as they dwelt on the banks of the Indus, they were a conquering militant people; but once settled in the valley of the Ganges, they became pacific and sacerdotal, and exchanged the nomadic life they had led among the Himalaya for a peaceful settlement in the midst of a magnificent country, where vegetation sprung up with unwonted splendour of colour and proportions; where Nature revealed her force in spectacles whose grandeur was overwhelming to human weakness. They were not now simply in presence of the cheering light of morning, of the sun sparkling over the mountain side, or of the swift-flying cloud that darkened the sky. The unity of Nature revealed itself to them in all its majesty; and they believed themselves to be in her temple when they entered those immense forests, where the summits of the trees, bound together and interwoven by the encircling ivy, formed a thick dome and a sort of sacred gloom.

Their religion, in its early form, bore the stamp of pantheism, but a simple, childlike pantheism, deifying what was admired or feared. Their personifications had in them something floating and indefinite—transparent symbols of the different aspects of the countries they passed through. As long as diversity preponderated over unity, the character of their mythology was that of a warlike polytheism—a constant struggle between two rival divinities; but when unity prevailed over diversity, they deified, not the opposing forces of Nature, but Nature itself, taken as a whole. Indra, the god of light, was no longer the supreme god; light being but one of the aspects of the life of Nature, whose totality they desired to symbolize. Accordingly, he gradually fell into the second rank, yielding his place to a god hitherto occupying a very secondary rank, but who had the advantage of being eminently sacerdotal. Brahma, or Brahmanaspati, whose name signifies the lord of sleep, increased in influence as the caste of priests, whose protector he was, predominated.[1] During the period of conquest the sacerdotal body had acquired considerable influence, victory being attributed to the scrupulous performance of the sacred rites. Exercising an immediate influence on their gods by sacrifices and libations, the function of the priests was as important in war as that of the military caste, and after the conquest it necessarily became the preponderating influence. Thus, when that religious revolution was effected which issued in an admirably constructed pantheism, the name of the victorious god was the sacerdotal god, Brahma.[2] Indra, and the other gods, who were but partial manifestations of Nature, and consequently inferior to the divinity that filled and pervaded the whole, were subordinated to him. But this triumph did not suffice: gifted in the highest degree with the speculative genius, the priests elaborated a subtle, complicated system, by which to explain the origin of the world. They thus arrived at totally opposite notions from those which characterized the earlier creed. Whilst, according to the *Rig Veda*, there was a good element in Nature—the element of life and light, which it was man's duty to make triumphant over the malignant element, which is the element of death and darkness,—the Indian priests laid all Nature under interdict. According to them, Nature was an emanation from Brahma. Brahma was the soul, the hidden genius, the deep source from which all life proceeded. But no being resembles him; none entirely reproduces him. When born into real life, the being issuing from him is necessarily born into an imperfect state of existence: the first emanation involves a diminution of the

[1] Lassen, t. i., p. 766. [2] Duncker, t. ii., p. 65.

divine life, the second a still greater, and so on; as beings multiply, the decline increases. 'Brahma, we read in a passage of the Vedas belonging to the Brahminical period, is the eternal, pure, supreme being. The world is his name, his image; but this first existence, that contains all in itself, alone really subsists. This universe is Brahma; it proceeds from Brahma, subsists in Brahma, and returns to Brahma.'[1] From this point of view birth itself is a fall, and the world of birth and change, a world under curse. This is the natural consequence of the dogma of emanation, which the Indian religion reduced to a rigid formula. Thus we find it to be a religion of asceticism and death, leading to the rejection of the natural element, to the destruction of finite and limited existences, and tending with all its might, not towards progress and life, but towards annihilation. In this Introduction we can only give an outline of its history; for Oriental studies have reached that point, that a complete exposition of this religion would require considerable development.

Brahminism, in its first form, before the idea of a trinity was introduced into the notion of the supreme god, was contained in the Laws of Manou. We cannot do better, in order to give an idea of it, than present a brief analysis of this religious code, the date of which is said to be 1000 B.C. The first book contains an essay on theogony, which is a development of the theory of emanation. 'By alternate waking and repose, the immutable being eternally causes the mass of mutable beings to revive or die. He makes all beings pass successively from birth to growth, from growth to dissolution, by a movement like to that of a wheel. He, whom the mind alone can perceive, who escapes all organs of sense, who is without visible parts, the eternal, the soul of all beings, whom none can comprehend, dis-

[1] Creuzer, traduit Guigniaut, t. i., liv. i., ch. ii.

played his own splendour, having resolved in his mind that all creatures should emanate from his substance.'[1] From the waters produced by him sprang an egg, which dividing, formed heaven and earth. At the same time a multitude of gods, of qualities, of virtues, took shape from these first emanations. Manou, produced by Brahma, created the universe by means of intermediary gods; but this world is the reproduction of an anterior world, for the creations of the divinity incessantly reproduce themselves.

The Laws of Manou show us the system of castes in full vigour. It was the result of the conquest. The ancient inhabitants of the country, under the name of Cudra or Soudras, became the helots of India, and constituted the despised and degraded class. The conquerors were divided into warriors and agriculturists; above both were the priests, who assumed the name of Brahmans. The sacred code endeavours to give an eternal basis to this organization. 'For the propagation of human life,' we read, 'Brahma produced the Brahmans from his mouth, the warrior from his arm, the labourer from his thigh, the Soudras from his foot.' The Laws of Manou place the Brahmans at the head of the social hierarchy, and constantly labour to exalt their dignity: they thus form a kind of Indian Levites. Nevertheless, especially in the latter book, the general organization of society is regulated by very minute prescriptions. Royalty is invested with despotic power. The king is compared to the gods, and thus placed in relation with the priestly caste. Despotism characterizes each degree of the hierarchy; and we can judge from certain prescriptions how harassing it became on the part of some of the subaltern authorities. The king is solicited to exercise justice in order that his kingdom may flourish like a well-watered tree. The Laws of

[1] Laws of Manou i. 57.

Manou are remarkable as a penal code. 'Punishment,' they say, 'governs the human kind; punishment protects it; it watches whilst the world sleeps.' Adultery and gambling are severely punished, but many crimes may be compounded for by graduated fines. Religious expiations are also frequent. But it is in the four books on the Brahmans that the real nature of Brahmanism is revealed. The Brahman should pass through four degrees—the novice, the father of a family, the anchorite, and the ascetic. The novitiate consists in celebrating the rites of purification: first, those intended to wash away the stain of birth; and to study the sacred books. 'It is not years, nor white hairs, nor parents, nor riches that constitute greatness. The saints established this law: He who is instructed in the holy books is great amongst us. Whilst the natural birth is purely human, the birth communicated to the novice by the sacred teacher is the true one: it is not subject to age or death.'[1] Already asceticism is apparent. 'Let a Brahman,' it says, 'stand in constant fear of worldly honour, and always wish for contempt as he would for ambrosia.'[2]

The third book introduces us to the novice as father of a family. Frankly accepting this phase in the Brahman's life, the Laws of Manou exalt in a high degree the family, and consequently woman. We find in them this fine passage: 'Wherever women are honoured, there the divinities are satisfied. The happiness of that family is secured in which the husband loves his wife, and the wife her husband.'[3] The wife's subjection to the husband is absolute. 'A woman,' it says, 'should never govern herself after her own fashion. The woman who has lost her husband should never pronounce the name of another man.'[4] In the house of the Brahman the

[1] Laws of Manou ii. 147.   [2] Id. ii. 162.
[3] Id. iii. 55, 60.   [4] Laws of Manou v. 147, 157.

family life should be essentially religious. 'Let the master of the house be always exact in reading the sacred writings, and in making offerings to the gods. A Brahman who has not studied the sacred writings, dies out like a fire of dried herbs.'[1]

But the highest degree of perfection for a Brahman is not the life of the family; on the contrary, it consists in the rupture of all natural ties. He prepares himself for it by leading the life of an anchorite in the depths of the forests. 'Free from all inclinations for sensual pleasures, chaste as a novice, having the earth for his bed, he lies at the foot of trees, practising all kinds of purifications, and disengaging himself from the bonds of the body.'[2] Quitting his house, always alone, without fire or domicile, he marches on in silence, fixing his mind on the divine being. 'Let him not desire death; let him not desire life; let him wait the moment fixed for him, as a servant waits for his wages. By mastering his organs he prepares himself for immortality.'[3] Finally, having renounced all kinds of pious practices, directing his mind to the sole object of his thoughts, exempt from all desires, having expiated his faults by devotion, he attains the supreme end, that is to say, absolute asceticism—image of and preparation for death.[4] Innumerable rites for purification are prescribed by the Brahmans. The whole system is crowned by the dogma of the metempsychosis. The migration of souls through different regions of creation, and through different castes, is proportioned in number and nature to the degrees of guilt. Thus we see Brahmanism ultimately leads to extreme asceticism, even to death: and nothing can be more logical; for matter is the *Maïa*, or eternal illusion, against which we must be incessantly on our guard. 'Brahma, seduced by Maïa,

[1] Laws of Manou iii. 75, 168.　　[2] Id. vi. 26, 32.
[3] Id. vi. 40, 45.　　[4] Id. vi. 96.

which is his emanation, united himself to her in the intoxication of passion, and the world was produced.' The mysterious veil she wove with her hands receives them both, and the thought of the eternal becomes fertile in falling on time; but its fecundity is, at the same time, the cause of the false, bad life of the finite earthly being.'

Speculation, so inherent in the Hindu mind, laid hold of the principle of this daring emanatism, and drew from it consequences of twofold tendencies. The philosophy called *Mimansa* teaches that Nature is but an appearance—a delusion, that it is nothing; and that the soul of the universe, or Brahma, alone exists.

The world is a dream of this soul. It is by illusion that the soul of man believes itself distinct from the soul of Nature, and it should free itself from this illusion by becoming absorbed in the great soul. The *Sankya* endeavours to re-establish individual existence against the *Mimansa*. According to this system, beside Nature, which is one, is the soul, which is parcelled out into a multitude of individualities, and only exists in multiplicity. The mission of each soul is to free itself from the fetters of the body, but it is dependent on no authority; for there is no universal soul of the world, no Brahma, no god: its followers must throw off the dominion of the priests. The disciples of Kapila, the author of the Sankya, thus arrive at absolute scepticism.[1] The task was reserved for a much less metaphysical system to clearly disengage the fundamental idea of Brahmanism, to separate it from all heterogeneous elements, and to realize it in all its consequences. Buddhism, whose origin goes back to six centuries before Christ, is the legitimate offspring of Brahmanism, its heir and conqueror.[2] It is difficult to distinguish

---

[1] Dunker, t. ii., pp. 166, 173.
[2] See on this subject the admirable commentary on the History of Buddhism, by Eug. Bournouf. Paris, 1844.

the true from the false in the legend concerning Buddha. It is probable that he was an adept of the Brahmans, who, combining their creed with the metaphysical ideas of the Mimansa, and practising the most rigid asceticism, was gradually led to the doctrine of annihilation, which is implicitly involved in Brahmanism. Buddhism was less a revolution than an evolution; and if it was subversive of the ancient religion, it was owing to the persecutions of the Brahmans.

According to the legend, Buddha, a prince of the royal blood of the Cakja, led the brilliant life of a prince destined to a throne, until, one day meeting on his road a sick man, an aged man, and a dead body, the thought seized him with overpowering force of the evils that desolate the world. To solve this lugubrious enigma of evil, he quitted his palace, abandoned his wife and riches, and gave himself up to the most absolute asceticism. It was in vain that he questioned the Brahmans, or the disciples of the Sankya: no light could they cast on the terrible question that absorbed his thoughts. At last, worn out by prolonged fasting, he received, as he sat beneath a fig-tree, the revelation of the truth, and set out in the garb of a beggar to communicate it to the world. He henceforward assumed the name of Cakjamouni, which signifies the hermit of Cakja. His success was slow at first, but he afterwards recruited numerous disciples. He came to die in the country, the throne of which he should have occupied, after having attained annihilation by contemplation. Whatever may have been the part of the presumed founder of Buddhism in the elaboration of the system bearing his name, the system itself is known to us, thanks to the numerous documents accumulated by European science.[1]

---

[1] M. Eug. Bournouf took the exposition he gives of Buddhism from Sanscrit manuscripts, which contain, with the Discourse of Buddha, the discipline and metaphysics of the sect.

It may be defined in one word: It is the system of annihilation. Four principles are first laid down:—1. Suffering exists. 2. It is the lot of all who come into the world. 3. We must rid ourselves of it. 4. This can only be done by science.[1] Now science teaches that suffering arises from sensation, and that sensation is but an illusion of the individual. The individual himself has no real existence, and all his ideas and all his sentiments should be immersed in the void. From all this results the annihilation of the world, which is but one vast mass of suffering.[2] When this absolute void is reached—this Nirvana, as the Buddhists name it—this quietism which consists in rejecting all sensation, all thought, all self-consciousness,—it may be said, 'The terrible night of error is dissipated for my soul; the sun of science is gone; the gates of suffering are closed. I have reached the opposite shore, the celestial shore of Nirvana.' In this way the ocean of tears and blood is dried up, the army of death annihilated. He who does not deviate from this way, escapes the whirl of a new birth and the changes of the world. He can boast that he has annihilated existence for himself—that he has attained liberty, and the cessation of all fear of a new life.

This aspiration towards the void and annihilation, although expressed with singular ardour in Buddhism, was at the root of Brahmanism. It was the first to pronounce a sentence of condemnation on the world, and upon the limited existence of the finite being. From this point of view, redemption for the creature is confounded with death, since evil is in birth itself. To be born again, however superior the degree of being, was to fall under the empire of evil; for it was to enter again into the world of change. To promise immortality to the believer in Indian pantheism, was to promise him an eternity of suffering; for in his eyes there was no

[1] Bournouf. [2] Bournouf.

other suffering, no other misfortune, no other sin, than that of living. Thus was kindled this passion for death, so energetically depicted in the sacred books of the Buddhists: 'It is for this the birds fly through the air, that wild animals fall into snares; for this men perish in combats, struck by the arrow or lance; for this it is that I, in the midst of a multitude of sins, have come so far.' We may attribute a great part of the success of Buddhism to the satisfaction given by it to the thirst for death and annihilation, already developed by Brahmanism. Moreover, it adroitly presented its doctrine under different aspects, reserving to the initiated all that was most arduous and extreme, whilst it was considerably modified in order to adapt it to the mass of its adherents. Buddhism preached charity and humility to the people, and the duty of repressing all violent passions. It thus lowered its standard in order to gain proselytes; and as it presented a striking contrast to the pride of the Brahmans, it gained by its mildness and beneficent action a multitude of disciples. What especially rendered it popular, was its eminently democratic character, which tended to remove the barrier of castes. 'My law, said Buddha, is a law of grace for all.'[1] Besides, its disciple escaped the law of a new birth, and the gradation of merit marked out by the system of castes.

We can understand the attraction such a doctrine must have had for these classes, which had been trampled down and despised by the Brahmans. Notwithstanding its success amongst the people, it was only in the monasteries founded by it that Buddhism was really carried out in all its consequences. The true follower of Buddha is the recluse, who, having shaved his head and beard, and clad himself in yellow vestments, quits his house, full of faith, to enter on the religious life, and begs from place to place.[2] His aim

[1] Bournouf, p. 178.   [2] Bournouf, p. 248.

is to gradually attain to total insensibility. Like the bird born of an egg, he must burst through his shell,[1]—that is to say, completely renounce terrestrial existence, break off every tie, look with equal eye on gold and on a clod of earth, turn his back on existence—on the joys and pleasures of men.[2] He does not live absolutely isolated, but associates with those who partake his sentiments. Vast monasteries receive the Buddhist monks, who, however, do not reside in them, but go from monastery to monastery begging along the road. They passed the degrees of a moral and scientific hierarchy, and rose in proportion to their progress in holiness and true science. Besides the regular monks, there were devotees, who were not subjected to monastic asceticism. Hospitality was abundantly practised in those monasteries, and any infraction of this duty severely punished. The Buddhist form of worship was characterized by extreme simplicity, and was connected with the constant memory of Buddha, whose relics were worshipped in the different convents. Offerings of flowers and perfumes accompanied the prayers addressed to him. There was no sacrifice in this religion. Thus, while Brahminical worship was called Yadjna, or sacrifice, the Buddhist was called Padja, or honour.[3] Buddhism was essentially a proselytizing religion. Placed by its favourite dogma above Nature, which it was its constant aspiration to destroy, it was arrested by none of the distinctions created by birth.

In its eyes, there was no more difference between the people of the various nations than there was amongst the castes. Hence the rapidity of its propagation from its very origin. 'For Bhagavet or the blessed Buddha, say the sacred books, there is no gift so precious as a converted man.'[4] Faithful to this principle, Buddhism

[1] Bournouf, p. 86.
[2] Bournouf 286, 288.
[3] Bournouf 327.
[4] Bournouf 327.

spread with incredible rapidity through India and the adjacent countries. It was led to organize itself, in order the more effectually to defend itself against its persecutors. The monasteries were united by a federative bond, and synods were convoked to regulate dogma. Three synods are mentioned: the first assembled after the death of Buddha; the second, 110 years after; and the third, 400 years later. The canon of the sacred books was revised in these sacred councils. The third revision alone has been handed down.[1] In presence of this formidable invasion of Buddhism, the Brahmans found themselves compelled to modify their religious system. The people had already imposed on them two new divinities: Siva, the successor or counterpart of the ancient Indra, the god of thunder and rainstorms; and Vischnou, the god of the serene sky and of abundant vegetation, the father of rivers, already mentioned in the Rig Veda, and adored on the banks of the Ganges under the image of a lotus. The Brahmans placed these two divinities side by side with Brahma, who continued to be god the creator, whence all emanations proceeded. Vischnou became god the preserver, and Siva god the destroyer. Sarasvati, Lakchmi, and Bhavani were introduced into this cycle as wives of these gods. Thus the Trimurti, or Indian trinity, was constituted. We may fix the completion of this mythological evolution about the year 500 B.C., since there are no traces of it in the sacred books anterior to this date.

But the Indian trinity was never generally adopted. Each of the three great divinities was the object of a special worship, and thus were formed three rival sects. Sivaism recalls the ancient religion of Nature, and the gross dualism of Phœnicia. The followers of Brahma pretend that their god, as god the creator, was a fallen

[1] Bournouf 448.

god, and must expiate by successive incarnations his having diffused himself through matter. But the most important of these sects was that of Vischnou. Considered as god the preserver and benefactor, he was opposed to Buddha. The great heroic poems of India, the *Mahabarata* and the *Ramayana*, were revised in his honour. He is represented as becoming incarnate to succour humanity; and, like Buddha, personifying all excellence.[1]

The perusal of the Ramayana is full of interest. We are carried away by this gorgeous poetry into the heart of the Brahminical world—into the deserts where the anchorites rule by asceticism over the gods themselves, and where, transfigured by macerations, their countenances are illumined as by the sun. The principal end of Vischnou's incarnations is clearly indicated in the following passage: 'Slayer of Madhou,[2] as thou lovest to draw out of affliction unhappy mortals, we, who are plunged in misery, pray to thee, august divinity, be our refuge.' 'Speak,' replies Vischnou, 'what shall I do?' Having heard the words of the ineffable, all the gods answered: 'There is a king named Daçaratha, who has embraced a life of severe penitence; he has even performed the sacrifice of an açwa-medha,[3] because he is childless, and prays Heaven to accord him a son. He is stedfast in piety, praised for his virtues; justice is his character, truth his word. Acquiesce then, O Vischnou, in our demand, and consent to be born as his son. Divided into four parts, deign, O thou who tramplest under foot thy enemies, deign to incarnate thyself in the wombs of his three wives, beautiful as the goddess of beauty.'

---

[1] See Mahabarata, fragments by T. Pavie; Ramayana, Sanscrit poem by Valmiki, translated by Hippolyte Fauche.
[2] Name of an evil spirit.
[3] The açwa-medha is the famous sacrifice of the horse.

Nârâyana[1] the master, imperceptible to the senses, but who then rendered himself visible,—Nârâyana answered the gods who invited him to this heroic avatâra: 'Once incarnate, what would you have me do? and whence comes the terror that troubles you?' To these words of the great Vischnou the gods answered: 'It is the demon Ravana, it is he, Vischnou, this desolation of worlds, it is he inspires us with terror.' 'Take upon you a human body, and draw out this thorn from the world; for none but you, among the inhabitants of heaven, can destroy this sinner. Know that he for a long time imposed on himself the most austere penance, and that he rendered himself agreeable in the eyes of the supreme father of all creatures. Thus the ineffable dispenser of all graces bestowed on him the signal gift of being invulnerable to all creatures, man excepted. Since thus endowed, death, the terrible and sure, cannot reach him except through man, go thou, powerful conqueror of thy enemies, go in human condition and slay him. For this gift, which cannot be resisted, exalts to the highest point the intoxication of his force. This vile being torments the gods and men sanctified by penitence; and although destroyer of sacrifices, lacerator of the sacred writings, enemy of the Brahmans, devourer of men, this incomparable gift saves from death Ravana, the wretched scourge of worlds. He dares to attack kings defended by war-chariots and elephants; others, wounded and routed, are scattered hither and thither before him. 'He has devoured saints, and incessantly in his delirium he takes pleasure in tormenting the seven worlds. As we have learned that he is mortal to the stroke of man,—for he did not deign to speak of him the day that this much-abused favour

---

[1] Nârâyana, the universal soul, one of Vischnou's names, means the spirit *that moves over the primitive waters*. This Sanscrit word naturally recalls the idea and expression of the Bible, 'Et Spiritus Dei ferebatur super aquas.'

was granted him,—enter thou into a human body: thou, who canst scatter thy enemies, cast lifeless at thy feet this proud Ravana, endowed with terrible force, immeasurable pride, the enemy of all ascetics, this worm that gnaws them, this cause of all their groaning."[1] It is curious to find the Ramayana opposing asceticism to asceticism. The struggle between Buddhism and Brahmanism may be reduced to a rivalry of annihilation.

The worship of Vischnou or Chrishna gradually became the most popular worship. Vischnou was the protective divinity, who, in order to succour man, lowered himself to his level—a god drawn near, not a god far off. Nothing can be more absurd than to compare his incarnations with that of Christ. They are, by their multiplicity alone, tinctured with the pantheistic idea. The human personality is destitute of reality, since it is taken up and laid down as a veil or mask, with which the divinity invested himself for a moment. Moreover, the degradation of the god was carried too far. He descended to evil, and participated in human corruption. Accordingly, his worship among the people is attended with gross, impure rites, possessing nothing moralizing in it. Finally, it is in its popular form a return to the divinities of Nature.[2]

The system of Joga, introduced into the Mahabarata, counterbalanced Buddhism by making from it copious borrowings. Vischnou, as the eternal soul of the world and emanation of Brahma, was opposed to matter. Man should seek to annihilate himself in him. In ordinary life, he is to be honoured by moderation, disinterestedness, and charity.[3] But it is in the Pouranas especially,

---

[1] Ramayana.
[2] See on this subject an interesting article by M. Theod. Pavie, in the *Revue des deux Mondes* of January 1858.
[3] Dunker, t. ii., p. 243.

the date of which is posterior, that Vischnouism is fully developed. The *Bhagavat-Pouranas*, although the most recent of Indian poems, bears evident trace of ancient pantheism. Bhagavat, or Vischnou the Blessed, is the god of gods, 'the cause and the effect, the soul and sovereign, of the universe.'[1] But this material universe has no reality. Nature is beautiful, admirably beautiful; but is not the less the eternal Maïa, the false delusion, the perfidious courtezan, whose embrace is to be fled from. She appeared in a wood, whose trees were covered with variegated flowers and yellow buds, the most beautiful of women. Her figure seemed as though it must dissolve while she stepped with nimble foot hither and thither, sweet as a tender bud. Her large eyes resembled the restless stars; the curls of her hair adorned her face; her charming hand gathered up her drapery. The magic charm that surrounded her shed trouble in the universe.[2] This enchanting Maïa is material life, the misery and slavery of man. Perfection consists in escaping from it by asceticism, and asceticism should be carried to the point to which Buddhism brings it. 'Action makes man live; inaction secures him immortality.' Let the recluse who sees truth sacrifice illusion in the consciousness he has of the spirit. Inactive, let him repose in the bosom of the spirit, and let him restore to their order the different elements of which his body is composed: let earth return to water, water to light, light to wind, wind to ether, ether into the higher principle of personality, personality into intelligence, intelligence into nature, and nature into the immutable spirit,—that, thus freed from duality, he becomes extinct like to a fire whose aliment is spent.

To lead men to this life of the spirit, was the purpose

---

[1] Bhagavat-Pouranas, trad. Bournouf, liv. iii., c. vii.
[2] Liv. viii., c. xii.

for which Vischnou became incarnate. His incarnations are multiplied to infinitude, because physical life is without reality and individuality, without value. At one moment he appears under the form of a man; next, under that of a fish, then of a wild boar, a lion; sometimes under that of a dwarf or of a hero. The supreme being assumes or quits noble or mean bodies, which have the attributes of heart, senses, elements: he does so by his own power, remaining distinct from these bodies.[1] In those incarnations he is like an actor who changes his costume.[2] The object of these incarnations is plainly indicated in the following passage:—The uncreated being abandons the body that he used in order to disencumber the earth of the burthen that overwhelmed it, as we use one thorn to draw out another.[3] The thorn is material life, which Vischnou apparently takes on himself that he may the more effectually destroy it.

Thus Vischnouism arrives at the sinister conclusion of Buddhism—death, annihilation: so fatally do all the religious ideas of India lead to the same conclusion. In vain Nature spreads out her grand magnificence: her splendid beauty is but a deceptive veil. The follower of Brahma, of Vischnou, or of Buddha, has pierced through it with pitiless eye, and seen the perdition it covers. We cannot better describe this sombre loathing of life than by quoting the most poetical of the allegories of the Bhagavat-Pouranas, which, with admirable art, reproduces the enchantments of the Indian forest as the brilliant image of human life, but mingled with dark symbols that recall the malediction. ' Led by illusion on a difficult road, the caravan of souls wanders in the forest of existence, thirsting for happiness, but unable to find it. Five brigands (the senses) pillage it.

[1] Pouranas, Bournouf, liv. vii., c. ii.
[2] Liv. viii., c. viii.   [3] Liv. i., c. xv.

Assailed in a forest, entangled with bindweed, grass, and bushes, the traveller flies, carried on by his desires. Tormented by the cries of invisible crickets, which torture his ears, and the voice of the screech-owl, that agitates his heart, he stops, exhausted by hunger, near poisonous trees, or rushes towards water which proves a mirage. Now wishing to ascend a mountain, he steps through thorns and stones, and stops at last, worn out. Here he is seized by reptiles. Now seeking honey, he is stung by the bees that produce it. Disputing with his companions, losing the goods they take from him, he falls down on the road overwhelmed with grief. Leaving behind those who fall, the caravan marches on, dragging in its course all those who are born. Not one ever goes back on his steps. Now the traveller clings to the branches of the bindweed, attracted by the songs of the birds hidden within. He carries his chain without hope of breaking it. No one knows the term of his voyage."[1] Evidently, under such conditions, the best that can be done is to break the chain one's self; and this leads us to the essential principle of the religion of India—asceticism and annihilation.

Is not this the final word of the religion of Nature, the conclusion of its dualism? It is no longer suffering which is the evil, as in Phœnicia, or sterility and destruction, as in Egypt, or physical and moral darkness, as in Persia. It is the world; it is creation as creation; it is the universe as opposed to its principle; it is the ever-changing diversity of life as opposed to the eternal and immutable. Thus, whilst in its first stage, in Phœnicia, the devise of the religion of Nature was, Enjoy; in its second, in Egypt, it was, Endure; in its third, in Persia, Combat and live; in its last, Die and become extinct. Evidently the cycle of the religions of Nature is filled up; but its influence on earth is im-

[1] Bhagav.-Pour. liv. i., c. xiii.

mortal; and we shall see later on by what large breach Oriental asceticism penetrated into the heart of the Christian Church.[1]

THE PELASGIC MYTHOLOGY.

Whilst in the vast monarchies—framed in the image of surrounding nature, that sprung up in those immense plains of Asia which are intersected by lofty mountains, and where none but the king rose above the level—religion never got beyond pantheism, sometimes monstrous, sometimes grand, but always fatalistic, because affirming Nature's triumph over man, the latter vindicated himself in a less favoured land—in one in which, being nearly encircled by the sea, man was constantly solicited to movement and action, and brought into the great current of ideas and civilisation. Bounded on the north by the Eastern Alps, the southern coasts of Greece are bathed by the Mediterranean, in a latitude nearly the same as that of Gibraltar, and facing one of the most fertile provinces of Africa. Separated by the sea from Italy, Africa, and Asia, it is linked to them by its islands. Its climate is temperate; and though it promises no excessive fertility, it amply repays man's labour. 'The Greeks,' says Thucydides, 'have learned from their fathers that they must pay the price of labour and effort in order to obtain any advantage.'[2] The interior of the country presents an animated variety: mountains of moderate height, and smiling valleys; while, in the distance, an infinitely undulating line of sea-coast forms fine natural harbours. It is not, then, surprising to find in Greece a blending of nomadic and agricultural life, and especially a great maritime development.

[1] Lassen, in the first part of his 3d vol., has treated this last subject in detail.
[2] Maury's Hist. of Greece.

If there is a fact acquired by cotemporary science, it is the community of origin of the first inhabitants of Greece and of the Aryans of Iran, whose traces we have followed in the great empires founded on the banks of the Euphrates and of the Ganges. The analogy of Greek and Sanscrit is established. The words most in common use in agricultural life are the same in both, proving that before their separation the family of the two peoples had already attained a certain degree of civilisation.[1] We know the *route* followed by the first migration which gave to Greece its first inhabitants and the germs of its civilisation. These primitive inhabitants were called Pelasgians, or wandering people; and the name is applied to all Aryan colonies before the properly called historic periods. The religious and national centre of these nomadic and warrior tribes appears to have been Dodona. It was there, according to some writers, that they took the name of Hellens, which was that of their priests, called *seers* or *illuminated*, because they adored the god of heaven. The designation was then extended to the whole people, and their country called the country of light. According to other writers, the *Hellens*, like the Pelasgians, were a tribe of Aryan origin, who drove the first migration towards the coasts and islands.[2] However this may be, it is certain that the Pelasgians and Hellens belonged to the same family, and were the first colonizers of Greece. This latter name, which was chiefly used by the Romans, was, according to Hesiod,

[1] Sheep among the Indians is *avis*; among the Greeks, *oïs*. The ox among the first is *gaus*; among the second, *bous*. House in Sanscrit is *damas*; in Greek is *domos*. Door in Sanscrit is *drara*; in Greek, *thura*. Vessel in Sanscrit is *naus* and *plara*; in Greek, *néus* and *ploion*.—DUNKER. *Maury's Hist. of the Religions of Greece.*

[2] The first opinion is held by Dunker (vol. iii., p. 13); the second by M. Maury (vol. i., p. 38). The last derives the word Hellens from εἶλυς, *marsh*, which refers to the marshy nature of their first dwelling-place. Dunker derives the word from ἕλη, signifying splendour of the sun.

derived from one of the fathers of the race, and had been given to a locality in the neighbourhood of Dodona.

The Hellens were divided into four families:—1*st*, The Achaians, or the good; 2*d*, the Eolians, or the mixed, formed of a mixture of different tribes; 3*d*, the Ionians; 4*th*, the Dorians. The two last form the two great Greek races, distinct in national genius and in dialect. The first, driven back by some unknown migration, inhabited chiefly the coasts of Elis and the islands of the Archipelago, and sent colonies into Asia Minor. It was a maritime race, and eminently susceptible to civilisation, but somewhat enervated by contact with the East. The second, after having sent colonies into Asia, ultimately established itself in the Peloponnesus, and there developed into a masculine, energetic people. It was at a later period that these decided national distinctions became apparent, when the character of each race was fashioned and moulded by events. It did not, however, prevent the formation of a common nationality.

It is certain that in the Pelasgic period the different tribes, notwithstanding their dispersion, held in substance the same religion, which was that they carried with them from the table-lands of Iran, and which is expressed in the fresh brilliant poetry of the hymns of the *Rig Veda*. It may have been slightly diversified in its passage from one tribe to another. The maritime divinities occupied amongst the Ionians the rank occupied by the solar divinities amongst the Dorians, but both professed the same simple pantheism that deifies whatever fascinates the childish imagination of humanity at a stage inferior to its religious development. The deep, luminous sky; the fertile earth; the now beneficent, the now terrible sea; the refreshing springs; the trees in their rich foliage; the victorious struggle of the sun against darkness;—such were the objects of this primitive worship; such were the varied aspects of this undulating divinity, still too much confounded with the life of Nature for the different types personifying it to be clearly distinguished one from the other. The fundamental idea of the divinity amongst the Pelasgians, as amongst the Aryans of the Indus, was that of light, splendour, as is indicated by the root of the word god in the two languages.[1] The supreme god in the old Pelasgic religion was Zeus, or the Jupiter of Dodona, identical with the Jupiter of Arcadia, the brilliant, luminous god. It corresponds with the Indra of the Rig Veda. Like him, he launches the thunderbolts and the lightning; like him, he dwells in pure air upon the tops of mountains; like him, he gathers the rain and produces the water in the fountains of the valleys of Dodona. Indra was the divine hero who fought against darkness and the clouds. Jupiter combats the malevolent powers of the black Tartarus, or the Titans, which are the spirits of darkness. The militant side of the divinity, so marked in the *Rig Veda*, reappears with singular energy in Pallas, the terrible virgin, the blue-eyed. She combats in the midst of the tempest. It was she that destroyed Gorgo, the horrible serpent,—emblem of the darkness of a stormy sky. Daughter of Jupiter, she is goddess of Athens. The Pelasgic Apollo is in all points like her. He also combats darkness, typified by the serpent Python, which he destroys with his victorious dart. This recalls to us the Vedic hymns which describe the triumph of Indra over the serpent Ahi, emblem of the cloud which spreads itself over the sky. 'He struck Ahi,' we read in the Rig Veda; 'he poured the waters on the earth, and let loose the torrents from the celestial mountains. He took the thunderbolt, which he launched forth as a

---

[1] *Deva*, in Sanscrit; *Daiw*, in the Avesta; *Theos*, in Greek.

dart ; and where his hand struck, the charms of the enchanter were destroyed. Thou seemest to give birth to the sun, the sky, to the dawn. The enemy disappears at your approach.'[1] Indra, after having rent the cloud, pours fertilizing rain, and lets loose the mountain torrents. Apollo is also the god of the Muses, who at first personified the sacred fountains. He is the god of Parnassus and Helicon, of the pure streams hidden in Olympus, where poets, his favourites, come to drink inspiration. The nymphs were another personification of the rivers, and filled the parts of subordinate divinities. The Dioscures, Castor and Pollux, sons of Zeus, heroes and tutelar divinities of sailors, dissipating the tempest by their prayers, appearing on white horses or golden chariots, were luminous divinities like the preceding. They are identical with the two first rays of the dawn, adored on the Indus under the name of Açvim, mounted on cars swifter than the wind. Hera or Juno, Artemisia, Selene, are feminine types of the luminous divinity. All seem variations of the primitive mythological theme.

If heaven was deified in the Rig Veda, the earth was not less so. 'They form the immortal couple—the two great parents of the world.'[2] The worship of the second primordial divinity, the earth, was more developed among the Pelasgic tribes than amongst the Indians : they thus began giving their own impress to the worship they carried with them from Asia. It is true, in a country like Greece, the earth, fertilized and moistened by the sweat and labour of man, was dearer to him than it can be in countries which are either barren as a desert, or so fertile as to need no culture. The Pelasgians worshipped the earth under the name of

[1] Rig Veda. See the interesting developments given by M. Maury to the Asiatic myth of the Serpent, compared with the Greek myth (p. 130, 144).
[2] Rig Veda viii. 2, 4.

Dêmêter, the nursing mother. She was a venerable divinity, a chaste matron, having nothing in common with the impure goddesses of Asia Minor. Rhea appears to have been the Demeter or Ceres of Crete. She was the wife of Saturn, who was the male type of the earthly divinities, Hermes or Mercury, who is often confounded with Pan. Aristæus or Priapus was the god of flocks and of animal fecundity. His name recalls that of the Vedic god Sarameyas, charged to assemble together in the heavens the flocks of fertilizing clouds, dispersed by the breath of the evil demons. The Pelasgians placed him on the earth, and made him the god of shepherds and messenger of Jupiter. The sea, which surrounded Greece on all sides, and whose varying aspects constantly fixed the attention of the inhabitants of the coasts, necessarily occupied a more prominent place in Pelasgic mythology than it did in the Indian myths. The god of the sea, Poseïdon or Neptune, becomes a sort of maritime Indra, more terrible and less helpful than the other, but possessing irresistible power. He sustains the earth, which he shakes at his pleasure. The wild Bacchus, god of the vine and of foaming wine, reminds us of *Soma*, the Vedic divinity personifying libations, and, in general, the liquid element in Nature. Agni, the god of fire, celebrated in the Rig Veda, we find in Vulcan, in Prometheus, and in Vesta, according as we consider volcanic fire, industrial fire which melts and fuses metals, or the fire of the domestic hearth. Such are the principal divinities of the ancient Pelasgic religion, brought, as we have seen, from the Asiatic cradle of the race into Greece, where they became modified in accordance with the new aspects of the country colonized by the Hellens. The divinities of earth and sea assume, if not the preponderance, at least a most conspicuous place. The winds or harpies, the high mountains, the souls of the dead, were all secondary objects of worship, admitted by the Pelasgic as well as the Vedic religion.

Nothing can be simpler or more nude than the worship established by the Pelasgians. Instead of temples, they had sacred enclosures for sacrifice, and grottoes and woods dedicated to certain divinities that were supposed to have made them their dwelling-place. The deep shadows of oak-groves formed the sanctuary of Dodona, and laurel-trees the temple of Delphi. Altars were reared out of the sod; and the gods represented by symbolical stones, sometimes square, sometimes lengthened into columns, or by coarsely carved pieces of wood. The Pelasgians did not confine their offerings to libations and the first-fruits of the field. Feeling the element of terror there is in Nature, they sacrificed to it human victims. Faith in oracles, or the endeavour to find out by material signs the will of the gods, appears at this early period to have taken root amongst these ancient inhabitants of Greece. They had doubtless received it from their fathers previous to their first migrations. Art at this remote period was clumsy and massive, hardly deserving the name, being applied to the useful rather than the beautiful, the type and proportions of which were then unknown. Walls, called cyclopian, composed of huge blocks of irregular polygon form, are the sole vestiges of those distant times. Their gigantic ruins bear the marks of primitive barbarism, and of the extraordinary but undisciplined force which characterized the childhood of humanity.

It is difficult to distinguish the historic groundwork concealed beneath the legends of the heroic age of Greece, on account of the additions and embellishments made by the imagination of its poets. Two of these legends evidently mark the important phases of the pre-historic period. The war of the Lapithæ and Centaurs (the latter, half man half horse, intended no doubt to represent the savage dwellers on the mountains) records the daily warfare that must have been waged between the pacific inhabitants of the plains of Thessaly and the nomadic tribes encamped on the adjacent mountains.

In order to defend themselves, arose the necessity for the former to build towns. The Lapithæ, whose name signifies constructor of walls, were in this way led to lay the basis of a more stable civilisation. Thus, about 1300 years before Christ, were built the towns of Orchomenes, Thebes, Ilissus, Argos, Mycenæ, and ancient Corinth.

The second of these heroic legends which throws some light over these dim times, is that concerning Theseus, the Athenian hero. He is said to have been the first to unite into one nation the small principalities of Attica. Whatever part he may have taken in this event, the fact is in itself of great importance; since it prepared the advent of that city, which was destined to reflect such glory upon Greece, and which pre-eminently represented its genius. But Theseus did not content himself with his triumphs in Attica; he slew the savage monster of Crete, the Minotaur, to which the Athenians had been condemned to make a yearly sacrifice of the flower of their youth. The historical fact underlying this myth is evidently the triumph of Greek genius over Phœnician civilisation; the latter, essentially maritime and conquering in its character, had struck root in the islands contiguous to Attica, in Cythera and in Crete. The female divinity of Western Asia, Aphrodite or Astarte, was worshipped there. The female warriors, the Amazons, were the priestesses consecrated to the service of this cruel and impure Asiatic goddess, who bore also the name of Ma. The Phœnicians had imported this worship into Athens, as well as into Thessaly, Thebes, and Orchomenes. Not far from this latter city, on Mount Laphystion, Moloch was worshipped under the name of Jupiter Laphystios, and human sacrifices offered to him. The Minotaur, to which Athens had to pay its annual cruel tribute, also typified this abominable divinity. Theseus, conqueror of the Minotaur and Amazons, was the ideal type of the Greek mind triumphant over the Asiatic, and achiever of that independence without which there could be no development for Greece. The cycle so rich in myths concerning the Trojan war, shows us the Greek genius pursuing Asiatic genius on its own ground, and establishing its pre-eminence.

DEVELOPMENT OF HELLENIC HUMANISM.

The two great events of the heroic age were the construction of cities, or the foundation of the different states of primitive Greece, and the victorious reaction of the Hellens against Asiatic pantheism. However great the obscurity spread over this period, it is certain it must have been a time of incessant warfare between all those small states. In the struggle, Greek nationality was forged, and powerful individualities, whose memory has been preserved in the national myths, then began to reveal the grandeur of the human character. Heroism laid the foundations of that bold apotheosis of humanity which was so long celebrated on the radiant summits of Olympus. Thus, when, about the year 1104 B.C., the Dorian invasion caused a movement of the populations, and planted at the same time the two great Hellenic races in the countries most favourable to their genius, all was ripe for the definitive advent of the national religion of Greece. The ancient religion of Nature was to be effaced by the worship of deified heroes. The Ionian race, owing to its more precocious development, stimulated by its colonies in Asia Minor, was about to give birth to that inimitable poet who, while giving a voice to the aspirations of the Hellenic conscience, created in the same breath the poetry and religion of his country; rather, let us say, the religion of poetry and art, for it was that alone that Greece ever seriously practised.

No trace has been found of any really literary works existing before Homer. 'Many centuries must have succeeded each other,' says Ottfried Müller, 'before speech found wings, and the first hymn was chanted.' Poetry was checked in its flight by the religion of Nature, which was oppressive to human sentiment. Strange that it should have been the mourning of earth in winter that first moved them to song, and that the first hymn sung in Greece should be a lamentation. It was called the *Linus*, from its referring to the tragical end of a demigod of this name, dying in the bloom of youth. It symbolized, like Adonis and Atys, the termination of the beautiful season, and the moment when winter began. The first accent of the Greek muse—the muse that was afterwards so serene—was an 'Alas!' 'Alas! Linus,'—thus began the mournful song. The *Pæan* was a song in honour of Apollo. Funeral or hymeneal songs, choruses or songs accompanying the dance, oracles in verse, sum up the poetry of these ancient times. It was essentially sacerdotal poetry, which, far from being a play of imagination, was a prescribed and monotonous ceremony. Its cradle was Thessaly, where flowed the sacred fountains of the muses. This sacerdotal subjection, perpetual in the East, did not continue long in Greece. The free fertile genius of the Hellenic race was roused during the heroic age. Grand figures stood out from a grand background, and the memory of the exploits of those heroes created a truly human ideal in the minds of their descendants. There was no longer that sterile bewilderment inspired by the spectacle of the irresistible forces of Nature. They had caught a glimpse of a higher force, the power of intelligence and freedom, which had been so often exhibited in the struggles that attended the formation of the different states. This power, concentrated on a narrower field, bore a deeper impress of the individual character than it did in the revolutions of the vast empires of Asia. It matters little that the victories of Hercules and Perseus belong to fable: the sentiment revealed by these myths is not the less an historical fact, surpassing in importance all others, since it was this sentiment that moulded Greece, its history as well as its religion. The idea of the hero—that is to say, the conception of a human ideal—was the landmark dividing the West from the East,—the land of light, the enchanting land of Hellas from that vast empire prostrate under the inflexible law of Nature. The wakening up of this human sentiment first manifested itself in the freedom of poetry, which broke away from the sacerdotal yoke, and became lay and warlike. The poet no longer confines his song to the praises of the divinity: he sings the glory of heroes; he sings at festivals when the cup circulates from hand to hand, and joy is in all hearts. The rhapsodist succeeded to the sacred bard. He becomes the harmonious echo of national traditions, and has a place assigned him at all solemn banquets and public ceremonies.

The Greeks loved to hear unfolded their grand heroic legend, and prizes were awarded to him who best succeeded. In this way, with the praises of the great deeds of their ancestors ever sounding in their ears, the descendants of those heroes conceived an enthusiasm for them which soon became worship; rather, let us say, it reformed the ancient worship.

The names or works of none of those early rhapsodists have come down to us. Their memory was eclipsed by the immortal bard who, 900 B.C., uniting the splendour of the Asiatic genius to the harmony of the Greek, constructed in two incomparable poems the real Pantheon of Hellenism—a temple of heroes built with dazzling marble, and inundated with all the joyous brightness of a morning sun. The Iliad and Odyssey are a complete apotheosis of humanity, or rather of Greek nationality. While the Aryans of India strove to strip their gods of all individuality, and were not satisfied until they had immersed them in the fathomless abyss of Brahminical pantheism, the Aryans of the West, starting from the same point, endeavoured with a firm hand to characterize the features of their first divinities, to reject what was vague, to give precise outlines,—to raise them, in fine, out of the impersonal life of physical nature to the rank and dignity of personal free beings. Homer, in attributing to the gods the qualities of heroes, was the most powerful religious reformer of his race; rather, he was its most admirable interpreter in the evolution accomplished by it after the heroic age. The life of the gods is represented by him as human life in its highest power. Olympus is an ideal Greece: the gods form a council of Hellenic kings, of which Jupiter is the Agamemnon. He no longer aims, as in the Pelasgic mythology, which was but an echo of the East, at symbolizing the ever-varying aspects of Nature, but rather gives a living picture of history, or the development of the free spontaneous forces. Jupiter is no longer the Vedic Indra, the sun vanquishing darkness, but a great king, which we may figure to ourselves seated on a throne, sceptre in hand. He deliberates, acts, interferes directly in man's affairs. It is the same with Juno, who, as his wife, has the sentiments of a woman and queen.

Minerva is an entirely intellectual divinity. The brightness of her blue eye is not simply the image of a cloudless azure sky, but is also the reflection of thought. She is the wise protecting divinity, who introduces order into the combat. It is the same with the other gods. The most brilliant Homeric creation is that of Venus, the exquisite daughter of the sea, image of soft beauty and bewitching grace. If Homer's gods were idealized human personalities, they had all our passions and weaknesses. They have their favourites and their enemies; sometimes they fight in one camp, sometimes in the other. They are susceptible of hatred, jealousy, sensual passion. They have neither omniscience nor omnipotence. They are taller in stature and more perfect in beauty than man, but their nature is the same; their body needs nourishment, their blood flows at the touch of the sword or lance; and if their cry shakes the earth, still it proves they were liable to pain. All were subject to the mysterious power of destiny. If they had the weaknesses of humanity, they had also its grandeur; for on one side—the moral—man touches God. Nor is this wanting in the Homeric mythology. The moral sentiments that preside at the constitution of the city and of the family we find amongst the gods. Jupiter is the great shepherd of the temple, the chief *par excellence*, the father of his subjects. With his awful frown he makes earth tremble, but he is appeased by the prayers of suppliants. He is the god of justice, of the domestic hearth; the protector of the exile, of the beggar; the vigilant guardian of hospitality. The religion of Nature never conceived this moral ideal; and, notwithstanding the gross legends that obscure it, yet it announces an undoubted progress. On the other side, courage, fidelity, frankness, respect of right, all those virtues which we may term elementary, are held up to honour.

The trials of Ulysses, the attachment of his wife and son, the whole drama of the Odyssey, in its touching simplicity, exalt the moral idea. We must confess, however, that these divinities, so constantly compromised in strange adventures, and so passionately mixed up in the quarrels of men, favoured impiety rather than the sentiment of veneration for sacred things. Such gods could only inspire the fear of a slave, or the baseness of a courtier seeking to buy the favour of a king more powerful but not better than himself. If the mythological evolution of Greece still needed a long purifying process before reaching its culminating point, yet had it made two important conquests. The gods appear as free personal beings, and, in spite of what is still impure and incoherent about them, the moral idea begins to manifest itself. The ancient personifications of Nature, which were numerous in the Pelasgic religion, were retained, and the ancient myths adopted; but were bound together as by the zone of Venus, of which the Iliad speaks, that image of light and delicate grace. In passing through the imagination of Homer, they were steeped in the freshest and most brilliant poetry—poetry that harmonized all it touched. Instead of the immense confused poems of Indian pantheism, we have a poem in which everything is linked together, and the parts of which form one harmonious whole. We are no longer in presence of grotesque creations, uniting the most heterogeneous elements. The types are moulded in the proportions of beauty, and are drawn with perfect clearness, introducing us to a world at once real and ideal. Heroes and gods move, speak, and act under our eyes. It seems as if the light and golden atmosphere of Greece breathed through this radiant poetry, such is the serenity and freshness of its colouring, such the fidelity and living splendour with which it reproduces the first dawn of the Hellenic race in the midst of combats and banquets. In the Iliad and Odyssey we breathe, as it were. the candour and health of childhood; but it is the childhood of the finest genius enraptured with the spectacle spread before its eyes, yet mastering it by thought. The æsthetic value of Homer's poems is more than a literary fact; it is a religious fact, for it announces a triumph over the religion of Nature.

But this perfect poetic creation has one sombre side. Earth only is beautiful: it is the present life only that is filled with the gifts of the gods. Hades, or the realms of the dead, inspires horror and fear. Achilles, the ideal hero, declares he would rather till the ground than reign in pale Elysium, carrying about him the regret of all he once possessed—glory, love, and power. Within Tartarus, the prison shut, with triple ramparts and gates of iron, are the Titans and Saturn, where the guilty hear the inexorable gates close down on them for ever. This melancholy view of the future life is the great imperfection of the Homeric religion,—we may say, of that of all Greece. We shall see that it was the desire of lighting up with a ray of hope these sombre regions which gave rise to the Mysteries, and to which they owed their success. Worship, as Homer described it, retained still its primitive simplicity: the priestly office was exercised by kings and by fathers of the family; and if there were priests and soothsayers, they did not form an exclusive caste. Libations, prayers, and sacrifices, intended to appease the anger of the gods by inviting them to sumptuous banquets, and offering what man most prized, constituted the rites of this worship, which was celebrated on altars placed on wooded hills. Rude temples now began to be reared.

Hellenism underwent its first purification in the hands of Hesiod. While Homer represents the brilliant, plastic, Ionian genius, Hesiod belongs to the severer and less flexible Dorian type. 'We shall not find in him,' says Ottfried Müller, 'the young imagination of Homer.

which painted the heroic age with such grace and splendour. Hesiod looked at human life with a melancholy eye. He did not, like the first, move in a world of imagination, but within the circle of toiling life, as his poem, " Works and Days," proves.'

We also find in Hesiod the influence of the philosophic poetry which had just appeared at Milet. His myths are essentially metaphysical, and his poems bear the trace of the mythological crisis which the Hellenic conscience had passed through in rising from the religion of Nature to that of humanity. The Titans represent the old religion; whilst the Jupiter of Hesiod, the young and conquering god, symbolizes the new evolution and the advent of humanism. Yet Hesiod eloquently expresses his regret of the past—' Would that I had not been born in the hard age of iron!'

The ancient gods appear superior to the new, although the latter indicate the progress of the moral idea. It is that the moral idea, powerfully excited, found it hard to adjust itself with the impure alloy that tainted the Homeric divinities. Conscience, forgetting that its first yoke was far more ignominious, flies back and bows before divinities that distance renders respectable. This was the eternal inconsistency in Greece, and one of the causes of the development of the Mysteries, which were a return to the old gods—to the gods of the earth and Hades, the elder brothers of the Titans. The moral idea is placed in bright relief by Hesiod. The wife of Jupiter is, not Juno, but Metis, or the Mind. Themis, or Justice, is also united to him, and by her he becomes father of the Fates, who were moral powers. Justice, he says, always ends in being triumphant in human affairs; and if her way is steep, if the gods placed sweat and pain in the path of virtue, the road grows easier along the heights.' Such words show how real

¹ Opera et Dies.

the progress made in the interval between Homer and Hesiod. It is still more evident in the period that followed, which extends to the reign of Alexander, embracing the time of the fullest maturity and the richest bloom of Hellenic civilisation. Everything contributed to prepare the way for this epoch, when Greece really attained the ideal she had proposed to herself. Man, for the first time in Paganism, arrived at the consciousness of his individuality, of his moral value as a free being. The democracy had almost everywhere replaced monarchy; the city governed itself; and as long as patriotism predominated, the Greek intellect derived fresh impulse from these new institutions. The constant contact of citizens amongst themselves, the agitations of the agora, the intestine struggles, and competition of city with city,—all these causes combined, favoured the growth of the national genius. The war with Persia, in which the East and West strove for pre-eminence, confirmed the triumph of Hellenism, and gave to it the legitimate exultation of victorious patriotism. Herodotus relates that, at the battle of Salamis, the phantom of a woman was seen to pass through the Athenian galleys, crying, Forward! This woman may be supposed to have been the genius, the soul of Greece, urging on towards their glorious destinies the descendants of heroes. Real heroism succeeded to legendary heroism. Miltiades and Themistocles inscribed with their swords an historical Iliad, almost as grand as the other, and which certainly flowed from it; for the genius of Homer had fashioned this handful of warriors, before whom retired the innumerable army of the Great King.

The Persian war had, besides, another result: it gave a centre and focus to Western civilisation. Athens, which had served the national cause with such courage and success, became the intellectual metropolis of Greece. It was admirably fit for this position. The

Athenians possessed the facile, brilliant genius of the Ionian race; but they were Ionians of Europe, and consequently endowed with greater vigour than those of Asia Minor.

Athens was placed in the most favourable conditions for the cultivation and perfecting of the Greek intellect. The beauty of its situation inspired its inhabitants with a deep enthusiasm, of which we find the expression in the famous chorus of Œdipus at Colonna. Its enchanting valleys 'are embellished, under the dew of heaven, with the richest vegetation, crown of the great goddesses: there the olive tree, with its ever-verdant foliage, grows; the murmuring fountains pour their inexhaustible waters along the fertile plains; and Aphrodite, with her golden zone, seems each moment rising out of the sparkling sea which bathes the city, and which heaves beneath the incessant oars of the boats that fly in pursuit of the Nereids. The chorus of the Muses never forsakes it.' This last stroke of the great poet recalls the chief glory of Athens. Eloquence, poetry, art, history, philosophy, reached under Pericles a degree of perfection we shall never see again; for nowhere else shall we find humanity endowed with such richness of youth, or with such wonderful gifts. But, if Athens was the centre of Hellenic culture, Athens never altogether absorbed it; each race furnished its contingent; and the Dorian genius united with the Ionian to increase the glory of their common country. A rapid glance at the history of literature and art during this period will enable us to follow the progressive development of Greece, and to comprehend the development of its religious conscience.

The epopée was long the only poetic form cultivated in Greece. Consecrated to the glory of heroes, and reproducing constantly the same cycle of legends, transmitted from rhapsodist to rhapsodist like a tradition, it was adapted to a period when human personality was imperfectly developed; for the epopée after Homer, when it passed from the greatest of poets to imitators, was essentially impersonal. As soon as individualism, fostered by democratic institutions, conquered its rights, a new form was created, in which the sentiments and impressions of the poet had fuller play: this was the lyric form. Tyrtæus and Simonides allowed their hearts to speak in the elegies they composed; and Archilochus employed his terrible iambics as a weapon of vengeance. The individual character is still more pronounced in the Lesbian poetry, such as we find it in Sappho and Anacreon,—a consuming fire in the heart of the first, a fine brilliant light and a voluptuous playfulness in the second. But it was the Dorian race that gave Pindar, the Homer of lyrists, to Greece. Pindar, the Bœotian poet, was the singer of all Greece, more than had been his predecessors Alcman, Stesichore, Ibichus. 'He belongs,' says Ottfried Müller, 'to that age of the Greek people which we may characterize as the full vigour of youth and the beginning of maturity, in which practical energy and the thirst for intense activity were combined, as they had been at no other epoch, with moral and æsthetic culture." Pindar was filled with the great Hellenic idea of the hero, of the Greek ideal. He reverts to it over and over again in his odes. It was, he says, a divinity that the people should worship. He never tires of going back to the heroic age; and the best homage he can render the victors in the Olympic games is to remind them of their heroic ancestors, and to celebrate their exploits. It is because they resemble those heroes that their bark has skimmed the last limit of bliss. Pindar thus effectively contributed to define clearly the fundamental creed of the Greek religion. Nor did he less contribute

[1] Ottfried Müller, t. i., p. 139. See also a fine passage from M. Villemain on Pindar (*Correspondent*, August 1857).

to purify it by exalting the idea of the divinity. He describes Jupiter as a just, wise god—'the blessed whom the souls of the just sing.' The judgment he passes on human life is profound: he recognises the misery and brevity 'of this dream of a shade,' attributing its misery to pride, and its fleeting joy to the benevolence of the gods. 'A god,' he says, 'is in all our joys.'

The advent of the great dramatic poetry coincides with the complete triumph of Hellenism over the religion of Nature. The drama is not possible as long as man is held to be the slave and sport of natural forces. While this notion prevails, there can be but one personage on the stage—Nature. All that art can then do, is to paint the regular revolutions of Nature in symbols more or less expressive, such as those of Adonis and Osiris. But it is otherwise when human personality comes into action; henceforth the chief interest is fixed on its destiny. It comes forth in all its solemn grandeur, and with it we are ushered into the moral world. But into this, Paganism never fully penetrated, held back as it was by the half-broken chains of dualism. The tragedy of the Greeks, like their religion, was still impregnated with the fundamental idea of the religions of Nature—irresistible fatality, the mysterious *fatum*, the Egyptian sphynx, that disturbed the harmony and serenity of Hellenism; but we are made to feel that it is upon a moral creature, partly conscious of his liberty, that this fatality weighs. It is this contrast between the grandeur of man, such as Æschylus and Sophocles portrayed him, and the wretchedness of his destiny, that constitutes the great pathos of these ancient tragedies. But even here all is not abandoned to fatality; it is invariably some latent crime that arms her avenging hand. The moral idea is still wrapped in obscurity, but it transpierces it with its radiance, and at times escapes altogether, appearing in its own serene beauty.¹

Æschylus is the great lyrist of tragedy. With him the chorus occupies the chief place. His nervous coloured language, condensing a whole picture into a metaphor, a long despair into an imprecation, is the inflexible instrument of a daring and almost Titanic genius. His national dramas, which, according to his own expression, breathe the breath of Mars, are filled with the martial enthusiasm that throbbed in every Greek heart on the morrow of the victory over the Persians. His religious dramas initiate us into the struggles and torments of the conscience, when placed between an ancient religion which becomes idealized because only seen in the past, and a new religion which, though in itself superior, is yet unsatisfying. His tragedy, entitled the *Eumenides*, is especially remarkable in this respect. We hear the complaints of the old divinities against the young new god Apollo. They pour forth savage imprecations against Jupiter, who held in chains old Saturn. Personifying the terrors of conscience, they protest in its name against the purely æsthetic religion of Olympus.

Is not this also the deep meaning of the strange sublime drama of the chained Prometheus? The old Titan's comforters are those who have been vanquished by Jupiter, from old Ocean to the nymph Io, the innocent object of his fury; and we note his mysterious prophecy of a new god, whose shaft would one day reach his persecutor. This is a sublime presentiment of the power of conscience. No writer of pagan antiquity made the voice of conscience speak with the same power and authority that Æschylus did. ' Crime,' he says, ' never dies without posterity.' ' Blood that is

---

¹ See M. Patin's beautiful work on the Greek Tragedy, the 2d edition of which has just appeared.

shed congeals on the ground, crying out for an avenger.' The old poet made himself the echo of what he calls 'the lyreless hymn of the Furies,' who, with him, represent severe Justice striking the guilty when his hour comes, and giving warning beforehand by the terror which haunts him. Æschylus was evidently influenced by the Mysteries, which were an attempt to calm the torments of conscience regarding a future life by the development of the worship of the Earth-divinities. Nor is it surprising that he should have been charged with having betrayed the secret.

With Sophocles, tragedy made a great advance. He created the human tragedy—the psychological drama. He, who in early youth was famous for his exquisite beauty, and who at the age of ninety-five compelled his judges to acquit him by reading in their presence the chorus of Œdipus at Colonna,—he represented all that was finest in the Greek genius, for he represented its ideal. His transparent, limpid language corresponds with the beauty, the serenity of his inspiration. While Æschylus reveals to us the sombre, terror-stricken side of conscience, personified in the Eumenides, Sophocles shows us the divine and luminous side. What an exquisite type of grace and purity he created in his Antigone!—born, as she says, not to hate but to love: who, after having accompanied her father into exile and poverty, refuses to return evil for evil upon her parricidal persecutor, and prefers death rather than be faithless to the inspirations of her heart. Antigone has the courage of a saint and the poetic weakness of a Greek virgin, who, while devoting herself a voluntary victim, yet mourns the loss of the bright sun and her own unwedded lot; but devotion and piety absorb her whole being. A divine breath seems to animate this sublime creation, in which the tenderness of woman is allied to the heroism of duty. It would seem as if the heaven of

Greece had opened, and a foregleam fell from depths which later on were revealed to humanity by the God whose sacrifice taught charity. No one has ever spoken with nobler eloquence than Sophocles of moral obligation—of this immortal, inflexible law, ' in which dwells a God that never grows old.' The religious inspiration that animates him breaks out with incomparable beauty in the last words of Œdipus, when the old banished king sees through the darkness of death a mysterious light dawn, which illumines his blind eyes, and which brings to him the assurance of a blessed immortality.

We can understand how great must have been the influence of an Æschylus and a Sophocles, from the religious point of view, in the Athens of Pericles. If Euripides obeyed a lower inspiration,—if in him we recognise the poet of the Sophists, who makes a jest of the gods and of the idea of divinity,—yet the pathetic development he gives to individual passions proves how completely humanism had assimilated to itself the Greek conscience. The keen satires of Aristophanes counterbalanced his influence, though manifesting in their way the triumph of human religion over the worship of Nature. Comedy is the result of the contrast existing between man as he is in reality, and man as he ought to be and might be. It presupposes his liberty : take away his liberty, and there is nothing shocking or ridiculous in avarice or cowardice. Nobody mocks the hare, but we all laugh at the coward.

Aristophanes carried the ancient comedy to perfection. His dramatic conceptions are as extraordinary for their daring and invention, as they are revolting for their cynicism. To a fancy full of originality, he unites the most literal portraiture of the actual world ; at one moment he wallows in obscenity, the next he rises to the finest lyrical vein, as in the chorus of the *Clouds*.

Aristophanes' fame balances that of Sophocles and Æschylus. Neither Cratinus, nor Menander the father of the comedy of manners and character, who with delicate hand painted the manners of the corrupt society in which the courtesans were the prominent figures, —neither of these equalled Aristophanes in power of invention.

The advent of literary prose was a fact of deep import, denoting more than any other the progress of Greek civilisation. Poetry, which is the essential product of inspiration, is more impersonal than prose; the latter being the deliberate, selected language of the historian, orator, and philosopher. It is the language of action. Fine prose supposes an advanced state of society, in which the individual finds all his rights recognised. Herodotus carried the epic spirit into his prose. With Pericles and Thucydides it became precise and energetic, but retaining, by the harmony of its periods and its logical construction, all its æsthetic value. The perfection of Plato's prose rivals that of the finest poetry; whilst Isocrates and the Sophists enervate and reduce it to a mere music of words that merely charm the ear. At a later epoch it rose to the full height of its power with Demosthenes, when from the tribune of Athens went forth the grand voice of a free people repelling the yoke of the foreigner.

An analogous development took place in art, which in Greece, more than in any other country, expresses and resumes the different phases of civilisation, and the different crises of religious thought.[1] Rude and shapeless during the Pelasgic period, it attempted nothing beyond temples of wood, without grace or symmetry; nor did the artist aim at producing any representations of the gods which were not distinct personalities, but vague personifications of the forces of Nature. They

[1] See Ottfried Müller's Archæologie.

contented themselves with symbolical signs, such as rudely cut stones or columns. Such were the antique Hermes, to which were afterwards added some impure symbols. Art continued to be long chained down, even after the heroic ideal had shone out in the poetry of Homer and his immediate successors. They endeavoured to represent the divinity by rudely carved images in wood, but they failed in giving life and movement to these early statues. The feet were not separated, the eyes were marked by a stroke, and the arms attached to the body. The artists of this remote period were styled Dædelus. The painting on the sacred vases bore the same character of immobility. During the period that followed (580 to 460 B.C.) artistic development corresponded with the development of Hellenism. Architecture, which had emancipated itself from its primitive barbarism, reached a high degree of perfection in the construction of temples: two of its orders express very significantly the twofold genius of Greece. Whilst the Doric column, springing immediately from the soil, and devoid of all complex ornamentation of its capitals, was the faithful expression of the masculine, energetic spirit of the Dorian race, the Ionian column, resting on a base, and with fluted pillar terminating in a convoluted capital, reproduced the grace and vivacity of the Ionian race.

The Greek temples, which at first only admitted columns in the façade, now began to multiply and dispose them round the *cella*—the immediate sanctuary of the god. They began already to assume that character of symmetry and unity which makes one harmonious plan, and not an edifice of indefinite proportions, as in Egypt, or a monstrous pagoda, as in India; but here the different parts of the building are each in its proper place, and so grow out of each other as to give the impression of a complete whole. The beauty of Greek architecture does not consist in gigantic forms, nor in profusion of costly materials, but in its proportions and symmetry, in the gracefulness of its lines and contours. It is an intellectual, not a material beauty. It would have been as impossible for Oriental pantheism to have produced this style of beauty as that it should have written an Iliad. Sculpture did not keep pace with architecture. Religious sculpture is more tardy, being more bound up with tradition. It contented itself with carving wood and overlaying it with ivory and gold, in which the æsthetic value was sacrificed to ornamentation. The gods were represented seated, with a solemn and austere expression spread over their countenances.

Lay sculpture had freer play. The human model, which now began to be copied, was supplied in its greatest beauty by the Hellenic race, and gymnastic games favoured the study. They began by ornamenting the friezes of their temples with statues consecrated to the memory of the heroic ages. The marbles of Ægina, now at Munich, belong to this period. They enable us to understand what was meant by the ancient style. This style is characterized by the regularity of the folds of its drapery; by the symmetrical curls of the hair, the tension of the fingers, and the general stiffness of the whole figure. Still the statue is not trammelled and motionless as in the preceding period. There is movement, though one of mechanical regularity. The features are strongly marked; but as yet no soul shines through them, no ray of beauty beams out from within. The period following this (from Pericles to Alexander, 560 to 330 B.C.) is the grand epoch of Greek art. While Æschylus and Sophocles gave in their poetry sublime expression to the ideal as it was conceived by the Hellenic race, Phidias carved it in marble, gold, and ivory, and found means to purify and ennoble while embodying it. The statue does not seem merely to move as in the preceding period, but becomes living under the chisel of the great artist. It has the suppleness, the easy motion, the liberty of life, and an indefinable serene grace which has never since been reproduced. *Incessu patuit dea.* These marbles breathe, as the poet says. We have only to compare the Greek and Egyptian statues in order to seize the difference between the two civilisations. Humanism emancipated the individual. Henceforth he walks and moves freely; his hands and feet are no longer bound; life animates the once inert body. Man steps as a conqueror over the earth, to which he is no longer a slave; and the lightness of his airy tread announces his liberty. His arm flings the dart, his hand lifts the spear, with heroic grace. We see he has thrown off the yoke of Nature. The young triumphant god which, in a celebrated statue, is represented in all the pride of his victory over the serpent Python, is the radiant image of this victory of humanity over the ancient divinities. What is most admirable in the great works of sculpture belonging to this period, is the union of beauty and majesty,—the sweet, grave serenity spread over features most noble and of exquisite outlines. ' The soul,' says Winckelmann, ' manifests itself as through the tranquil surface of water,—no impetuous movement. In the representation of the greatest grief, the grief is concentrated; and joy flows like a zephyr that gently touches the leaves.' No nation ever more fully expressed its genius through its works than did the Greeks. We may figure to ourselves Greece itself in the representations of its favourite goddesses, exalting in the human being both dignity and beauty, at once serene and majestic, possessing grace and grandeur, ready for the combat as for the feast,—rather making all life a feast in honour of its gods, and placing its glory in preserving this august calm, this *ataraxie,*—image, but delusive image, of real peace. In Greek art there is no contrast to shock between the real and the ideal, because the ideal was not sought beyond earth. The artist found what was most beautiful in the actual world to represent this limited ideal. Thus we find no signs of torment in his style; he breathed into his work the felicity he felt within his own soul, and which was kept alive by the facility with which he created these incomparable types. We feel that such a moment could only be experienced once in the course of the progress of humanity, and that that moment must necessarily have been brief.

We have already named the supreme artist. The *Pallas* and *Olympian Jupiter* of Phidias are his two masterpieces, and the masterpieces of sculpture itself. These statues, executed in the most costly materials and in colossal proportions, give a sublime expression of majesty and beauty to the divinity, and helped to purify the religious idea. The fragments of the friezes of the Parthenon prove that the great sculptor knew as well how to represent the fury of a battle as the supreme calm of the divinity. But, whatever the subject he treated, he was always faithful to his high ideal, and preserved the exquisite beauty of form. Polyclete of Sicyon, the author of the Juno of Argos, was the worthy rival of Phidias; after him, Praxiteles and Scopas. Not less skilled in the sculpturing of marble, but obedient to a less noble inspiration, it was the voluptuous beauty of Aphrodite that they loved to reproduce. The Venus of Praxiteles breathes voluptuousness: not a gross voluptuousness which would exclude it from the domain of art, but a refined, delicate voluptuousness, not the less dangerous. We feel that the reign of the courtesans has begun, and that Greece has fallen from the serene heights she had for a moment reached.

Still, some of the works of Scopas belong to the grand period. It is sufficient to cite the Pythian Apollo and the Niobe group. In this latter work the representation of the most cruel anguish takes nothing from the calm beauty of the figures. Lysippus, continuator of the school of Argos, devoted himself to the reproduction of athletes: Hercules is his favourite type. Painting shed its light over this period. Zeuxis and Parrhasius, and the painters of the school of Sicyon, of whom Apelles was the chief, united brilliancy of colouring to grace of execution. Still, Greek painting was necessarily inferior to Greek statuary. Christianity alone could carry it to perfection, by opening up the inner world of the soul, and offering to the rich resources of the palette the infinite scale of human sentiment. But architecture, the elder sister of sculpture, profited by the progress, and reached at the same time its apogee. It suffices to mention the Parthenon, which is to Greek temples what the Jupiter Olympus is to Greek statues. The Parthenon was dedicated to the intellectual divinity adored at Athens. This edifice, which borrowed from the Doric order the simplicity of its columns, had a character of serious beauty in harmony with the worship of the immortal Virgin. The most exquisite elegance reigns throughout. The Corinthian order, substituting the acanthus leaf for the Ionian convolution, dates from this period of unequalled artistic fecundity. The temple of Jupiter Olympus, ornamented with Phidias' celebrated statue, is a sample of its grandeur. It is the imposing temple of triumphant humanism, and consequently the central-point of Hellenism.

Religion was so intimately interwoven with art that it shared its growth, and passed through the same purifying influences. But we must bear in mind that there was always a double current of religious ideas in

Greece—one spiritualist, the other tainted by impure legends. Unfortunately, these contradictory divinities, in which conscience and the passions may recognise themselves, stood historically on equal footing. Jupiter at this period became more and more the sovereign god—the leader of all things, creator of heaven and earth. He sees the guilty actions of men, and accordingly is the god of justice. If he strikes, he can also console, and is the refuge of mortals. 'The god of supplicants,' says Æschylus, 'is moved to anger when the cry of the unhappy is not heard.' He is the god of the city—the protector of the domestic hearth—the vigilant guardian of the sacred rites of hospitality. He is pre-eminently the Greek god: all Greece bowed with equal respect before the sublime image of Jupiter Olympus, the most majestic representation of humanized divinity. The other divinities underwent the same transformations. Juno is the legitimate wife of Jupiter, and shares his attributes. She is the ideal matron. Athene or Minerva occupies a leading place in this transfigured Olympus. She represents the intellectual side of the supreme god—his wisdom and prudence, accompanied by the calm courage that secures success in battle. Thought shines from her pure lofty brow. She is armed with the warlike spear, and protects both artist and labourer. The savage Ares or Mars is eclipsed by her, and falls into the second rank, though the attribute of justice is allowed him. Neptune, equally with Mars and Vulcan, retains his ancient attributes. Idealization was a more difficult process in the case of divinities so bound up with the life of Nature. Neither Mercury nor Pluto underwent any important modifications. Aphrodite or Venus, although lowered by Praxiteles to the rank of a courtesan, represents in Pindar what is most delicate and noble in woman. The Venus of Milo suffices in itself to prove that the goddess of beauty personified something higher than a life of pleasure and voluptuousness. Pride and chastity are stamped on her features. She represents youth and grace far more than sensual love. But we can already foresee that the voluptuous Aphrodite will soon outstrip the ideal Venus, and that the ancient Oriental Astarte will eventually efface the Hellenic goddess.

The purifying process becomes most manifest at this period in the special veneration paid to two divinities which, anterior to it, possessed no importance. Apollo and Bacchus are placed immediately after Jupiter and Pallas. The former, adored at Delphi, and at first the god of light, now becomes the god of purity, and claiming from man holy ablutions and sacrifices. He himself, according to the myths of the country, had to undergo purification for having shed the blood of the serpent Python. Accordingly, it was at Delphi that the purifying rites were performed which cleansed from blood shed by violence. A whole system of purification was elaborated by the priests, and gave a more serious character to a religion which was essentially æsthetic. Apollo was regarded as the mediating god between heaven and earth: by his oracles he reveals the will of the gods, and reconciles man by sacrifice to Jupiter.[1]

We know the perils that attended the infancy of Bacchus, son of Jupiter and Semele, who was pursued by the jealousy of Juno; also his victorious progress into India, and his return to Thrace. 'Bacchus,' says M. Maury truly, 'is the last of the gods of ancient Greece. In the legend, he preserves both the character of the hero and that of the god,—that is to say, man deified and superior to man. He constitutes the link that binds the old Olympian gods of Homer to the modern gods—heroes that take their place beside them, and who at times usurped their attributes. Hercules

[1] Dunker iii. 542.

is in many respects a god like Bacchus; but being more closely connected with earth, his deification was a more definite apotheosis. With him the Greek more boldly scaled Olympus, and claimed his share of divinity without passing through the idealization of a Jupiter or an Apollo. Hercules became the saviour-god, the future conqueror of Jupiter. Nothing could be more logical: the real gods were the heroes; they were destined to supplant the ancient personifications of the forces of Nature. At this period the Hellenic mythology is encumbered with heroes and demigods claiming worship. The fundamental religious idea of Greece becomes more and more clear. Whilst the East calls on the divinity to descend from heaven and unite himself with man in order to absorb him, Greece invites the ideal man, or the Greek hero, to rise from earth to heaven and replace the ancient gods, by manifesting not only æsthetic or intellectual beauty, but moral beauty. This religion could not satisfy even him whom it deified. It had both too much grandeur and poverty to last long. The noble instincts of the soul were at the same time kindled and crushed by it. It was doomed to perish by this irremediable contradiction.

The Mysteries were a proof of the insufficiency of the official religion. We have already said that the most important of the Mysteries were connected with the ancient divinities of earth. Those relating to the adventures of Bacchus embodied a kind of metaphysical doctrine. According to an Athenian legend, Bacchus was torn to pieces by the Titans, and then miraculously saved by Jupiter. The mutilation of the young god symbolized the subdivisions of being at the creation, as his resurrection was the emblem of universal renovation, or the restoration to unity of all individual existence. The love Mysteries, interpreted in hymns called Orphisies, also inculcated the doctrine of individual restoration to unity by means of love, causing all discord to cease. The myth relating to Psyche was elaborated in this sense. But these Mysteries, which were rather philosophic than religious, had neither the importance nor the popularity of those of Eleusis, which were intended to remove fear inspired by the idea of death, and to give peace to the troubled conscience.[1]

The testimony of ancient writers is positive on this point. These Mysteries, says Isocrates in his panegyric, secure to those admitted to them the most blissful hopes, not only for the duration of this life, but for ever. Cicero says of them, We have not only received the means of living joyfully, but of dying with better hopes. If these Mysteries were connected with Ceres and Proserpine, it was for reasons made accessible to us through the famous Homeric hymn to Demeter, containing the sacred legend that was dramatically represented at Eleusis. Ceres, disguised as an old woman, seeks her daughter Proserpine, who had been carried off by Pluto. She arrives, overwhelmed with fatigue, at Eleusis; and there received by the daughter of King Celeus, she devotes herself to the education of his son Triptolemus. In order to confer immortality on him, she throws him into the fire, on which his mother uttering a cry, the charm is broken, and Triptolemus, instead of being a god, becomes the heroic benefactor of his country. Such was the declaration of the goddess, who suddenly revealed herself, and to whom a temple was dedicated at Eleusis. Furious at not finding her daughter, she strikes the earth with sterility, and, in spite of the supplications of Jupiter and all the gods of Olympus, only consents to be appeased when Pluto promises to restore her daughter for nine months of the year.

[1] See for details the *Mémoires sur les Mystères de Cérès et de Proserpine*, by M. Guigniaut, Member of the Institute, 1856; also the chapter on the Mysteries in M. Maury's 2d vol.

The Mysteries of Eleusis began by a series of purifications, designated as the Lesser Mysteries, to distinguish them from the Great Mysteries, and were a kind of dramatic representation of the legend of Ceres, which took place in autumn and spring. The first referred to the painful search of Ceres in quest of her daughter; the second represented the happy moment when her daughter was restored. The supreme initiation was the last and most solemn act of this religious drama. The initiated saw in the midst of darkness the image of the goddess suddenly appear in bright light, accompanied by the gods, who were represented by the priests. To penetrate the sense of these Mysteries, we must recollect that Ceres and Proserpine were two of the ancient divinities of earth. The first represented the earth, the second the grain of wheat. As the seed remains shut up within the earth during the winter, in order to germinate and reappear in spring, so Proserpine goes down three months into the realms of darkness. The Mysteries of Eleusis were, then, first of all agricultural fêtes; but their complex symbolism did not stop there. Greece could not, even when returning to her old gods, rest satisfied with seeing in them merely the personification of the forces of Nature. Proserpine, reigning in hell, was the tutelar divinity of those who after her should descend there. Her reappearance to the light of day was prophetic of immortality. Man, like the grain, must die, in order that he may again rise to life. Finally, the peregrinations of Ceres symbolize the wanderings of the soul which has lost the right path, but which, after much labour, finds it again.

Two dogmas we then find contained in these obscure symbols,—namely, that of evil or sin, and immortality. The purifications were intended to operate the desired salvation. The great goddesses alone could restore souls to their pristine purity. Thus, while the national religion was supposed to have broken the yoke of the religions of Nature, the Mysteries in turn, while proclaiming its powerlessness, endeavoured to express the deep aspirations of the soul, which, charmed and dazzled by the splendour of the ceremonies, still found its real wants unsatisfied.

However, those momentary stings of conscience did not suffice to cast a lasting shadow over the serene sky of Greece. Surrounded with the masterpieces of art, with poets such as Sophocles and Æschylus, with temples like those of Jupiter Olympus and the Parthenon, Greece may for a moment have believed that she had rid the world of the malediction which the gloomy mythologies of the East had drawn upon it. Every four years the celebration of the Olympic games drew together, on a plain bordered with olive trees and plantains, the flower of Grecian youth. There their courage derived fresh stimulus, their supple bodies acquired strength, and displayed all the beauty of form. Extraordinary importance was attached to these games, which were regarded as the school of heroism. They bore a sacred character in the eyes of Greece, ever ready to worship heroes and human beauty of every kind. In the interval between the great Olympic games, each city exercised the *élite* of its population in the gymnasium. Hellenic life was essentially public life; women alone passed their lives in private, shut up in the gynæceum.

Man lived solely for the State; the individual being absorbed in the collective but not abstract being which daily met at the Agora,—noisy, agitated, and sovereign even in its caprices. What a contrast between ascetic India, solely bent on destroying the natural and human element, and Greece, accepting it in all its phases in order to ennoble it! Greece conceived no ideal beyond Nature : there she sought it, or rather, there she placed it; thus combining the real and the ideal, preventing the former from becoming gross and vulgar, and the second from becoming lost in vagueness. Nature embellished —this was the Hellenic ideal. Hence that plastic perfection, with its marvellous harmony, which has become the true classic ideal; but hence also its incompleteness and insufficiency. The day humanity feels its want of something more than being embellished and ennobled, that day it feels its need of being saved and restored from the consequences of its fall. It is then true, that what constituted the glory of Greece, also led to its ruin. A rapid glance at its philosophic development will confirm this position.

GREEK PHILOSOPHY TO THE TIME OF ALEXANDER.

A people's philosophy is the highest and truest expression of their development. Philosophers, falling back upon their own minds, disengage from all *impediments* the fundamental idea which rules a nation's destiny. In this way the Brahmans of India, in their refined speculations, boldly pursued to their consequences the premises contained in the national creed, and concluded by reducing to a definite formula the doctrine of annihilation. Greek philosophy fulfilled a similar mission, and gave an exact formula to the essential principles of Hellenic Paganism.

It would be difficult to overstate the importance of Greek philosophy, when viewed as a preparative to Christianity. Disinterested pursuit of truth is always a great and noble task. The imperishable want of the human mind to go back to its first principle, suffices in itself to prove that this principle is divine. We may abuse speculation; we may turn it into one of the most powerful dissolvents of moral truths; and the defenders of positive creeds, alarmed by the attitude too often assumed by speculation in the presence of religion, have condemned it as mischievous in itself, confounding in their unjust prejudice its use and its abuse. But, for all serious thinkers, philosophy is one of the highest titles of nobility that humanity possesses; and, when we consider its mission previous to Christianity, we feel convinced that it had its place in the divine plan. It was not religion in itself that philosophy, through its noblest representatives, combated, but polytheism. It dethroned the false gods. Adopting what was best in Paganism, philosophy employed it as an instrument to destroy Paganism, and thus cleared the way for definitive religion. Above all, it effectively contributed to purify the idea of divinity, though this purification was but an approximation. If at times it caught glimpses of the highest spiritualism, yet it was unable to guard against the return and reaction of Oriental dualism. In spite of this imperfection, which in its way served the cause of Christianity by demonstrating the necessity of revelation, men like Socrates and Plato fulfilled amongst their people a really sublime mission. They were to the pagan world the great prophets of the human conscience, which woke up at their call. And the awakening of the moral sense was at once the glory and ruin of their philosophy; for conscience, once roused, could only be satisfied by One greater than they, and must necessarily reject all systems which proved themselves impotent to realize the moral ideal which they had evoked.

But to perish thus, and for such a cause, is a high honour to a philosophy. It was this made the philosophy of Greece, like the Hebrew laws, though in an inferior sense, a schoolmaster that led to Jesus Christ, according to the expression of Clement of Alexandria. Viewed in this light, it was a true gift from God; and had, too, the shadow of good things to come, awaking the presentiment and desire of them, though it could not communicate them. Nor can we conceive a better way to prepare the advent of Him who was to be the Desire of nations before being their Saviour.

Rigid consistency binds together the different systems of philosophy. Logic reigns sovereign in the domain of pure speculation, and is at once the cause of its grandeur and of its insufficiency. A doctrine dies out owing to what is false or incomplete in it; and the incoming doctrine is its natural refutation, by either drawing ultimate consequences from the premises laid down, or by substituting a new principle for an erroneous one. The great problem ancient philosophy had to deal with, was how to get rid of the opposition between mind and matter; it being the eternal mission of speculation to restore unity to the conceptions of the human mind. This great problem was also the great stumblingblock of Greek philosophy, and one it never succeeded in solving. To do so, a higher light was necessary. As long as the dogma of creation was not accepted, but three solutions were possible: either the two terms of the problem were to be eternally laid down in the presence of each other, affirming the most decided dualism; or one of the terms was suppressed, leading to materialism or to idealism; or refuge was sought in the theory of emanation.

If all systems split on the same rock, they did not all split in the same way; and some amongst them, though erring in one capital point, yet mixed such an amount of truth with their error, that they exercised a most beneficial influence. Mainly preoccupied with the moral action of the different doctrines upon mind— convinced that this action does not always absolutely depend on the metaphysical point of view—we shall carefully abstain from pronouncing a summary judgment upon the whole philosophy of Greece, but point out the purer current discernible through these troubled waters, and which acquired such power and limpidity in the Platonic philosophy. It is this system that evidently has most affinity with Christianity, and which was most efficient in preparing hearts for its reception, —such hearts as did not find in it full satisfaction. Accordingly, we shall always bear it in view in the summary we now proceed to give of the philosophic development of Greece.

We shall find under a new form, in the successive philosophical systems, the succession of the different mythological creations of humanity. Nor should this surprise us, since there is nothing arbitrary or accidental in the order of the religions of the ancient world. They are connected with each other by a hidden but irresistible logic. Humanity was not compelled to take this path; but, the first steps once taken, necessarily pursued it to the end. *Naturism*, or the glorification of the forces of Nature, fatally led to a more and more decided dualism, as dualism led to Brahminical pantheism and Buddhist annihilation. Such were the inevitable phases of religious thought, till it attained the higher sphere of humanism. Philosophic thought passed through the same series of ideas; but, as reflection never precedes but follows imagination, philosophic development did not keep pace with mythological development. Accordingly, we find that the periods of Greek philosophy do not coincide with those of its religious history. Naturism was banished from the religious sphere while still dominant in speculation; and it was long after it had triumphed in the temple that humanism was taught as a formula in the schools.

Speculative thought, once excited, follows the course of religious thought, and seeks in Nature the first principle of all things. Overpowered, since his fall, by Nature, man began by proclaiming his own defeat; but to proclaim it, and to endeavour to account for it, is already in a degree to repair it. The thinking reed, to use Pascal's term, rises in presence of the blind forces of Nature which bowed it to the earth. The philosophy of Naturism is already an enfranchisement, in being a philosophy. The most ancient of the Greek schools of philosophy, the Ionian school, succeeded, towards its decline, in attaining glimpses of spiritualism. It was divided into two branches — the Dynamic and the Mechanic branches. The first held that there was an inherent force in Nature presiding over its developments; the other attributed the order and government of the world to a principle outside and above it.

It is evident that that branch of the Ionian school which sought in Nature itself the germ of life and the principle of organization, was nearer to absolute materialism than that which sought this germ and principle out of Nature. Thales of Miletus supposed water to be the first principle of things. Anaximenes maintained that air was the primal essence; while Heraclitus attributed the origin of all things to fire. These philosophers represent, in philosophy, the gross Naturism that predominated in Asia Minor. If Diogenes of Apollonia attributes divine intelligence to air, we must regard it but as a noble inconsistency, which leaves undisturbed the materialistic character of the Ionian school.

The Mechanism tendency, which, as we have said, admitted a principle of organization outside and above Nature, approached, without attaining, spiritualism. Anaximander of Miletus supposed the great primary essence to be the *Infinite*, whence existences became disengaged by the separation of antagonisms. Anaxagoras taught that a supreme intelligence presided over the creation. 'All things were confounded together, and mind reduced them to order.'

This was but the crude beginning of spiritualism, still tending to dualism; for if intelligence orders the confused world of matter, what then is the origin of matter? What were those chaotic elements organized by the great Intelligence? Anaxagoras does not answer this question. Hence we are not surprised to find the Pythagorean school, which succeeded the Ionian rather in the order of logic than of time, accept dualism and rigorously formalize it. The famous theory of numbers evidently bears the dualistic character. Unity, whence all flows, comprehends the material principle, which is the unlimited, the indefinite, and the spiritual principle, which is again the element of limitation and determination. The number, which is at once the essence and type of all beings, results from the reciprocal penetration of these two elements: it is neither simply the unlimited, nor the determining element, but determination in the unlimited—in other words, confused matter receiving form, precision, and harmony from the spiritual element. The laws of symmetry are strictly observed in this penetration of matter by intelligence. Mathematical relations express the union of mind and matter. Contained at first without distinction in the great whole, the limited and the unlimited, mind and matter became disengaged in order to unite and form an harmonious world, of which heaven is the most perfect representation. The Pythagorean school was a school of mathematicians and astronomers. To us it appears to correspond, with sufficient exactness, with the mythological evolution accomplished in Iran in the time of Zoroaster. Accordingly, whilst the Ionian school, in this respect like the religion of Phœnicia, only admitted one blind, confused principle, uniting in itself the contrary forces of Nature, the Pythagorean doctrine, like the Avesta, recognised two principles, opposed one to the other, but requiring the material principle to be subordinated to the spiritual; and, like the Persian religion, tending to moral development by commanding that man should always strive to make right and harmony predominate; but also, like Parseeism, it remained bound in the trammels of dualism. 'Unity,' says the Pythagorean school, "results from duality."[1] Dualism leads to annihilation. The human mind cannot long preserve the equilibrium between the material and spiritual principle, but endeavours to get rid of one of the terms of the great antithesis. As soon as the sentiment of unity is revealed, all is sacrificed to it. Diversity, movement, individual life, all appears an evil; and all that has an existence separate from the great whole must be annihilated, and lost in the abyss of the one absolute being. This tendency was called Brahmanism in the mythological evolution of the East; in the philosophical evolution of Greece it produced the school of Elea. We know with what courage Xenophanes and Parmenides taught the doctrine of idealism. 'The divinity,' says Parmenides, 'has neither beginning nor end. He is without parts; for he is always one and identical.' He is without movement, adds Melissus, for the great being is unalterable; and what is unalterable neither diminishes nor augments. There is no plurality; for there is only one true being which is unalterable. It is impossible not to recognise Brahmanism in this doctrine; but as it was the product of Greece, and not of the banks of the Ganges, it received a deeper stamp of idealism.

The one immutable being, according to Parmenides, is endowed with reason and intelligence. 'He is a holy, ineffable spirit: the plenitude of being is in thought.' High as they exalted him, still they failed to range the external world under his law, and were compelled, in order to vindicate their doctrine, to deny all contingent existence. The production of individual existences, and of the world containing them, was to their eyes, as to

[1] Τὸ δ' ἓν ἐξ ἀμφοτέρων. Aristot. Metaphys. A. 5.

the Brahmans', a malediction. They pronounced the same anathema on Nature as was passed in India. According to Empedocles (ranked erroneously by Brandis amongst the Ionian philosophers), the world was created under the influence of the principle of hatred, which broke the bond of love that in the beginning bound together all beings in the bosom of the one absolute being. Hence the incurable sadness that casts its sombre hue over all that is born, lives, and moves. Empedocles poetically expressed this feeling when, powerless to triumph over this dualism, which ever presented itself in spite of the daring negations of the school of Elea, he cries out: 'I am an exile from truth, obeying furious discord; O wretched race of mortals, of what discords and sighs are you not born!' Buddhist asceticism is tacitly conveyed in this lamentation; and if it did not practically flow from it, it was that the serene Hellenic temperament effectively counterbalanced this sombre Oriental spirit.

The extreme idealism of the Elean school led to a violent reaction, of which Democritus was the organ. Parmenides had denied movement and plurality. Democritus replied by denying the supernatural world—the world of intelligence and unity. He explains the formation of things by the doctrine of atoms, drawn in an eternal vortex, and blending and separating at the sport of chance. He seeks no first principle, no god, no morality. To the idealistic excesses of the school of Elea he opposes an equally absolute materialism. Tossed from one to the other of these two exaggerated tendencies, convinced by each in turn of the errors of the antagonistic school, the Greek mind, whose inherent subtlety already disposed it towards scepticism, abandoned itself unreservedly thereto towards the close of this period. It was then the Sophists sprang up, making a sport of philosophy, and a traffic of the noblest preoccupations of the human mind, which in their hands became a profession without higher aims than the gratification of vanity or self-interest. Bringing into collision all the contradictory solutions proposed by the different schools upon the ontological problem, refuting Parmenides by Democritus, and Democritus by Parmenides, they concluded from all these discussions that it is impossible for man to arrive at truth—rather, that there is no fixed absolute truth—that upon every question two equally plausible answers are possible, and that man's own fluctuating thought is the measure of all things—such was the doctrine of Protagoras and Gorgias; and they sought to establish it by a subtle, sapping dialectic destruction of all rational and moral evidence. The Sophists, who were at the same time great rhetoricians, inaugurated the reign of false elegance. As in their eyes all was but appearance, they solely aimed at effect, pomp and harmony of language. They delighted, as Cicero tells us, to plead the opposite sides of a cause with equal force. We can conceive the fatal influence this must have exercised upon the young, whose moral sense became falsified or destroyed by such a process. Nor did they less effectually destroy the religious sense; for the Sophists were noted for their atheism and impiety. They thus undermined the very foundations of the State, and inspired with a legitimate inquietude the minds, not only of religious men, but of such as were preoccupied about the welfare of the republic. Thus, through their fault, philosophy long fell into discredit, and he who rehabilitated it, died victim of the unpopularity which its deadly enemies had stirred up. His life and death were needed to restore it in the estimation of Greece. No mission could have been nobler; and this was the mission of Socrates. For our part, we do not hesitate to say that he was a great servant of the God whom he had but glimpses of, and whose will he accomplished in the measure of the light and strength given him. He was faithful 'over the few things entrusted to him;' that is to say, he was faithful to the full measure of truth he possessed. What is remarkable in Socrates is not the system, but the man. The memory he left behind him amongst his disciples, although idealized, the affection blended with reverence which they never ceased to feel for his person, bear sufficient testimony to the elevation of his character and to his moral purity. We recognise in him a Greek of Athens—one who had imbibed many dangerous errors, and on whom the yoke of pagan customs still weighed; but his life was nevertheless a noble life; and it is to calumny we must have recourse if we are to tarnish its beauty by odious insinuations, as Lucian did, and as has been too frequently done, after him, by unskilful defenders of Christianity, who imagine that it is the gainer by all that degrades human nature. Born in an humble position, destitute of all those external advantages which the Greeks so passionately loved, Socrates exercised a true kingship over minds. His dominion was the more real for being less apparent. No man more utterly rejected all vulgar artifices for producing effect upon men: no mere parade of dignity, no magisterial pomp of words, but out of the free interchange of familiar talk he allowed his lessons of morality and philosophy to flow; his speech affected not the accent of authority, but took the easy tone of conversation, seasoned with fine irony, the capricious course of which it sufficed him to direct in order to gain his end. He instituted no school. All hours and all places were good where instruction could be imparted: the market-place, the shop, the banquet-hall, the interior of a prison. His power consisted of three things,—his devoted affection for his disciples, his disinterested love of truth, and the perfect harmony of his life and doctrine. 'He was surprised,' says Xenophon, ' that men could dare to earn their living by teaching virtue, as if the greatest gain were not the possession of a virtuous friend. He would have feared by so doing to diminish the gratitude he wished to inspire.' Comparing truth to a young virgin he adored, he would consider himself as much dishonoured by selling truth, as if for a sum of money he should sell a young girl entrusted to him. When he spoke of loving, he did not refer to the external person, but always to the soul and virtue. He placed friendship above all the blessings of earth. What blessing is there that is not second to a true friend! It is easy to understand how he, who ranked friendship so highly, should have inspired his disciples with such warm and profound affection; and their esteem was equal to their affection, for what he taught he scrupulously practised. If he recommended temperance and sobriety, he also set the example: poorly clad, satisfied with little, he disdained all the delicacies of life. He possessed every species of courage. On the field of battle he was intrepid; and still more intrepid when he resisted the caprices of the multitude who demanded him, when he was senator, to commit the injustice of summoning ten generals before the tribunals. He also infringed the iniquitous orders of the thirty tyrants of Athens.

The satires of Aristophanes neither moved nor irritated him. The same dauntless firmness he displayed when brought before his judges charged with impiety. ' If it is your wish to absolve me on condition that I shall henceforth be silent, I reply, I love and honour you, but I ought rather to obey the gods than you. Neither in the presence of judges nor of the enemy is it permitted me, or any man, to use every sort of means to escape death. It is not death but crime that is difficult to avoid; crime moves faster than death. So I, old and heavy as I am, have allowed myself to be overtaken by death, while my accusers, light and vigorous, have allowed themselves to be overtaken by the more light-footed crime. I go then to suffer death; they to suffer shame and iniquity. I abide by my punishment, as they by theirs. All is according to order.' It was the same fidelity to duty that made Socrates refuse to escape from prison, in order not to violate the laws of his country, to which, even though irritated, more respect is due than to a father. ' Let us walk in the path,' he says, ' that God has traced for us.' These last words show the profound religious sentiment which animated Socrates,—that faith in the divinity which made him say it was a god that had given him to the Athenians, and that a god or goddess guarded him in all things. Superstition here mingled with truth, but did not stifle it. It is impossible not to feel that there was something divine in such a life, crowned by such a death.

As regards his teaching, it is difficult to disengage it from the commentaries of his disciples. Still, by comparing Xenophon with Plato, and judiciously availing ourselves of their testimony, we can seize some of its general features. When Cicero declares, in an often quoted passage, that Socrates drew philosophy down from heaven to earth, he perfectly characterizes his work; for Socrates was the first to lead philosophy from the path of hypothetical speculations on the world and its origin to that of psychological observation. He not only made it descend from the mythic heaven of the Pythagoreans, and the vast solitude of the Eleans, where the Being immutable and alone was as it were lost,—he made philosophy enter into man, gave her his mind and conscience to study,—he made human nature the principal field of his explorations, and substituted the philosophy of humanity for that of Nature; thus accomplishing in the domain of speculation the evolution already realized in that of mythology.

Socrates was the first philosopher who reduced to clear formula the fundamental data of Hellenism, eliminating at the same time the impure elements which alloyed it in the popular religion. He was in philosophy what Pindar and Sophocles were in poetry, and Phidias in art; like them, he purified the Greek ideal, and humanism, in passing through his hands, received the impress of high spirituality. He raised it far above the idle fables of mythology. Already the Elean school had rejected the gross anthropomorphism of the Homeric religion. 'God,' Empedocles had said, 'has not a human head nor limbs like ours; arms do not descend from his shoulders, nor has he feet to run with.' But this school had gone into the other extreme, by condemning the absolute being to eternal immobility, by representing him as an impassible intelligence holding no relations with humanity. Socrates was equally removed from both these errors. His god, though not the Jupiter of fable, subject to all our passions, is a god in close relations to man—his protector and model. Socratic humanism is no presumptuous apotheosis of humanity; if he proclaims it divine, it is in the name of the superior element it possesses. Hence the science of sciences that it imports man to acquire, is self-knowledge—introspection. In gaining deeper insight into his own nature, he learns the inutility of the vain, false science of the external world, and finds out his ignorance of the subject most essential for him to know. Hence the principle of all sound philosophy is embodied in the inscription on the temple of Delphi, 'Know thyself.' In knowing himself, man knows also the true good; for it is revealed in these eternal and unwritten laws of which Socrates, as well as Sophocles, speaks with reverential eloquence. Good is inseparable from truth—truth and good are one and the same. Science and virtue are intimately joined, inasmuch as the first object of science being the good, and the good being inaccessible to an impure heart. Socrates draws no distinction between the idea of the good and the idea of the divinity, nor does he admit a separation between morality and religion. The august type of good should be sought amongst the gods, who not only reveal it to us and counsel us to it, but who aid us to accomplish it. Once on this path, we can understand how Socrates was led to the notion of the immortality of the soul. If he did not go so far as to affirm it, the hindrance arose from his mode of dialectics, and not from any tergiversation of his conscience. It was because he believed in the divine element in man that he employed the famous inductive method, which consisted in eliciting from the conscience, by a system of skilful interrogations, what was there hidden and inherent. He has been unjustly accused of having founded eudemonism, or the selfish morality of happiness. If Socrates loved to enumerate the happy results to man of temperance, simplicity of manners, and virtue in general, we can only regard it as the legitimate condescension of a philosopher making himself all things to all men, and endeavouring to render virtue attractive to his hearers without making the happiness it procures the chief motive of morality. We would equally deceive ourselves were we to suppose that Socrates, in dwelling on the practical side of philosophy, condemned real science. It was that frivolous curiosity he condemned which seeks its aliment in the spectacle of the universe, while neglecting the human soul and the treasures it contains. But the best proof that Socrates did not proscribe real metaphysics, is the fact that he had Plato and Aristotle as disciples. It is true he left no complete system after him, but this was not his mission. His greatness consisted in what he inspired rather than in what he himself taught, although we do find in his fragmentary teaching the solid foundations on which Platonism was built, and that moral character which enables us to mount from the divine in man to the absolute and eternal. Socrates breathed new life into conscience and thought; and if the moral impulse imparted by him was more energetic than the intellectual, it was because the time, in which the influence of the Sophists was in the ascendant, most needed it. Besides, it was his profound insight into the true and good that constituted the originality and power of this noble philosopher, who more than any other laboured to destroy polytheism. From the point of view of ancient Greece, Socrates accordingly deserved death.

For the same reason, Christianity, instead of gathering up the calumnies and outrages of a Lucian, should accept Socrates as one of its precursors. Socrates was, no doubt, incapable of filling the place of Christianity; but it was his vocation to make the world feel the necessity of Christianity, by developing wants and aspirations which the Hellenic religion could not satisfy. He represented in Greece the moral law—that law which Saint Paul declared was written on the heart of the heathen, and which filled a part analogous to that of the Mosaic law. Notwithstanding the inferiority of philosophy compared with revelation, all that Socrates did and said to establish the obligations of conscience, had the same pedagogic results in relation to his people as flowed from the positive institutions of the Jews. The 'Know thyself,' taken seriously, must end in the invocation to the Unknown God, which is none other than the Christ.

The minor schools that sprung from Socratism, such as the Cyrenaic and Cynic, we shall not dwell on, for they neither comprehended nor developed their master's doctrines. The first was an anticipation of Epicureanism; the second, a foretaste of Stoicism, without its grandeur or influence. We shall proceed at once to that noble Platonic philosophy which has at all times exercised so powerful an action upon all elevated minds, and which, with the exception of Christianity, may be regarded as the greatest event in the history of thought. It has even been maintained that it superseded the necessity of a revelation, by giving to humanity, in the form of speculation, that pure morality which the Gospel, at a later period, promulgated; but to refute this assertion, it is only necessary to state Plato's system, the merits of which it is needless to exaggerate, in order to do justice to this glorious school of spiritualism in antiquity, as great by virtue of what it destroyed, as for the sublime ideas it ushered into the world.

Born towards the close of the age of Pericles, connected by kindred or friendship with all the most illustrious men of the republic, Plato began life by cultivating that poetry which he afterwards would have proscribed from his *Republic*, but of which he never succeeded in divesting his own mind; for, if we admit that poetry exists independent of rhythmical syllables, Plato was then one of the finest poets of Greece. From the moment he became the disciple of Socrates, he consecrated himself to philosophy. His vast studies and travels (which a judicious criticism must reduce to reasonable limits[1]) put him in possession of all the treasures that science and religion had hitherto accumulated. In the most beautiful of all languages he possessed the most pliant instrument of the intellect. Uniting, as M. Cousin says, the sublime and graceful; by turns ingenious and brilliant; endowed with a creative, plastic imagination, which enabled him to invest his thoughts in transparent forms; as inspired

[1] See Ritter, *Histoire de la Philosophie Ancienne*, t. ii., p. 129.

an artist as he was a profound metaphysician,—Plato left in his *Dialogues* one of those perfect works, such as humanity produces but at rare epochs. When he says in his *Republic* that one of the most rapturous spectacles would be that of a soul and body equally beautiful, 'in unison with one another, in which all qualities should be in complete harmony,' he unconsciously defined his own style; for Plato's thought found in his style a form equal in beauty to itself.

Like Socrates, Plato loved truth with fervour. 'If anything,' we read in the *Banquet*, 'gives value to human life, it is the contemplation of absolute beauty. What would be thought of the mortal to whom it was given to contemplate beauty, pure, simple, and unmixed, divested of all human alloy, and all other perishable accessories—divine, homogeneous, absolute beauty? Would we not believe that this man, who here below perceived beauty by the organ to which beauty is perceptible, could alone conceive true virtue, since it is to virtue that beauty belongs? Now to him who gives birth to and nourishes virtue it belongs to be beloved by God; and if any should be immortal, he, above all, should. To attain this great good, human nature will find no more powerful auxiliary than love.' 'He, who in the mysteries of love has risen to this point, after having traversed according to order all the degrees of the beautiful, reaches the final initiation, and suddenly perceives this marvellous, sacred, imperishable beauty.' Plato gives us the highest and most austere idea of this love of truth and beauty, when he declares that he who possesses it should rise completely above corporeal life, and never forget that what is pure only belongs to the pure. The true philosopher is he who loves to contemplate truth for its own sake. 'He,' he says, 'who makes the contemplation of truth his sole study, has no time to bend his thoughts down to the conduct of men in order to censure it, and to fill his mind with bitterness; but, having his mind ever fixed on objects which observe amongst themselves a constant and immutable order, he applies himself to imitate this order. Is it possible to admire the beauty of an object, to love to draw nearer and nearer to it without endeavouring to resemble it?' We shall now seek out the grand lines of a system of which we already know the generous inspiration.

Plato begins by defining science—true science, that which is worthy of the name. It is to be distinguished not only from ignorance, but from opinion, which is a premature conclusion of the mind, based, not on thorough examination, but on our transient fugitive impressions. In opinion there is nothing certain or absolute. If it escapes the shallowness of ignorance, yet it knows not real being; but is, to speak the language of Plato, a compound of being and non-being. Science, on the contrary, rises above what is accidental and conditional, and attaches itself to the pure, immutable, and eternal being. 'It fixes its eyes on objects enlightened by truth and being—it sees them clearly; but when man turns his eyes on what is mixed with darkness, on what is born and dies, his vision becomes disturbed and obscured: he has then only opinions.' Under its higher form, science takes the name of logic, which is distinguished from physics, morals, and politics, in that it seeks, not the different manifestations of being, but being itself, and only stops when it has attained the absolute, beyond all contingence. Science, thus understood, intrenches upon morals; for pure being in itself is inseparable from pure good in itself. To know it, is to know the good. What is pure, being only for the pure, can alone be penetrated by loving and practising purity. Science in this high sense is virtue: ignorance brings evil. Sin is another name for error. Plato in this point is the faithful disciple of Socrates. In order to define real being, he had to guard against a twofold exaggeration : that of Xenophanes and Zeno, who denied movement and change ; and that of Democritus, who denied unity and the absolute. Plato first of all endeavoured to establish that we must admit unity as well as plurality and movement, and movement as well as unity ; and in this way reconciled the contradictions which had made the fortune of the Sophists. One is amazed, in reading the Parmenides and the Théétites, at the ingenuity of his arguments, which frequently turn upon subtle grammatical analyses. Plato shows that human language implies both unity and plurality; that isolated words have no meaning, and only become intelligible to the mind when joined to each other. The phrase thus contains multiplicity and unity.

The laws of knowledge lead to the same result. In all knowledge there is duality : a subject and an object ; he who knows, and that which is known. We thus get rid of the abstract and absolute unity of the Elean school without falling into atomism. This subtle logic, besides being perfectly appropriated to the adversaries Plato had to combat, concealed a profound view that pervades the whole system of his philosophy. Adhering to the grand movement of Hellenic humanism, he admits, like his master, that man was made in the image of the divinity. His reason is divine. Consequently the laws of his reason, manifested by the laws of language, are those of being in general. Grammar, from this point of view, has an important bearing ; and we are no longer astonished at the revelations evolved from it, which at first appear puerile. Thus, in presence of absolute being, we find a contingent being, multiform and endowed with movement. This is not the contrary of being. because it has an existence of its own ; but neither is it the being *par excellence*. It occupies an intermediate position—it is the eternal OTHER, always mingled with the absolute being. It is the element of change, of plurality, of contingence, or, to give it its true name, it is matter; not the gross matter palpable to the touch, but a subtle matter everywhere diffused and attached to absolute being. Here we come to the fundamental error of Platonism, which is that of Paganism itself. Humanism does not succeed in his hands, no more than in those of any other philosopher of antiquity, in disengaging itself from the trammels of dualism.

Evil is inherent to the condition of the finite and multiform being, because it is inherent in matter. Eternal, like Being, the Non-Being has no end, as it had no commencement. This is the primal error of Platonism, whence flows all his errors in physics, in morals, and in politics: it logically tends to pantheistic annihilation, were it not permeated by the most admirable moral sentiment. Real Being is then everywhere mixed with the contingent being; it constitutes the element of unity, whilst the contingent being represents diversity and multiplicity. The element of unity in each thing is its prototype or idea. There is a world of prototypes or ideas of all that exists—a higher sphere of being, to which we have access by means of logic, which helps us to rise from the contingent to the absolute, from diversity to unity.

'Ideas,' we read in the *Parmenides*, 'subsist as the models of Nature; things resemble them and are copies of them. The participation of things with ideas consists in the resemblance of things with ideas.' The idea in Platonism performs the same part that the element of limitation did in the Pythagorean school; effectively, it is limit or outline that marks the form of things and approximates them to an intelligible type.

Moreover, those ideas of things are bound together, forming one harmonious whole; and are all merged into one supreme idea, which contains them in itself— the idea of the Good. It is this that sheds light and truth on the objects of science, and gives the faculty of knowing to the soul. 'Its beauty must be unspeakable, since Good is the source of science and truth, and is more beautiful than they are. This idea of the Good may be compared to the sun, which not only renders visible things visible, but is the cause of their birth, growth, and nourishment; in effect, intelligible beings derive from the Good, not only their intelligibility, but also their existence.' This absolute Good is the God of Plato. He says of God that He is the source of all good, and the principle of all ideas. He is the Spirit that sees in Himself the idea of each being, and that realizes it in each being.

Plato applies the principles of his logic to physics. 'The world is formed,' we read in the Timeus, 'after an invisible model, conceived by reason and intelligence. The Creator did not draw it out of the void; for, matter being eternal, He had only to reduce to order the scattered elements; and, seeing that all visible things were not in repose, but agitated by a confused, disordered movement, He drew them from disorder and subjected them to order, thinking that it was preferable.' Thus we see Platonism does not admit the creation: its god only introduced order and harmony into a chaos, eternal as he was eternal; and which is the non-being, the element of diversity and divisibility, which the philosopher can no more explain than he can suppress. 'The supreme God, not being a jealous God, desired that the world organized by Him should be the best possible. Nothing is more beautiful than an intelligent being. He made it, accordingly, a being endowed with soul and intelligence; the soul being the bond between matter and reason. The universe, taken in its totality, is a god whose intelligent soul circulates in an immense body. It is, to speak in Plato's words, a divine animal, formed after the perfect idea of the animal, or according to the animal type and ideal, which includes in itself as parts all individual animals, from the highest in the scale of beings to the lowest; for perfection always resides in unity. 'Thus the world is an animal visible and alone, comprehending in itself all animals, which have a natural relation with it. In order that this animal should, by its unity, resemble the perfect animal, its author did not make two worlds; and produced but the one heaven, which is and ever shall be alone. He gave it the form appropriated to it; and as it was destined to contain all beings, this form was a spheroid. The nature of the animal in itself being eternal, it was not possible to confer this attribute on the animal which had been produced; He therefore created in time a mutable image of eternity.

From this one divine animal, called the world, God caused to proceed all the species of animals that intelligence sees comprehended in the ideal animal which is the prototype of creation, in its details as in its grand features. There are four kinds of animals: the celestial race of gods, the winged species that fly in air, that which dwells in the waters, and that which walks on the earth. Each star is a divine, eternal animal—a real, though secondary divinity. These brilliant gods, whose mysterious movements in the heavens our eye can follow, were charged with the creation of inferior beings. They constitute the Greek Olympus. The supreme God furnishes the divine immortal part which is to be united to the mortal in those beings which, like man, reproduce, in one side of their nature, the type of absolute good. Each is in relation with a particular star, to which he will return, if by virtue he makes what is divine in him predominate over the material; those, on the contrary, who yield themselves up to evil, will, after death, go through a series of migrations under inferior forms of existence till their complete purification. The predominance of the divine element over the inferior element is not possible as long as the disorderly movements of the body remain unregulated by reason.

Plato distinguishes his three parts in man:—first, reason, which proceeds from the supreme God; the body, which is the material element; and the soul, which is the intermediate link. The human being is thus formed in the image of the world, of which he is, in a manner, a reduced model. By his higher nature, he approximates to God; by his inferior nature, he is bound to incoherent matter, the matrix of all beings. His reason reflects the divine world of ideas, the world of beauty, of harmony, and of good. This part of man is immortal; but this immortality is nowhere clearly defined, and it is impossible to say if it be personal. Besides, a vast interval separates man from God. The divine nature never being in communication with man, it is through the intervention of demons, who act as ministers between heaven and earth, that the divinity converses and speaks with us, either in our waking or sleeping state.

Such are the general features of Plato's physics. It is enough to have pointed them out. We find in them the grandeur and the imperfection of his dialectics,— that is to say, a powerful effort to resolve all things into the unity of the divine thought, yet constantly baffled by an invincible dualism. The god of Plato suffers, through all spheres of life, the torment inflicted by Mezentius on his victims; he being eternally attached to matter, which he neither produced nor can destroy. The idea of the Good, principle of unity, is, as it were, riveted to incoherent diversity, which it only partially subdues. Evil is mixed up in all his most beautiful creations; and the more his works are multiplied, the more evil abounds,—beings form a descending scale: man has degenerated from the gods, woman is a degeneration from man, and so on. Thus we see that Platonic dualism arrives at Indian emanation, without, however, reaching its ultimate conclusions, from which it owes its escape to the development of the moral element.

We have already seen that Plato, while admitting the necessity of evil, admits man's capacity to overcome it, at least in part; thus recognising his liberty. Earth is in his eyes a place of probation, even of expiation; for Plato is far removed from superficial optimism. Our present condition he describes as a fall and a punishment. 'Formerly,' he says, 'in the anterior life, our soul contemplated essences. Its beauty shone in all its splendour, when, mingling with the celestial chorus, we followed in the train of Jupiter, as other beings followed other gods; when enjoying a ravishing view and spectacle, we were initiated into mysteries which may be called the blessed, and which we celebrated, exempt from the imperfections and miseries that awaited us in death; when, having attained the highest degree of initiation, we admired these perfect objects, which we contemplated in a pure light, pure ourselves, and free from the grave we call the body. Pardon this diffuseness,' adds Plato, 'to the regret inspired by the recollection of the spectacle we then enjoyed. This happy life we forfeited by our fault.' Led away by dangerous attachments, our soul forgot the sacred things it had contemplated. We now resemble those captives, so poetically described in the seventh book of the *Republic*, chained in the cavern which serves as their prison, their backs turned to the light, and seeing, consequently, but the shadows of the objects which pass behind them, without once seeing the objects themselves. Nevertheless, these pale fugitive shadows suffice to revive in us the reminiscence of the higher world we inhabited, if we have not absolutely given the reins to the impetuous untamed horse, which, in Platonic symbolism, represents material life. Man, who is still full of the recollection of the holy mysteries, is transported, by the imperfect beauty he sees on earth, towards the perfect beauty he formerly contemplated; his soul recovers the wings which formerly bore it through the serene regions of essences. Detached from earthly cares, and solely occupied with what is divine, he is blamed by the multitude, who treat him as a madman, and who do not see that he is inspired. Beauty—splendour of truth, radiation from God, and which, altered and fragmentary as it is on earth, recalls sovereign beauty—is not to be the object merely of our admiration. The philosopher is not invited to a sterile contemplation; he should realize the good: all Plato's ethics are intended to teach how this can be attained. We already know the nature of the real good,—the real good is God. To practise good, is to resemble God. But God is the One and Absolute Being. Evil, as we have seen, is identified with change and diversity—with material life. To resemble God, is accordingly to aspire after unity, and to fly from contingence; it is to reject as much as possible all that partakes of contingence, to avoid diversity, to combat it within us and outside us.

Such a system of morals, intimately connected with Platonic metaphysics, necessarily demands the sacrifice of individuality; it tends to absorb the parts in the whole, and to refuse all value to the individual. This explains how, with Plato, the moral doctrine must be inseparable from the political; and both were, in fact, unfolded in the same treatise. In a system where the good is unity, society is everything — the individual nothing. The first of duties is to divest oneself of it as soon as possible; it is then only in the social sphere, or the republic, that it is possible for man to realize the good, because the State alone corresponds to the world of ideas, which is the world of unity. Thus the type of the good for the individual is borrowed from the State, which reduces all classes of society to a unity. Evil in us is a schism; it is the revolt of one faculty, breaking the internal unity, and destroying the equilibrium of the soul, and causing the insurrection of one part against the whole. Justice consists in binding together all the elements which compose the human being, in such sort that from their assemblage there may result a well-regulated, well-harmonized whole. Plato distinguishes four virtues: temperance, courage, justice, and reason. To these four virtues correspond four orders in the State: the slaves, the warriors, the magistrates, and the philosophers,—the government of the State should belong to the last. Justice is incumbent especially on magistrates, courage on warriors, reason on philosophers. Temperance, which in the individual consists in subjecting the lower part of man's nature to the higher, is realized in the republic by maintaining the social hierarchy; thus it may be equally practised by the lower classes as by magistrates and warriors. By this virtue, harmony is preserved in the State, which may arrive at reflecting in some degree the harmony and unity of the world of ideas.

The errors with which we reproach Plato in the plan he has traced of his ideal republic, flow from the fundamental error of his system. If he suppresses property, if he puts an end to family by sanctioning community of women, and opposes all domestic education, he is only consistent with the general tendency of his logic, which implies the sacrifice of the individual to the

phantom of unity, and which allows no value to the
parts composing the whole, compared to the whole
itself. The barriers behind which private life takes
refuge, must be removed, since community of goods is
the ideal of a really philosophic republic. Logically,
Plato should have gone further; he should have gone
the length of absolute asceticism, the germ of which is
latent in all dualism. But Greece, and above all Greece
after the days of Pericles, was not the East. The air
breathed there made men free and strong, it impelled
to activity. Plato did not therefore profess universal
annihilation, but the effacement of the individual. As
he saw in time the mutable image of eternity, he wished
his ideal republic to be a mutable image of the unity
of the higher world. However we may regret his
errors, we cannot but acknowledge that an admirable
spiritualism breathes through the picture he has drawn
of his ideal republic, where, from gymnastics and music
to philosophy, all should tend to a resemblance to God.
We cannot but be touched at the elevated manner in
which he treats of the education of youth, whom he
would remove from all corrupting influence, and the
wings of whose soul he would nourish with the luminous substance of truth and beauty, which alone they
can assimilate.

We have finished our sketch of this great philosophy,
which has fulfilled so important a part in the intellectual and religious history of humanity; and it is now
easy to measure the distance which separates it from
Christianity. It is impossible to set aside his metaphysics, treating them as of no account, in order to confine ourselves to his moral doctrine; for we find as
great a difference between the moral doctrines of Christ
and Plato, as there is between the Christian dogma and
the lofty speculations of the Academy. Nor could it
be otherwise; for the total separation between dogma

and moral doctrine is an invention of that vulgar philosophy which supposes man can rest satisfied with aplications without going back to principles.

More especially would this be impossible in the case of the great idealist of antiquity, who only lived for the ideal and supernal world. Such as your God is, such will be your duty; as is your doctrine, will be your morality. The distance that separates Plato's god from the Christian's God, separates the two systems of morals. In the one, dualism leads to the annihilation of the individual; in the other, spiritualism, triumphant, consecrates human individuality, and makes it the corner-stone of the edifice. Plato, like the Gospel, says to man that his duty is to resemble God; but, while Plato's god is only a sublime idea, a being of the reason which does not enter into communication with man, the God of Christians is the living God, the most holy and the most good—the God revealed by Jesus Christ, whose name is Love. Hence the riches and fecundity of the moral doctrine of the Gospels.

If we point out these imperfections in Platonism, it is in no spirit of depreciation; far from it. We rather aim at preserving to it its true mission. If we regard this sublime philosophy as a preparation for Christianity, instead of seeking in it an equivalent to the Gospel, we shall not need to overstate its grandeur in order to estimate its real value. It was this philosophy that gave the death-blow to polytheism, against which it never ceased levelling its victorious polemics. Plato, the poet-philosopher, sacrificed Homer himself to monotheism. We may measure the energy of the conviction by the greatness of the sacrifice. He could not pardon the syren whose songs had fascinated Greece, the fresh brilliant poetry that had inspired its religion. He crowned it with flowers, but banished it, because it had lowered the religious ideal of conscience. Plato admitted humanism, but he spiritualized and transformed it. Nor was it the whole of humanity he deified : he only recognised divinity in the higher part of our being. He thus carried Hellenism to the highest point it could reach. He gathered up its noblest elements in order to purify and harmonize them. He was thus, after Socrates, the inspired apostle of the moral idea,—not, it is true, understood in all its depth, but nevertheless presented in all its sanctity and in all its inflexible rigour. When we read the *Gorgias*, the *Philebus*, and, above all, the treatise on the *Republic* and the *Laws*, with what noble joy we are filled on hearing the grand voice of human conscience sweeping away all the sophisms of personal interest and the tumult of passions! If he calls us to witness the triumph of the wicked in the first part of the *Republic*, it is in order that, at the conclusion of the book, we shall see the deceitfulness of this triumph. 'As to the wicked,' he says, 'I maintain, that even if they succeed at first in concealing what they are, most of them betray themselves at the end of their career. They are covered with ridicule and opprobrium ; and present evils are nothing compared with those that await them in the other life. As to the just man, whether in sickness or poverty, these imaginary evils will turn to his advantage in this life and after his death, because the providence of the gods is necessarily attentive to the interests of him who labours to become just, and to attain, by the practice of virtue, to the most perfect resemblance of the divinity that is humanly possible. It is not natural that a man of this character should be neglected by him whom he endeavours to resemble.' Plato rises high above all eudemonism, and declares distinctly in the *Gorgias*, that it is better to suffer injustice than to commit it. 'I maintain,' he says, 'that what is most shameful, is not to be struck unjustly on the cheek or to be wounded in the body; but that to strike and wound me unjustly, to rob me or reduce me to slavery, to commit, in a word, any kind of injustice towards me or to what is mine, is a thing far worse and more odious for him who commits the injustice than for me who suffer it.' It is a great combat, he says; greater than we think, that wherein the issue is whether we shall be virtuous or wicked. Neither glory, nor riches, nor dignities, nor poetry deserve that we should neglect justice for them. The moral idea in Plato had such intense truth, that, as has been remarked, the expression he gives it has at times a singular analogy with texts of the Holy Scriptures. What is most striking in his ethical point of view, is its freedom from the dry frivolous Pelagianism which is at the root of all purely philosophical doctrine of morality. He admits that man cannot by himself rise to good. 'Virtue,' we read in the *Menon*, 'is not natural to man, neither is it to be learned, but it comes to us by a divine influence. Virtue is the gift of God in those who possess it.'[1]

Plato, in laying down such a system of morals, followed up and completed the work of Socrates. The voice of God, that still found a profound echo in man's heart, possessed in him an organ which all Greece gave ear to; and the austere revelation of conscience, this time embodied in language too harmonious not to entice by the beauty of form a nation of artists, they received it. The tables of the eternal law, carved in purest marble and marvellously sculptured, were read by them. This fact is of immense importance as an element in the work of preparation going on in Paganism. Besides, Plato, in order to waken up and develop the sentiment of man's fall, did not limit himself to painting in purest colours an ideal morality. He affirmed the fall in most emphatic terms, as the

[1] See the conclusion of the *Menon*.

fragments prove which we have quoted from the *Phedre*. The soul in its actual state appeared to him more disfigured than was Glaucus the seaman, 'whose primitive form was not recognisable, so disfigured had he become by his long dwelling under the ocean.' It was not possible that, in insisting as he did upon the miserable condition of man upon earth, he should not have contributed to excite an ardent aspiration towards a better state, and to develop a thirst for salvation. Unfortunately, while he woke up this feeling, he gave it a false direction, since he taught salvation by science, rather than salvation by redemption. The salvation he saw was through the intellect, and, consequently, essentially aristocratic, and ill adapted to the mass of mankind. This was its weak point, and must be the weak point of all philosophy, which can only find its completion in revelation. Philosophy may discover that which is necessary for man, but has no power to supply it. A system cannot save man, for salvation is an act. Still a most precious service was rendered the fallen race by wakening up its profoundest wants, and giving them a form of expression that must be immortal.

Moreover, Platonism was the most energetic protest of the spirit against the flesh heard in the ancient world. We cannot better sum up our appreciation of this glorious school than by applying to it what Plato so poetically says of love in the *Banquet:* it desires what is sovereignly beautiful, without possessing itself what it pursues.

We shall not dwell long on the philosophy of Aristotle,—not that we underrate its value, for it exercised an influence equal to that of Plato; it created an immortal method, and accumulated precious materials; it was the most scientific of all the ancient systems of philosophy;—but its relation to Christianity was far less direct; its service in the work of preparation consisted in perfecting the formula of humanism, and continuing the work of undermining polytheism. It formed, as we know, a striking contrast to Platonism, though proceeding from it. Aristotle, who had been during twenty years the disciple of Plato, remained faithful to him in one point: he admitted with him, and perhaps even more, the analogy between the higher elements of human nature and the divinity. The god of Aristotle is thought—the Supreme Mind. It was for this he studied the human intellect through all its manifestations with such minute care, hoping through this means to arrive at the universal laws of being. We can understand from this point of view the importance he attached to logic. Whilst Plato rose at once to ideas in order to construct from thence the universe, while attaching himself to what is general and eternal, Aristotle concentrates himself on the particular, the individual, the contingent, in order to frame by patient induction his whole system of logic. We shall not follow him in his close analysis of the forms and modes of our judgments, whence he drew the great principles of his philosophy. As in the syllogism, which is the ordinary mode of our judgments, we proceed from the known to the less known, so science, according to Aristotle, should take as starting-point what is most immediately known to us,—that is, sensation. This by repetition produces recollection, recollection experience, and experience produces science. The human mind is composed of two kinds of intelligence: the passive intelligence, which is, as it were, the receptacle of sensation; and the active intelligence, which impresses the seal of thought on the data furnished by the senses—thence disengaging first principles and those eternal truths, the type of which it contains within itself. This active intelligence is the divine part of the mind. It is this that impresses an intelligible character, a definite form, on the incoherent, indistinct elements that reach us through the channel of sensation. Thus we find already this duality of matter and form which pervades the whole system of Aristotle. Matter is passive, indeterminate, general; form, on the contrary, is active, determinate, particular. The mind on its passive side is related to the sensible world—on its active side, is connected with the divine world. Aristotle exalts these conclusions of logic to the height of universal principles. He proves that the essence of a thing does not consist in what it has in common with other things, but in what distinguishes it from them—that it is by this essential difference it is to be defined. Consequently, the essence of beings is not to be sought in the element of unity and generality, or in the idea, as Plato taught, but in the element of diversity and speciality. It is not possible to be in more direct opposition to Platonism.

Thus the opposition of matter and form, with Aristotle, corresponds to the opposition between the element of generality and the element of the particular. On one side is pure passivity, the non-being; on the other, activity, being, thought. Matter and form are the two great causes whence proceed all beings. The formative cause is at the same time the motive and final cause; for it is evidently the element of determination which impresses movement on passive matter while determining it; and it also is the end of being, since being only exists really when it has passed from an indeterminate state to a determinate. Movement is the universal end of all beings: it is eternal and permanent. If movement be universal and eternal, there must exist an eternal unchangeable motive cause that produces it. This primeval cause of movement alone, because absolute, is Aristotle's god. 'This motionless cause of movement,' we read in the twelfth book of his *Meta-*

physics, ' is a necessary being ; and by virtue of such necessity, it is the all-perfect ; consequently, a principle. This all-pervading principle penetrates heaven and all nature. It eternally possesses perfect happiness: its happiness is in action. This primeval mover is immaterial ; for its essence is energy—it is pure thought, thought thinking itself, the thought of thought.' The activity of pure intelligence, such is the perfect, eternal life of God. This prime cause of change, this absolute perfection, moves the world while itself remains motionless, powerfully drawing to itself all beings. The principle of movement is found in the universal desire for absolute good. 'The world is moved by the attraction exercised on it by the eternal mind, the serene energy of the divine intelligence.'

Those principles are applied to physics. Heaven is the first force moved by the divine mover, and all things move after it. Movement is the final end of each being. The soul, or the rational energy, is the end, or, to speak as Aristotle, the *entelechy* of the body. Morals, from this point of view, become a kind of spiritual mechanics : as all is reduced to movement, it is a science of equilibrium in the higher sphere of life. We are not to expect here the sublime effort of Platonism : it is too near earth. The aim and end of life is happiness, and happiness is to be sought in activity in conformity with virtue. Virtue is defined by Aristotle as a *mean* between two extremes. The great peripatetic philosopher, like Plato, sacrificed everything to the State. The family is the end or *entelechy* of the individual, and the State is the end of the family. The dignity of the individual is entirely overlooked. Consequently, we find Aristotle professing the most unscrupulous principles on the subject of slavery and the slave trade, as practised by antiquity. Ingeniously applying his ontological principles, he sees in the soil and population of a country the material element of the State. To impress a form on this, is the duty of the social constitution. On politics his genius casts most penetrating light. His love for the *mean* betwixt extremes in all things led him to give the preference in government to the middle classes.

If we now appreciate as a whole the philosophy of Aristotle, it will appear on one side to pass the line of the great Hellenic period. It does not inaugurate, but it prepares, the decline. In it we admire the most powerful effort of the human mind in antiquity: it left permanent results in psychology and logic; it perfected the instrument of human thought, giving to it delicacy and precision. Yet, taking all things into consideration, it appears to us inferior to its predecessor. In combating what was exaggerated in Plato's theory of ideas, Aristotle's philosophy was a reaction against the ideal itself, and prepared the way for the sensualist schools. Leaving the problem of duality quite as unsolved as did Platonism, he laid stress on the side sacrificed by the other: contingence, the particular. It is easy to foresee that the successors of Aristotle should neglect the elevated portion of his system, that which concerns the eternal cause of change, and attach themselves too exclusively to sensation. But it is in the moral point of view that Aristotle's inferiority is most palpable. His god, as he himself says, is above virtue; it is pure thought, rather than moral perfection. Indifferent and alone, he takes no cognizance of man. Morality has no divine basis, no eternal type, no aid to look for from above. Consequently, Aristotle's philosophy had but little influence on conscience. Its chief merit consists in having given to Hellenic humanism its most perfect formula, in defining God as the eternal reason—thought contemplating itself. By this, Aristotle completed the destruction of polytheism in the higher regions of intelligence. 'For several to command,' says Aristotle in his Metaphysics, 'is not good; there should be but one chief. A tradition, handed down from remotest antiquity, and transmitted under the veil of fable, says that all the stars are gods, and that the Divinity embraces the whole of nature. All the rest is but a fabulous recital, invented to persuade the vulgar, and to serve the cause of laws and human interests. Thus they give human forms to their gods, or represent them under the figure of certain animals, and a thousand other inventions derived from such fables.' This passage in itself suffices to prove that we have reached the term of the period of progress and glory of Paganism. From the East to Greece, the idea of God had become purified and clearer; man began to understand that union with the Divinity was something else than the pantheistic absorption, or an apotheosis of humanity. He caught glimpses of a holier union; a reparation worthier God and himself. But at the same time he knows not where to find it. The purifying of the religious idea, and the progress of the philosophic idea, evoked a new ideal; but this ideal was vague and remote. Nor has he the means of realizing it. He knows sufficient to make him renounce his ancient religion, but not enough to found a faith which can satisfy him. Wherefore we are not to be surprised that the grand philosophic period of Greece should be followed by one of incredulity, moral collapse, inaugurating the long and universal *decadence*; which was, perhaps, as necessary to the work of preparation as was the period of religious and philosophic development.

II. GRECO-ROMAN PAGANISM.

TRANSFORMATION OF ANCIENT PAGANISM FROM THE TIME OF ALEXANDER, AND UNDER THE ROMAN DOMINATION.

GREECE UNDER ALEXANDER AND HIS SUCCESSORS.

The decline of Hellenism began at the time of its greatest external glory. We may date it from the conquests of Alexander; for to undergo the influence of the East, was synonymous with decline, a step backwards, a partial relapse from humanism to the old religions of Nature. This gathering together of all creeds and all gods necessarily tended to their mutual destruction; and from the wrecks of all their altars we find erected the altar to the unknown God, the mysterious inheritor which the old world so long looked forward to. From the time of Philip and Alexander, the old democratic type, which had been so favourable to the development of Hellenic genius, became gradually effaced. It disappeared as an institution disappears that possesses immense vitality,—not suddenly, but gradually, and with frequent efforts at restoration. Athens still cast a vivid light on expiring liberty. In this city of the Muses, political glory was inseparable from literary fame. Demosthenes, while defending the Republic, gave to the world the finest models of eloquence, and conferred immortality on orations of ephemeral interest by impressing upon them the perfection of form.

After the death of this great citizen, Athens rapidly sank; and, notwithstanding a few feeble efforts to recover its independence, gradually adapted itself to a foreign yoke. The same citizens that had applauded the orations of Demosthenes, marched out to meet King Demetrius, some years after his heroic struggle against Macedon, carrying crowns of laurel, and chanting songs such as this: 'Other gods are too far off, or are deaf; they either do not exist, or are indifferent to us; but thee we see before us. Thou art not an effigy in wood or stone, but a body of flesh and blood.' The different states of Greece were subjected to the same fate. Handed over from one domination to another in the struggles of Alexander's lieutenants, they endeavoured to reconquer their independence by forming themselves into confederations, but were powerless to unite even in defence of a common cause. The Achæan and Etolian leagues were weakened by internal discords; and it was in vain Sparta tried to recover her supremacy. Divided amongst themselves, the small states invoked the aid of dangerous allies, at one time appealing to Macedon, then to Egypt. They prepared in this way the total ruin of Greek liberty, which Rome was destined to put an end to for ever.

With the decline of Athens coincided the rising glory of Alexandria, which at this period became the centre of Greek civilisation. Athens had been the brilliant focus of Hellenism; the intellectual metropolis; the seat of a civilisation strong without hardness, graceful without effeminacy, combining in one harmonious whole all the qualities of the Hellenic race, which made this little country the classic land of liberty and art. The beautiful, through all its manifestations, was there wrought out in most exquisite proportions, and clad in inimitable perfection. Athens was truly the republic of letters, the ideal democracy wherein intellectual distinctions prevailed over all others—where intellectual gifts developed themselves with marvellous facility, and were nobly tempered in the fruitful struggles of a free people. Alexandria, the new metropolis of

Greece, was in all points the opposite of Athens. Built by a great conqueror, whose dream was to unite the world under his sceptre, and who had selected it as the point of junction between the East and West, temples were erected there to the divinities of Egypt as well as to the divinities of Greece. It continued faithful to the idea of its founder: the genius of the East and the genius of the West were there blended and fused, and mutually modified each other. Considerably enlarged by the Ptolemies, containing in its immense library all the treasures of ancient culture, the emporium of universal commerce, Alexandria was rather a city of the world than the capital of a kingdom. Representatives of all religions met there. Beside the temple of Jupiter rose the white marble temple of Serapis; and close by stood the synagogue of the Jew. Universal scepticism sprang up in Alexandria, and rapidly effaced the distinctive characteristic of the Greek intellect. From Athens to Alexandria we can follow the transformation it underwent at this period, in religion as well as in philosophy, in art as in literature. The fall of liberty was necessarily followed by vast results in the ancient world, where morals and politics were so nearly identified,—where the individual was so completely effaced by the State. The State once humbled and enslaved, the moral ideal was veiled, and demoralization, which invariably follows discouragement in a society to whom all higher consolations are unknown, made frightful progress. In religion the mythological purifying process, which had been so successfully pursued by the great artists and poets of the age of Pericles, completely ceased. We have already noticed the dissolvent action of Greek philosophy on the national creed. It had destroyed faith in the Olympian gods, in the name of a higher ideal, but an ideal too vague to replace the ancient popular faith. On this delicate point the language of philosophers had always observed a certain ambiguity; the death of Socrates had taught them prudence; and they therefore adopted no definite position. Polytheism was undermined, but not swept off; its carcass was still left standing. Faith in Homer's gods was gone; but the carcass was there, and before it many had to prostrate themselves. Greece knew too much and too little: she knew too much to have complete faith in her gods, and too little to adore another divinity. Accordingly, we are not to be surprised to find that the period of mythological purification was succeeded by a period of religious degradation. Apotheoses were multiplied; worships and festivals in honour of powerful kings instituted, such as those of Demetrius Policrate in Athens, Attalus in Sycion, Antigone in Achaia, Ptolemy in Rhodes. At the same time, contact with the East led to a restoration of the ancient worship of nature: the worship of Bacchus rapidly increased, assuming a more and more Asiatic character. Impiety took advantage of this degradation of the religious idea; and Evhemere of Messina, 300 B.C., openly declared that the gods were ancient kings deified by fear or superstition after death. Aphrodite, he maintained, had been a beautiful courtesan; and Harmonia a Phrygian dancer, seduced by Cadmus.

The philosophic movement of this period followed the same downward path. After what has been said of Aristotle's philosophy, it is easy to foresee the danger that necessarily followed in the track of his disciples. If the vigour of his genius kept him from sinking down the inclined plane of sensualism, towards which his system tended, his successors were incapable of the same effort. The noble part of his Metaphysics, concerning the changeless cause of movement—the all-perfect God deriving happiness in the contemplation of his own perfections, the thought of thought—all this grand side of his philosophy was forgotten or ignored; and the counsel which, in opposition to Platonism, he gave his disciples, that they should attach themselves above all to sensation, being misinterpreted and exaggerated by them, necessarily, in a time of moral collapse, opened the way to sensualism. Already had his immediate disciples, the peripateticians Dicearchus and Straton, deliberately set aside the god of philosophy, affirming that a divinity was unnecessary to the explanation of the formation of the world. Thus we see, as at all times of social degeneracy, scepticism appeared, covering its bitter sadness with an ironical laugh: it rose up to proclaim cruel deceptions, and its triumph was marked by the ruin of all greatness. In the same way that the first sceptics set atomism and the docrine of the Elean school against each other, the new sceptics opposed Aristotle to Plato, and Plato to Aristotle. They found an ignoble pleasure in seeing these two illustrious philosophers mutually stab each other, and finally fall with philosophy itself, whose most powerful representatives they had been. Timon and Pyrrhon declared, that of each thing it might be said to be and not to be; and that, consequently, we should cease tormenting ourselves, and seek to attain absolute calm, which they dignified by the name of *ataraxie*. Spectators of the disgrace of their country, surrounded by examples of pusillanimity and corruption, they wrote this maxim—one worthy of a time when liberty dies betrayed by the senses: 'Nothing is infamous; nothing is in itself just; laws and customs alone constitute what is justice and what is iniquity.' Having reached this extreme, scepticism dies out in the vacuum it creates around it. Pyrrhon declared that even negation too definitely affirmed, implied the possibility of certainty, and that therefore we should abstain from it.

Were we to estimate the importance of a school by

its duration, no glory would be comparable with that attached to the Epicurean and Stoic schools. Yet these two systems implied a *decadence* in philosophy—first, because they profess disdain of all high speculation; secondly, that they are based on sensualist principles.

It is unnecessary to enter largely into Epicureanism. According to Epicurus, philosophy is essentially the art of making oneself happy. It is therefore a system of morality. And what morality! Its leading principle is, that we should fly from suffering and seek happiness, which, according to him, is identical with pleasure. We should be guided in our choice of pleasure by the consideration of avoiding suffering. It is on this account that virtue, which consists in moderation, is desirable. Epicurus distinctly says that the beginning and root of all good is in the pleasures of the table. He adds, that we should avoid injuring our neighbour, so that he may not injure our interests. In logic, all is referred to sensation; pure atomism is the principle of the Epicurean system of physics. Bodies were formed by the combination of atoms; the soul is composed of lighter atoms, and will perish as soon as they separate. The gods are material beings, like our souls. Impassible, taking no cognizance of us, it is needless to weary them, rather ourselves, by praying to them. Such a system of philosophy condemns itself: it may suit a time of degradation and corruption, by inculcating the impunity of injustice and the lawfulness of sensuality. There can be no surer means of enslaving a free people than by degrading them.

Stoicism, founded by Zeno, and completed by Cleanthus and Chrysippus, set out from logical principles identical with those of Epicureanism, and concluded with a system of morals diametrically the reverse. It also takes sensation as the starting-point of all science. Ideas are inscribed upon the soul by sensation, as on soft wax prepared to receive the impress. Certainty is founded upon sensible evidence, and truth itself is corporal. The Stoics professed the most decided pantheism. According to them, the two principles of the universe are matter and reason; the latter being a subtle fire, called the artistic fire, the active principle diffused through the universe, like blood through our veins. This is their god, the universal Jupiter, that penetrates all things. The world, taken as a whole, realizes the good; evil is but relative and apparent; it consists in particularity and passivity. Besides, all things are subject to the laws of fatality. The soul is not immortal, being corporal. The portion of the universal soul that animates it, becomes finally merged into the active principle of the world. The universe is to be destroyed by fire, but to be recreated after the combustion. From this materialistic physical system the Stoics educed a severe moral system, but one impossible to realize, and often inconsistent. The first maxim seems, at first sight, to belong to Epicureanism. 'We should,' says Zeno, 'conform ourselves to nature.' But nature here means the active principle, reason. To conform to nature, is therefore to give the ascendency to the rational, active element; to rise above passivity; to triumph over emotion, over suffering, over pleasure. Since pleasure is a passive state of the soul, its aim is to attain impassibility. Virtue is identical with reason, and is inculcated as a system. It is absolute in its nature, and is possessed, or is not possessed,—the rational principle being one and indivisible. There are no degrees, no shades, in moral life. Stoicism, in its early form, did not profess the rigour it afterwards assumed in Rome. In Athens it never reached the same height. It would appear that the early Stoics, under pretext of impassibility, unscrupulously tolerated some of the most shameful vices of Paganism.

At a later period, the philosophy of the Porch underwent a notable purification, and rallied to itself all great souls who desired to react against the frightful moral degradation of imperial Rome. It became the refuge of all noble spirits; but, as we shall see, though it carried its severity to the farthest limit, it was never able to neutralize the consequences of its fundamental principles. It could not rise to spiritualism. Denying both God and immortality, morality was left without its true basis, reducing all to the Ego; it was, in spite of appearances, tainted with an incurable egotism. Pride takes from it all disinterestedness. Disheartened by its metaphysical impotency, it concentrated itself upon practical applications. If Stoicism was powerful as a protest against the worst infamies of Paganism, all it could do was to bear testimony to that decline, without being able to arrest it.

Scepticism, unable to find for itself a master either amongst Stoics or Epicureans, reappeared under a new garb, and, sheltering itself under the name of Plato, pretended to renew the chain of true Socratic traditions. The New Academy, at first moderate and prudent under Arcesilas, taught through Carneades that certainty upon any subject was impossible. Adopting the tenet of the Stoics, that sensation is the source of our knowledge, Carneades had no difficulty in proving that sensation can yield no criterion of truth, and hence concluded that we must rest satisfied with the probable. The natural consequence of such a principle is eudemonism, and to it Carneades was led. Thus we find that once philosophy deserted the heights of Platonism, it fell into materialism and scepticism, and was condemned to play the miserable part of reducing to maxims the practices of a most corrupt period.

If from philosophy we turn to literature, we shall be still more struck by the transformation which Greek genius had undergone. Creative inspiration had died out; it no longer breathed the vivifying air of liberty, was no longer fortified by the manly struggles of public life. Accordingly, in all that implies development of political existence, the decline is remarkable. The two forms of composition which at this time attained any real distinction were the New Comedy and the Idylle. Menander to paint the vices of private life, and Theocritus to celebrate the charms of solitude, needed not the noble inspiration of patriotism. Nothing can replace this in the higher walks of poetry. The splendid hospitality with which the most eminent representatives of letters and science were received at Alexandria failed to rekindle the inspiration that animated Æschylus, Sophocles, and Pindar. Tragedy is no longer the solemn representation of the national myths, but a literary exercise—an academical competition, where the king distributes the prizes. The seven poets of the Pleiades, in spite of their ambitious appellation, did not rise above mediocrity, and were mere declaimers and erudites.

Epic poetry ran into dissertations, and became didactic and scientific. Callimachus of Cyrene does not sing of heroes, but of causes. Dicearchus writes a geographical description of Greece, and Aratus composes a poem on phenomena. The *Argonauts* of Apollonius of Rhodes, though often attaining to real beauty of form, is rather the production of an erudite than of a poet: belief, simplicity, enthusiasm, are wanting. Occasionally we meet a passage of poetry—a fine verse may surprise us—a brilliant descriptive passage; but reflection predominates, and with it coldness. The time is not yet ripe for a new source of poetry to spring up out of the dried, exhausted soil,—the poetry of melancholy, enlightened by prophetic presentiment. The old world was not yet sufficiently humbled. It had ceased to add to its wealth, but went on making its inventory, and enjoyed a keen satisfaction in the task; and this satisfaction, unlike enthusiasm, is most adverse to poetry. If poets are not forthcoming, grammarians and commentators abound—they fix the canons of Greek literature, and carefully determine the really classic works; thus acknowledging that the great literary epoch is past, and that they and their successors were henceforth to be reduced to the necessity of imitating those immortal types of the beautiful without making an effort to create others. Zenodotus, Aristophanes of Byzantium, and Aristarchus hold the first rank amongst critics and grammarians; but, though able dissectors of the grand school of poetry, they could not resuscitate it. History alone profited by the new conditions in which literature was placed; its horizon was enlarged, and it was no longer confined to exclusively national topics. With Polybius it began its researches into the hidden chain of causes and effects. Eloquence, on the contrary, rapidly declined: it had lost the nervous, passionate language of public debates among a free people; and the more shallow and empty it became, the more it assumed ample forms and affected false majesty. Cicero admirably characterizes it by the word Asiatic, thus painting by one word its frivolous pomp and meanness.

One might suppose, that with Alexander a new and wider extension would have opened for Greek art. Its first contact with the East gave new stimulus to inspiration without deteriorating it. Hellenic nationality had still too much vitality to abdicate: it was possible that the Greek artist, while captivated by Oriental grandeur, would still cling to the traditions of the Greek schools. Nevertheless, the new order of things inaugurated by the conqueror, precipitated the decline of the plastic arts. Amongst the intelligent democracies of Greece, the artist had to seize the spirit and imagination

K

of a whole people who were themselves artists. He had, consequently, to attach himself to a point of view, at once elevated, universal, and truly human; hence the religious and patriotic character of his inspiration. But this ceased when princes became the protectors of artists. Henceforward their preoccupation was to flatter their patrons' tastes and pleasures. All the grand ideas of Hellenism had been expressed by the glorious artists of the time of Pericles. But they, and the poets their cotemporaries, carried away with them the noble inspirations which they had obeyed. Their successors were initiated into all the secrets of art, and wielded the chisel with unsurpassing skill; but they had no grand ideas, certainly no religious ideas, to express. Art became a courtier, and performed its functions with wonderful distinction; but nothing could redeem it from the consequences of the vile condition it had accepted. Palaces rather than temples were constructed. The brilliant and useful became the aim of the artist, as the monuments of Alexandria and Antioch testify. The decoration of man's dwelling-place was more the subject of preoccupation than how to confer an imposing character upon religious edifices. The Corinthian order had universally dethroned the Doric; mechanic arts received extraordinary development; chariots, warlike instruments, were luxuriously ornamented; sculpture multiplied the statues of princes, and marbles personifying famous cities. Statues of the gods, being less profitable, became rarer. The school of Rhodes, founded at this period, produced such *chefs-d'œuvres* as the Laocoon and the Farnese Bull. But the preoccupation about effect is already evident. There is something in them theatrical, though the rules of beauty are still faithfully adhered to. In proportion as true inspiration fails, the greater will be the search after effect, and greater the distance from pure, calm, classic beauty. Precious stones were elaborately worked, as was all that pertained to luxury. Painting followed the same course as sculpture: it became a trade, became degraded and prodigal. Mosaic work, contributing to the decoration of palaces, assumed an unfortunate prominence. Thus in religion, as in philosophy and art, the decadence is prepared,—retarded for a time, and concealed by the splendour of a refined civilisation, but spreading with irresistible sway, owing to the increasing corruption, and the destruction of all moral bases in the ancient world. A notable event was about to hasten on this degeneracy—the conquest of Greece and of the world by Rome, and the formation of the Empire.

ROME BEFORE AND AFTER THE CONQUEST OF GREECE.

While Greece was wasting strength in intestine struggles, a new power was rising in Italy, of which it was easy to prognosticate that it would one day become the successful inheritor of the conquests of Alexander. Its origin had been obscure and humble; its cradle, a small town in Latium, inhabited by a rude, wild population, composed of shepherds and brigands. But this rude tribe, that in many respects deserved the name of barbarian, which the Greeks so lavishly bestowed, possessed a hidden force which is the secret of great things, and which enables man to achieve the impossible. It had faith in its destinies; and this faith was indomitable, for we find it reappearing after each defeat with increased energy. The Roman people allowed themselves no respite till their destiny as conquerors was fulfilled, but marched on with heroic, indefatigable perseverance. No victory satisfied their ambition; no defeat shook their courage. Defeated, they waited the return of fortune; conquerors, they marched onwards. Never did the unity and *solidarité* of the different generations of a people appear more evident. One might suppose them to be the same man animated by the same idea. The task undertaken by the fathers was continued without hesitation or delay by the sons, from the point at which it had been dropped. This vigorous Roman race was nerved and tempered by the struggles of the democracy, as well as by their foreign wars. Violent disputes between patricians and plebeians make up the internal history of Rome, giving to its people that character of pride and hardness which marks their genius. They grew up in the atmosphere of stormy liberty, in which too many passions were stirred for it to be bloodless. In agricultural labours the Roman sought repose from the toils of war and the forum; the plough and sword were his constant companions. Hence a simplicity of life verging on austerity; a something grand and serious permeating his whole existence; purity of morals, and dignity of the domestic hearth; but, at the same time, an implacable severity towards the vanquished and the stranger. The Roman of the republic, it has been truly said, was pre-eminently the expression of natural right: he represents what is inexorable in it, and embodied it in formulas with incomparable clearness and practical sense; but he was unable to understand that rights implied duties. He considered himself master of mankind, assuming them to be his legitimate property; whilst in return he owed them nothing but proconsuls to carry out their fiscal relations. This inflexibility and pride still breathe in the language of this conquering race, which is precise as a military order, brief as a word of command in battle; neglecting all those delicate articulations which give grace and pliancy to speech, and with which the Greek idiom abounds. *Festinat ad res.* It is the language of action, hard and cutting as a sword. Not contented with painting thought, it carves and chisels it.

We can easily conceive that the religion of such a

people must have differed profoundly from that of the Greeks. Their first creed was a mixture of old local traditions. In their religious ideas we find traces of the religion of Nature—adoration of its forces and laws. The hidden gods worshipped in Etruria represented the inexorable and mysterious power of Nature. The Indra of the Vedas reappears in the Etruscan religion, which, like the early Vedas, sees the highest manifestation of the divinity in the roar of thunder and the brightness of the lightning. The Etruscans sought in lightning the signs of divine will; the science of augury was much cultivated amongst them. Their religion was essentially an art, the art of discovering the designs of the gods, and exercising an influence upon them by means of various rites. Much importance was likewise attached to divinities of an inferior order—demons or genii, styled Lares, which were regarded as protectors of the household hearth and family. This singular religion, blended with the various worships of Latium, and in a slight measure enriched with Hellenic traditions that reached them through Magna Grecia, was the ground-work of the national religion of Rome. But the proud city was not long in stamping religion with the same impress it left on all it touched. In every respect Roman genius was a contrast to that of Greece, being entirely devoid of that rich imagination which could create myths, and make the history of the gods one brilliant poetry. Till the day Greece, subjugated by Rome, conquered it morally, and spread over it its entire civilisation, nothing could be more poor or nude than the Roman mythology. Without any ideal character, it is the most prosaic of religions. Never seeking to invent poetic legends, it made no attempt to glorify the founders of the race under the name of heroes, but deified real life without endeavouring to transform it. Essentially agricultural, it took hold of all the details of field-life, in order to consecrate and sanctify them. The gods are simple abstractions of Nature, without any real analogy with man, but impersonal as the laws of the physical world, and indefinitely multiplied, although the worship of Jupiter Maximus maintained a kind of monotheism at Rome. 'The whole Roman mythology,' says Benjamin Constant, 'was not only moral, but historical. Each temple, each statue, each festival, recalled to the Romans some danger from which the gods had saved Rome. Each divinity had some special virtue under its protection: Jupiter inspired courage; Venus, conjugal fidelity; Neptune prepared for prudent resolutions; Hercules, for inviolable vows.' Juno Sospita was worshipped for having granted the Romans a signal victory over the Gauls; Jupiter Stator had arrested their flight; Castor and Pollux had fought with them; Jupiter Latial presided over the alliance of all the Latin tribes. The Roman priesthood was elective, and not the fief of certain special families, as in Greece; and enjoyed considerable political influence, one of its functions being to pronounce on the legality of adoptions and of wills. The name of Pontiff comes from the bridge (pons) which Ancus Martius built across the Tiber, and which was placed in the custody of the priests. The festivals celebrated at Rome were almost all consecrations of its history. The *Lemuries* were solemn expiations for the murder committed by its first king; the Quirinals perpetuated his apotheosis; the Sabian dances were celebrated in honour of the buckler which the gods had thrown down from heaven to the Romans. Thus we see the human and national idea prevailed over the religious idea. The characteristic feature of their worship was the complexity of its ritual, and the multiplicity of its sacrifices. The science of the aruspices and augurs was cultivated at Rome as at Etruria. The gods, lares and penates, were worshipped with especial predilection.

A profound change was wrought in the constitution and spirit of the Roman people from the time when, masters of Italy and conquerors of Carthage, no further obstacle stood in the way of their ambition. The spoils of conquered provinces gorged Rome with wealth; insolent luxury superseded ancient simplicity of manners. The middle classes, from which had been recruited the heroic legions that had secured Roman preponderance, now gradually disappeared. There remained but a corrupt aristocracy, and a turbulent, imperious herd of beggars, who became the tools of the different factions.

The conquest of Greece, completed 146 B.C., more than any other event, hastened the decomposition of ancient society. The contact of two such opposite civilisations was equally fatal to both,—each communicating to the other its share of corruption. The Roman retained his rudeness, but had lost his primitive austerity of manners, and pursued with savage greed the acquisition of wealth and pleasure. Suddenly transported into the midst of marvellous artistic treasures, he became, as it were, intoxicated; and, though unable to feel their value, he at once set about appropriating them. But Greek culture was not as easy to conquer as Greek provinces. Its precious marbles might be carried to Rome, but not its delicate grace. Its vices were more easily borrowed, as were the doctrines of the schools which justified them, such as the Epicurean and Sceptic. Greece was to Rome what we might imagine an intelligent slave to be, who seeks to dominate her master by flattering his passions. She degraded herself more and more by this shameful game, without raising to her own level her formidable disciple, who was at the same time her tyrant. The Roman mode of reciting the lesson taught, completely changed its nature. The political Greek mythology, transplanted to Rome, lost all its ideal character: it became naturalized, and underwent a thorough alteration. We shall see in the ensuing period the depth of degradation which humanism reached.

Roman literature copies Greece with Ennius and Livius Andronicus; but their hand is too rude to reproduce the grace and freshness of colouring of the original. Roman genius at this period shone only in comedy—in works such as those of Plautus and Terence; the ridiculous abounding at this intermediate phase, when new manners were at war with old national traditions. Greek artists filled the city, carrying with them their facility, elegance, and pliant manners; but as they toiled for the oppressors of their country, we may judge how completely all noble inspiration must have been wanting. Nevertheless, they were still too near the grand artistic epoch not to have produced admirable works. Rome was embellished by them and their disciples. There was nothing henceforward to arrest the tide of luxury.

But the most active agent of corruption was the Greek Sophist, the representative of the New Academy, the used-up Sceptic who, like Carneadas, came to teach Rome contempt for all sacred things, and to undermine the moral bases of society. All these combined influences led to the fall of the republic. Nothing better prepares humanity to acquiesce with docility in the designs of brute force than unbridled scepticism. Between incredulity and despotism there is a secret but sure understanding. The day Rome ceased to believe in her gods, she ceased to believe in herself; the same blow that struck religion struck the republic, and henceforward power became the disputed prey of ambitious men without fear and without scruples. Neither the virtue of Cato, nor the eloquence of Cicero or the dagger of Brutus, could save liberty. Rome was ripe for the empire of the Cæsars, and was worthy of it, ere it was inaugurated by Augustus. In spite of the splendour that surrounded its opening, augmented by the splendour of a great literary epoch,—in spite of the repose it for some time procured the world, it nevertheless inaugurated, let Gibbon say what he will, that universal decline which was to demonstrate the radical incapacity of Paganism to accomplish the work of restoration. Fortunately for humanity, this incapacity became more and more felt: all eyes were turned towards the East; some lifted them higher. The ancient world, thus sinking back upon itself, was thrilled by a mysterious anticipation. It is this contradictory state that we have now to paint, carefully collecting all the signs of decline, and all the sighs for deliverance that burst from many hearts. No period of history presents so many contrasts, so many subjects for sadness and indignation, and so many reasons for hope. All the elements of good and evil are in a state of fermentation. The great preparation is being consummated. If the night is dark and thick, the horizon is brightening with prophetic light.

THE GRECO-ROMAN WORLD.

Universal Decline and Universal Aspiration.

It may appear strange to speak of universal decline at a time when the ancient world, almost entirely united under one single domination, presented all the appearance of power and prosperity. Including Spain, Gaul, Britain, Italy, Illyria, Greece, Asia Minor, Egypt, Africa, and the islands of the Mediterranean,—or, in other words, 600,000 square leagues of the most fertile countries,— the Roman Empire all but realized the dream of all great conquerors; that is to say, the empire of the world. It was defended by a regular army of five hundred thousand men, ranged in the order of the famous legions, which constituted the most skilful military organization known. Imperial despotism, resulting from the concentration in the hands of a single person of all the functions of the republic, transformed the whole of the ancient constitution while it preserved its semblance. It might be supposed that it would have given peace to the worn-out world. Augustus introduced some slight order into the mythological chaos of Rome, and endeavoured by means of decrees to effect a religious restoration. Literature and arts reached their apogee. The language, rendered flexible by Horace and Virgil, united precision to elegance, and attained that classic beauty which is so transient in all literatures, but which fixes the rules of beauty by being in itself its most perfect type. However, the religious restoration, like the literary restoration, was but a pause in the downward course,—rather, we should say, masked it for a moment without arresting it. The religious restoration was purely political, and in nowise concealed that contempt for the gods which had become universal. Of the two great poets of the Augustan age, one was an Epicurean; and the other found his finest inspiration in a strange melancholy, which he expressed in verses such as have not since been written. Virgil is not the poet of a young race, but the poet of a time of sadness: he sings at that evening hour when, as he says himself, the shadows of the mountains lengthen; but the evening was illumined for him with mysterious lights. There are radiant distances in his sweet, sad poetry. He sings in his own fashion the approaching renovation. With the exception of Virgil, the theme the poets most loved to celebrate was voluptuousness. Ovid's Metamorphoses reduce the history of the gods to a series of love adventures, of which the charm of the style can hardly atone for the impiety of the theme. The literary restoration enables us to estimate at its true value the worth of the religious restoration. We are therefore justified in considering the age of Augustus as an episode in the history of the decline of Paganism, which began anterior to it and continued after it; and, if we look closely, we shall see that the process of social decomposition was not for a day interrupted. In the picture we present of this time, which must necessarily be one of a summary character, we shall include the time immediately preceding the empire and that which followed.

Beheld from the point of view of luxury, Roman life was a grand life at the close of the republic and at the outset of the empire. The houses, Seneca tells us, were refulgent with gold; slaves, attired in gorgeous vestments, circulated through them; opulence shone out in every corner; fountains shot up in sparkling columns in the banquet-rooms. The palace of a wealthy Roman frequently contained four dining-rooms, twenty bed-chambers, and a hundred other rooms besides, and was surrounded by a double portico of marble. The luxury of the public edifices exceeded that of private dwellings. Divided into fourteen districts, Rome was covered over with countless temples and aqueducts. The forums were surrounded with thousands of statues: the principal forum was inclosed within a double portico of richly ornamented columns, under which the people majestically beguiled their weariness. The warm baths, destined for their use, were decorated with pictures, paved with marble from Alexandria, and ornamented with precious mosaics; the water was poured out from silver cocks. The circuses were not inferior in magnificence. Caligula carried this extravagance so far as to scatter the circus over with gold dust. Rome was truly the royal residence of the sovereign people of the world. The imperial city shed such splendour, that, according to Pliny, it seemed as if another sun had risen on earth. Apuleius calls it the holy city. Pleasure and festivity constituted their whole existence,—the people passing incessantly from the Campus Martius to the circus and the forum. Yet nothing could be more precarious than this sumptuous existence. The Roman people did not live by their own labour, but by largesses. Mechanical arts and trades they left to slaves, whilst their masters fed and amused them. Their food was brought from Egypt; and their lives, as Tacitus says, were thus at the mercy of the hazards of the sea. The fortunes of the wealthy classes were swallowed up by fiscal extortions, and the enormous expenses of the most unbridled luxury. Population diminished at a frightful ratio. The family instinct died out. Men no longer cared to marry. It was in vain Augustus promulgated the Pappia Poppæa law, punishing celibacy, and granting recompenses to parents with large families; but it was evaded by the subterfuge of adoptions. Italy, which now numbers seventeen millions of inhabitants, then numbered but ten millions at the outside. Thus we see, even from the most superficial point of view, that this much vaunted civilisation was but a gorgeous mantle covering over utter decrepitude. We may guess what it must have been, viewed in its moral and political aspect. Historians who, like Gibbon, stand in admiration before the grandeur of the empire, forget the price paid for it, involving as it did the ruin of the noblest hopes of the ancient world. For a society that had sacrificed all to public life, the empire proved the cruellest deception. Servitude, though set off by glory, and securing public peace, as it did under Augustus, was already an irreparable calamity, for which no great citizen could find consolation. From servitude to baseness there is but one step, and we know how quickly that is taken. The Romans had to bend beneath an ignominious, stupid, cruel domination. If some, by a dignified, prudent retreat, escaped the shame, they could not escape the hideous spectacle of the degradation of Rome, and of seeing, as Tacitus tells us, senators and knights rush into servitude, vying with each in proportion to the rank of each. We need only read this implacable historian to understand the indignation, wrath, and bitter sadness accumulated in those hearts that remained untainted by the universal baseness. He not only chiselled the hideous features of the Cæsars, but he engraved the image of those debased generations that supported them, and who, though capable of assassinating them, were unable to give the death-blow to the institutions represented by them. He paints the Romans of the time, pale with terror, becoming informers and executioners to escape being victims, and finding a word of approbation and flattery for each of their masters' infamies. This great avenger of the human conscience, while scourging the past, had no faith in the future. He had the soul of a Scipio in the Rome of Nero and Vitellius. If he utters an immortal protest against tyranny, he does so with the tone of discouragement of a man who knows its inutility. Let us not forget that this tyranny spread its ramifications over the whole empire; and that where the Emperor was not, the proconsul was all the more arrogant in the provinces for being servile in Rome.

The social condition was on a par with the political. We have already alluded to the disappearance of the middle class, which was replaced by an idle multitude ever eager after gross pleasures, and who supplied the Emperor, whoever he might be, with as many partisans as he could feed parasites. This was constantly recruited from the slave class: thousands of freedmen swelled the ranks of the Roman plebeians. The opprobrium attached by antiquity to the artisan class, and to manual labour, perpetuated the imperial mendicity of a people at once poor and proud. Cicero expresses the prejudices of his cotemporaries against the useful arts, when he says, 'The gains of mercenaries and labours that have no connection with the fine arts, meaning those who sell their work, are illiberal and sordid; their salary only increases their servitude. All artisans cultivate sordid arts.'

All that can be said of slavery, as it was constituted in imperial Rome, has already been expressed. The slave was purchased for five hundred drachma. He possessed no rights: even his children belonged to his master. He was nominally allowed to purchase his freedom at the end of six years; but there were a thousand ways by which his owner could frustrate his purpose. His life was held to be of such little value, that he was sacrificed on the slightest suspicion. All the slaves in the house of a master who had been assassinated were put to death, and hundreds perished to prevent the murderer escaping. In short, as Seneca says, everything was permitted towards a slave. In trials, he was examined by means of torture. For trifling offences he was condemned to have his legs broken; and the most cruel treatment inflicted if he had the misfortune to spill water while serving at his master's table. A slave on one occasion was flung to the fishes for having broken a crystal goblet. Obliged to pass the whole night standing and silent round the banquet-tables of their masters, if they coughed or stirred, they were roughly chastised. 'We treat them,' says Seneca, 'not as men like ourselves, but as beasts of burden.' Would to Heaven the Romans had confined themselves to the abuse of the physical force of their slaves, without making them subserve their infamous pleasures. They were forced into those horrible seraglios where the worst iniquities of the old pagan world were enacted. If they fell ill, they were frequently left to die, to escape, as Suetonius tells us, the trouble of tending them.

Seneca sums up in a phrase this social condition, when he says, 'We have as many enemies as we have slaves.' What aggravated the situation, was the increasing number of these domestic enemies. As Tacitus says, 'They multiply at an immense rate, whilst freemen diminish in equal proportion.' The danger resulting from such a state of things was keenly felt. Pliny the Younger writes, 'By what dangers we are beset! No one is safe; not even the most indulgent, gentlest master.' The slaves avenged themselves for the cruel treatment they had been subjected to, by actively contributing to the general demoralization. The education of children was confided to them; and they sought to gain protectors for themselves by flattering all their evil propensities. They, in this way, obtained ascendency which, later on, when they were enfranchised, made them in a degree a sort of *maires du palais*. A considerable number of slaves figured as gladiators in the public games; thus contributing not only to their masters' amusement, but to that of a ferocious people, whose favourite pleasure was to see human blood flow copiously before their eyes.

Beside the multitude of citizens who lived on imperial alms, were a vast number of poor excluded from all participation in them. These were strangers and enfranchised slaves, who lived on public charity, and who consequently fared ill. It is true there were some institutions for official charity; but, like all such things, they were powerless. No feeling was more alien to the ancient world than that of compassion for the poor and unfortunate. 'What is a beggar?' scornfully asks one of the guests of Trimalcion in the *Satyricon* of Petronius. Cicero himself, who is generally so nobly inspired, declares alms should only be given to a stranger when involving no privation to ourselves. Plautus makes one of his personages say, that by giving to a poor person, we lose what we give, and only prolong a miserable existence.

If we now penetrate into the interior of the Roman family under the Cæsars, the scandal of private life will appear at least equal to that of public life.

The family at the time of the republic was better constituted at Rome than in Greece. Woman in the latter country always held a low rank. Shut up within her gynæceum, she exercised no influence, and diffused no charms over her husband's life. Home had no existence. The sole object of marriage was to favour and regulate the propagation of citizens for the republic. Man sought in other relations, which were always guilty and often abominable, relaxation from the toils of public life. It was otherwise in Rome during the period of republican austerity. The conjugal tie was held sacred, and polygamy prohibited. It is true that woman, during her whole life, was in a state of complete subjection either to her father or husband. In the first case, she belonged so entirely to her father, that he might at any moment resume all he had bestowed upon her. In the second case, she was, according to legal phrase, under her husband's hand. He possessed the right of life or death over her; he alone was competent to possess. Still, under the republic, women were protected by the censorship and public opinion. The sanctity of marriage was long maintained. Dionysius of Halicarnassus tells us that five centuries elapsed without a single divorce taking place in Rome. It is true that the disorders which are the inevitable concomitants of slavery partially relaxed the conjugal tie. Yet, if we compare this period with the ensuing, we may safely affirm that manners were then relatively pure. Marriage was the first institution undermined by the influx of corruption that marked the close of the republic, and which exceeded all bounds under the empire. Constantly dissolved by divorce, the marriage tie no longer imposed any obligation: it was virtually annihilated by the right of severing the tie at the first caprice. Seneca mentions a woman who computed the years, not by the names of the consuls, but by those of her husbands. According to the energetic expression of Martial, woman was legally an adulteress.

The Roman family, while sinking into corruption, still retained its old harshness: the father retained his right over his children, and largely used it.

No colours are strong enough to paint this corruption. We shall not attempt it, but merely indicate some of its characteristics. They who desire a clear insight into the iniquities of those times, have only to read Juvenal, the Tacitus of private life. Women vied with men in licentiousness. They were for the most part bold-faced courtesans, having everything except pure souls. Not satisfied with lovers of her own class, the patrician woman sought out others from among the dregs of the people, among slaves and gladiators. Women were sometimes to be seen combating in the arena. Juvenal, in an image of horrible beauty, paints in one trait the infamy of the woman of his time, describing her laughing as she passes by the altar of Modesty. Clement of Alexandria describes the pagan woman with a chaster pen, but the idea he conveys in his *Pedagogue* perfectly corresponds with Juvenal's sixth Satire. Sumptuously clad; steeped in exciting perfumes; painted; not satisfied with indecent pictures covering her dwelling, she reproduces them in the ornaments about her feet. She lives in the midst of obscene luxury; taken up with idle defiling gossip, or listening to the suggestions of old panders; surrounded by buffoons and exotic birds; sometimes parading the town in a litter, going to the public baths, or to the shops where idlers congregate. Her nights are passed at banquets whence all decency is banished, and where excesses are carried to the length of drunkenness.

Thus, this elegant woman, chained to vice by golden links like Venus, hides under her brilliant exterior the most shameful corruption, 'like those Egyptian temples, magnificent to look at, but hiding in their deep sanctuary some hideous divinity.'

It would not be possible to attempt giving any idea of the morals of the men of the time. Unnatural vice, that incurable plague-spot of Hellenic Paganism, assumed unbridled proportions at Rome. All classes were infected. Licentiousness, accompanied as it always is by cruelty, illustrated on a gigantic scale the connection between debauchery and murder, which we have already indicated as a feature of the religions of Nature. Tacitus tells us of a Roman of his day, who finished a night's orgie by assassinating the courtesan who had presided over the feast. This mixture of blood and pleasure is the expression of the whole of the imperial epoch, and explains the popularity of the circus, where courtesans might be seen standing close to the arena, the sand of which was steeped with blood, that flowed in torrents from the gladiators. Slaves did not suffice. Soldiers and centurions were compelled to fight. In the morning the people repaired to the circus, and remained there at noon during the interval of the games; in the afternoon took place nautical combats on mock seas, which cost the lives of hundreds. To see death was the supreme pleasure. The writers of the time denounce the corrupting influence of the circus. 'You meet there,' says Seneca, 'as many vices as there are men. Everything is full of vice and crime: infamy circulates through the people, and so takes possession of all hearts, that innocence is not only rare, but is nowhere.'

There is a feature in the corruption of those times which it is important to remark;—there is a something feverish in it, that denotes the profound moral *malaise* with which the world was tormented. Benjamin Constant has eloquently said, 'that earth separated from heaven feels as a prison to man, in which he strikes his head against the walls of the dungeon that shuts him in.' This noble thought, which was suggested by the spectacle of imperial Rome, explains the instinct, then so general, of exaggerating all things, carrying everything to excess in voluptuousness as in luxury. When the immortal soul has lost that faith which opens to it the supernatural and ideal world for which it was made, it seeks the infinite in this lower world, where it is not to be found: it seeks it in the life of the senses, and, not finding it, yet still seeking, it obtains the monstrous. Hence an extravagant refinement, a false grandeur blended with eccentricity, in pleasure as in pomp;—hence the grasping after the impossible in material things. 'The aim of luxury,' says Seneca, 'is to triumph over contradiction, and not only to feel distaste for what is reasonable, but to do the very opposite. To desire roses in winter, to plant trees on the top of towers, is not this living in opposition to nature? Is it not being in opposition to nature to lay the foundations of public baths in the middle of the sea?' Heliogabalus, at a later period, in obedience to this craving for the impossible, had the tongues of peacocks and nightingales served up at his table, and loved to see mountains of snow in summer gardens, and to turn day into night and night into day in his palaces. Suetonius says that Caligula cared for nothing but what he was told was irrealizable, such as constructing dikes in the most dangerous seas, levelling mountains and elevating plains. The heart of the Roman world was devoured by *ennui*. It was, Seneca says, like the hero of Homer, who kept sometimes sitting and sometimes standing in the restlessness of his malady. The Roman world was sick, not only from the shocks it had received, but from a profound disgust of all things. Surfeited, it said, with Petronius, 'I don't wish to obtain at once the object of my desire; the birds of Africa please me because they are not easily reached.' Their malady has been well styled, weariness of ordinary life. Satiated with all they had seen, with all they possessed, they asked in scorn, 'Is it to be always the same?' In search of novelty they tortured Nature, but could not escape monotony and satiety, and ended by plunging into the mire. They abandoned themselves to the most hideous gluttony, consuming the treasures of the world at their gigantic repasts, which earth and sea had been scoured to furnish. They sought a remedy by exaggerating the evil. Crime alone could excite sensation; and, as Tacitus says, by the greatness of the iniquity is measured the height of pleasure. The same author mentions a suicide from no other motive than disgust of living at such a time. This suicide may symbolize the moral suicide of a whole world. Rome, according to the simile of an unknown writer, may be compared to a gladiator, who, after having vanquished all his adversaries, concludes by turning his sword upon himself. And this was the end of the serenity, the ataragic of the ancient world, of which Greece was so proud. Inaugurated by a poetic banquet to the music of inspired lyres, the pagan world closes in an orgie. They felt a consciousness that they had entered upon an age of effeteness and death. Juvenal declares his age was worse than the iron age, and cries, with the accent of a soul in despair, 'Earth feeds only wicked, cowardly men; and the god, whoever he may be, that contemplates them, must laugh at them and hate them.'

Literature, under the emperors that succeeded Augustus, was the faithful image of this degraded social state. Seneca, in his 114th Epistle, eloquently complains of the corruption of the language, which, according to him, is the inevitable result of the corruption of morals.

If literature declined, it was not that it had fallen into discredit; for never in its best days did it excite a more universal interest. 'It is the characteristic of a futile decrepit age,' says the younger Pliny, 'to bestow the more interest on letters, being the less preoccupied about action. We find our joy and consolation in letters.' Thus the separation between literature and national life became daily wider: the former, serving but to amuse the leisure hours of intellectual men, ended in being merely a play of intellect. It was only by reacting energetically against the spirit of the times, as did Tacitus and Juvenal, that it was possible to escape the pedantry of the *bel esprit*. Real literary merit could only be achieved by getting, as it were, at a distance from the age, and being in direct opposition to it. The great writers of this epoch might all truly say it was indignation had made them orators and poets. But even in their indignation the influence of their cotemporaries is visible. The language they spoke, however nobly they may have handled it, was no longer the classic language in which every word is weighed and graduated. Antitheses abound, and at each line we feel a straining after effect. Nevertheless, noble genius and a noble heart raised Tacitus to that degree of distinction which, when a writer attains to, he no longer belongs to one country and to one period, but becomes a recognised organ of all humanity. The younger Pliny, on the contrary, essentially belonged to his age; a refined, intellectual man, avoiding all excesses, but censuring none, and perfectly combining the philosopher and the courtier. With no passion but the one for literature; never without his tablets; hunting or walking, they are always at hand to note down each inspiration, each trifling effect of style that occurs to him. We feel he was just the man to have the courage to read Livy at Pompeii during the eruption. Still, Pliny the Younger is not the perfect type of the literary man of the *decadence*,—his talent was too fine and too genuine. Apuleius rather represented it, who, though he lived a little later, only carried to extreme a tendency existing before his time. We need only read his *Florides* to appreciate the shallowness and bombast pervading a literature written without passion and without ideas. These pieces, which were ingenious and florid, obtained considerable vogue in those public readings which were the fashion of the time. Apuleius excused himself from delivering one of these discourses at a place where a rope-dancer had been performing his exploits. We think no better place could have been selected for his platform; for literature, as he understood it, is almost identical with the feats executed on the tight-rope.

The fine arts shared the destiny of literature. Public monuments under Augustus, Trajan, and the Antonines showed forth an air of grandeur and majesty; but the different orders of architecture began to be mixed and confounded with each other; there was a profusion of ornamentation. Sculpture became colossal, and painting obscene. Petronius himself complains of the decline of the fine arts, which, neglecting the noble traditions of the past, sought to flatter the vices of a corrupt age. Still, if art reflected but too faithfully the ignoble side of imperial Rome, it expressed its aspirations also. The sarcophagi especially reveal this higher inspiration, expressing that longing for a universal revival and restoration, now beginning to be felt. The subjects represented on them are chiefly selected from the myths of Ceres and Bacchus. The myth of Eros and Psyche is frequently treated in a most admirable manner,—the artist representing the anguish of the soul deprived of true love. The Eastern element began more and more to invade the domain of art. Everything relating to the worship of Mithra was particularly the object of predilection; a pantheistic spirit began to predominate; even India and Egypt were looked to as sources of inspiration. Sometimes art confined itself to the mere fabricating of amulets, which popular superstition brought into demand. Thus we find art reflecting and expressing all the contrasts of this age of transition.

We can imagine what religion must have been in such a social state. The profound degradation of the preceding period had become more manifest. The gathering together into the Pantheon of all the gods of the world, placed them all in equal peril. Had they had intelligence, as popular superstition believed, they would have experienced the same difficulty the augurs did in looking in each others' face without laughing; since the mere fact of this assembling together of so many supreme gods was for each an irremediable discomfiture. The mysterious voice, which, according to the poetic legend related by Plutarch, was heard out at sea, crying, 'Great Pan is dead,' rose up from every heart, the voice of an incredulous age proclaiming the end of Paganism. The oracles were silent. 'They are no longer what they were,' says, sadly, the same Plutarch. 'In all sacred places the same sadness and silence prevail.' We should be wrong, in accounting for this abandonment of Hellenic Paganism, were we to attribute it alone to the diffusion of philosophy; but philosophy possessed a formidable rival in the increasing progress of Oriental Paganism. A double current was at work: on one side, the current of impiety; on the other, that of superstition. We shall endeavour to analyze this complicated religious condition.

Let us first of all observe that the official national religion had ceased to satisfy any one; it had sunk too low. Humanism ended in the worship of the Emperor. The official god, who could with a sign or frown command land, sea, war or peace, was the Emperor; that is to say, the chances were that he was either a furious madman, an actor, or a monster, or all these together. The god was at one time a Caligula, 'the cruellest of masters, after having been the most abject of slaves;' then a Nero, 'who had not neglected any one crime.' To-day, an imbecile old man, like Claudius; to-morrow, a sanguinary buffoon, such as Commodus, polluted with every vice. It was no longer allowed to wait the death of the god in order to celebrate his apotheosis. In the case of Augustus, the completion of the temple of Jupiter, which had been begun in his honour, was postponed until after his decease; but his successors insisted that their altars should be erected in their lifetime. Caligula, according to Suetonius, mutilated some of the finest statues of antiquity in order to surmount them with his bust, that his own head should be adored in place of the god's. This sacrilegious action is a faithful representation of the transformation humanism had undergone: humanism, that had the Jupiter Olympus of Phidias as its symbol, now ended with the hideous bust of a Caligula. Apotheoses by flattery were indefinitely multiplied. Proconsuls were deified by their provinces, in the hope of being less robbed and mulcted. Adrian built temples to the beautiful Antinoüs, the object of an infamous passion, and instituted his worship. Such deification degraded the idea of divinity. The old gods, which, in the grand period of Greece, had been invested with a certain majesty, were now debased, and placed on a level with the new gods, which in increasing numbers were taking their seats beside them. The Roman emperors and this degraded Olympus were in keeping with each other. The temple of Venus at Corinth was guarded by a thousand courtesans; and the young virgin who desired to preserve her purity was warned to fly the temple of Jupiter. Nothing proves more clearly the low idea formed of those gods than the prayers addressed to them—prayers by which, according to the satirist Perseus, the suppliant sought to buy their favour, and to seduce them. It was impossible to utter aloud what men prayed for in whispers,— the satisfaction of guilty passions, or the possession of unlawful gains. So that, if there was venal justice on earth, it was but an imitation of the venal justice of the gods, who, instead of making men better, rendered them more cowardly and base. If a crime was committed by a prince, it was understood beforehand that solemn thanksgiving would be offered up to the gods. The conduct of the priests, too, contributed to their discredit. Their morals were infamous; their frauds began to be seen through; and their false prophetic inspiration was now freely talked of. Apuleius describes in vivid colours the profligacy of the priests of Cybele, a species of favoured beggars, who fattened on public charity, who speculated on devotion, and were altogether most audacious robbers. In the presence of such scandals, incredulity and impiety necessarily assumed frightful proportions. Cicero had said, in speaking of ancient mythology, 'Do you suppose me so insane as to believe in such fables? Is there any old woman silly enough still to fear the monsters of hell?' Vespasian, dying, cried out, 'Woe to me! I am going to become a god!' If in the time of Cicero incredulity had reached this point, we can imagine what it became during the two succeeding centuries. Lucian, whom later on we shall find in the ranks of the most perfidious enemies of Christianity, began by turning against the religion of his fathers the pointed shafts of his irony. In the history of the second century of the Church, we shall make a study of this original character, this unswervingly mocking pagan, this implacable castigator of Paganism, pursuing with his cynical laugh all the glories of the past, philosophical and mythological. Evidently the current of ideas he had most affinity with, was that which we have just been tracing. It only sufficed to see how new gods were made, to know how to unmake the old. From the apotheosis of a Cæsar to the degradation of an Olympic god there was but a step. It took so little to create a new divinity, that men naturally were led to demand no more of the ancient. The element of poetry and ideality once taken from the ancient mythology, the gods appeared but as corrupt men; and such they were to Lucian. Mercury is a dexterous robber; Hercules, a rough gladiator, threatening Esculapius with the weight of his blow; Juno and Latona, two sharp-tongued, jealous women; Jupiter, a licentious king, seeking to plant on earth the mistresses he had tired of. Lucian had only to collect in his writings the blasphemous raillery that was current before his time. This incredulity was not confined to the cultivated classes, but reached the lower classes equally. If a great calamity occurred, temples and altars were destroyed, and the penates often flung into the public road. When the disaster at Pompeii took place, voices among the crowd of fugitives were heard to say that there were no gods. Plutarch describes the sceptic, with his bitter smile, assisting at the solemn festivals, and ridiculing all he saw. It is true the same Plutarch describes also the poor superstitious wretch, wrought up to the highest pitch of fanaticism, pale with terror at the thought of being an object of hatred to the gods, rolling himself in the dust and refusing all consolation; terror haunts him in his troubled sleep, and the phantoms of his dreams beset his waking hours. Superstition, says Cicero, pursues and oppresses its victim, compassing him about wherever he goes. Meeting a priest, hearing an oracle, the sight of a sacrifice, the flight of a bird, a clap of thunder, lightning,—everything revives it. Superstition often appeared in the character of the grossest fetichism. Many believed it was possible by means of some sort of sorcery to shut the gods up within their own statues. Magic arts were much practised, and we are told with what avidity these counterfeit wonders were run after. Magicians and necromancers grew rich upon this credulity. They pretended to possess charms having the power to draw down heaven and to lift earth up to the clouds, to harden water, to evoke the spirits of the dead, to vanquish the gods, to put out the stars, and to illumine Tartarus. Thessaly was the birth-place of magic, from whence it spread over the world. Nothing was more natural than this preoccupation about magic arts in a pantheistic age, when, under various names, the forces of Nature were alone believed in. It was connected, too, with that vague longing for salvation and deliverance that was gaining ground in human hearts.

All that had been hitherto worshipped had proved insufficient. The only hope was now in the unknown; above all, in the occult forces of the mysterious Isis, who, as containing the principle of universal life, effaced other gods. It was this same aspiration towards the unknown that inclined men's minds towards foreign superstitions. Cotemporary writers constantly allude to the invasion of these singular rites, which were the more curiously sought after for being singular. Tacitus, the representative of the old Roman mind, bitterly laments it. The new religions had particular attraction for women and slaves. Strange to say, it was towards the East, and towards Egypt, that expectations were directed. The Jews, who up to this time had been abhorred, now made such multitudes of proselytes that the emperors found it necessary to issue decrees against them. Claudius laid a positive interdict upon all foreign superstitions, and published a decree of proscription against the Jews of Rome. But those efforts towards religious restoration were powerless to resist the current.

The worship of Serapis and Isis, that of Cybele, the great mother, and the Asiatic Aphrodite, were everywhere established, and testify at once to the corruption of the time and to its religious wants. Solemn purifications, called *Taurobolies*, were connected with the worship of the Magna Mater. They consisted in the individual being sprinkled from head to foot with the blood of a bull. No expiation was equal to this in value; and he who obtained it could communicate its virtues to those about him, to his native town, or even to the Emperor. This anxious search after unknown worships, this look of hope turned towards the East, and especially towards Judea, are all so many symptoms of a supreme religious crisis. 'There is an idea throughout the East,' says Suetonius, 'that it is destined that the domination of the world shall fall to men belonging to Judea.' This idea must have passed from the East to the West, else how shall we account for the strong leaning towards the Jews which we have indicated? However this may have been, it was the same restlessness, the same weariness that generated the frightful sensuality of the old Roman world, making it seek the help of the monstrous to escape from satiety, that urged it on to the development of foreign superstitions. It knocked at every door, questioned every altar, at once disabused of its own creeds, and thirsting after truth. 'I have had myself initiated,' says Apuleius, 'into almost all the mysteries of Greece. I have investigated all kinds of religions, rites, and ceremonies, urged on by the desire for truth, and by my veneration for the gods.' In thus speaking, he spoke in the name of the age he lived in. In such a state of minds, none was so welcome as he who pretended to bring something new. All religious quacks found ready followers. This explains the singular history of Apollonius of Tyana, recorded by Philostratus, and who, born at the same period as was Christ, was sometimes opposed to Him by the enemies of the new religion. His birth, according to tradition, was accompanied by various prodigies, and had been foretold by Proteus the diviner. After having studied at Tarsus, he settled at Aege, in the temple of Esculapius, where it is said he performed many miracles. He voluntarily devoted himself to a life of poverty. After having exhausted all that Greece could teach him, he travelled through Asia, stopped at Babylon, and proceeded to India to learn magic from the Brahmans. His return was a triumph: he presented himself as a prophet; announced the plague of Ephesus; resuscitated a young girl at Rome; and afterwards travelled over Egypt. He was arrested and imprisoned by Domitian on an accusation of conspiracy. Immediately after his liberation he repaired to Ephesus, where he announced to his audience the death of the tyrant at the moment it was happening at Rome. Shortly after he disappeared, and his disciples pretended that he was carried off by the gods. Through this tissue of fables we can distinguish all that was calculated to please expiring Paganism: Oriental gnosis blended with Greek subtlety, magic united to asceticism. Apollonius of Tyana was just the character adapted to a time of confused aspirations and of syncretism. This clever magician, who claimed the title of liberator and prophet, owed his success to the fact that the Greco-Roman world was, in its vague fashion, waiting for the Deliverer who was about to come, rather, who had already appeared amongst a despised nation. False messiahs only succeed in an age when the true one is expected.

Nor was philosophy more successful than religion in

restoring vigour to this worn-out society. Imported, like art and literature, to Rome, philosophy was too hastily developed. The Roman intellect reached at its first bound the ultimate conclusions of Hellenic philosophy, without having passed through the intermediate stages. Less subtle than the Greek mind, without its delicate perceptions, loving only decided colours, it translated at once into its clear prose the dialectic which so artfully combined heterogeneous elements,— fused together Platonism and scepticism, Epicureanism and temperance. At Rome each school was constrained to manifest at once all the consequences of its principles, at the risk of being itself the cause of its own death-blow. The transplantation from Athens to Rome succeeded with but one school—and with this because it harmonized with the fine side of Roman nationality—the Stoic school.

Outside the schools, properly so called, a certain philosophic spirit was diffused through all cultivated classes. It was a practically sceptical spirit, professing an ironical scorn of all noble preoccupations of the soul, and treating as frivolous whatever rose above the sphere of pleasure and material interests. This resolved indifferentism was perfectly expressed, but not without cynicism, in the ironical question addressed by Pilate to Christ, 'What is truth?' The influence of this practical scepticism was counterbalanced by that of another tendency, which was becoming more and more general towards the decline of the old pagan world: this was the pantheistic tendency, leading back humanity by a roundabout way to the starting-point of all idolatries. It reigned, as we have seen, side by side with gross superstitions in the degenerate Paganism of the time, which was saturated with Oriental ideas. It had gained the upper classes, and infected many distinguished men who would have refused to worship the great goddess, or to associate with her dissolute priests. Thus we find Pliny the Elder declaring in his great work, which was the Encyclopædia of his time, that the world is a divinity, eternal, and immense, without generating cause and without end. Varro, whom St Augustine refutes in the 7th book of his *City of God*, appears to have professed a pantheism identical with that of Pliny. He recognised a soul of the world, the different parts of which had received the names of the different gods.

If we now turn to the schools of philosophy, the first that presents itself is the New Academy, imported into Rome by Carneades towards the close of the republic. This school was well adapted to prepare the transition between the stormy liberty of those times and the servile stagnation of the empire. It had the honour of numbering amongst its disciples the greatest orator and the finest intellect of that period, Cicero, of whom the elder Pliny so eloquently said that he had enlarged the moral boundaries of his country. Cicero was not one of those frivolous sophists of Greece who sought in philosophy their own material interest; he loved it for itself, proclaiming it the physician of the soul, and declared his wish to live retired beneath its shadow: he asks aid and protection of it. He loved truth, but it ever escaped him. Initiated too abruptly into the results of Greek speculation, he drank of an intoxicating cup. More the scholar than the philosopher, he sank beneath the weight of all those systems which he delighted to enumerate. He knows not where truth is; finds absolute truth nowhere,—for what doctrine has not been refuted? Accordingly, he accepts the conclusions of the New Academy, declaring that it is impossible for man to rise beyond the probable. He elsewhere speaks of the sad necessity of renouncing the discovery of truth. His curious work on the nature of the gods is a refutation of Epicureanism by Stoicism, and of both doctrines by the system of the New Academy. In his work on divination, Cicero lays bold hands on Paganism, which he attacks piecemeal, and ridicules unsparingly; but out of all these accumulated ruins he is unable to find the materials to build up a new edifice, and cries out bitterly that he doubts of all and of himself: *Et mihi ipsi diffidem*.

In morals he is less negative. His *Treatise on Duty* abounds in admirable passages impregnated with the true Platonic spirit. In his sublime protest against tyranny and usurpation we have the dying accents of Roman liberty. Nevertheless his moral point of view is limited, and far below the Platonic principle of conformity with God. Cicero's defective metaphysics permeates his moral system. His intellectual conclusion having been scepticism, the clear idea of God is absent, and with it a divine, immutable type, superior to ourselves: hence the standard of life must necessarily be sought below, not above—in man, not in God; the obligation imposed will not be holiness, but honesty; in other words, what is generally esteemed among men, consequently the strongest moral motive, will be love of glory.

Cicero more than once falls into a happy inconsistency; as when, for example, he recognises the divine element of conscience, and proclaims the universality of the sentiment of justice, from which even the wicked cannot escape. Still, upon the whole, we must rank him amongst the disciples of Carneades; his eloquence, combined with his moral elevation, having failed in filling up the void of scepticism.

The philosophy of Epicurus so perfectly coincided with the instincts of Rome, now gorged with the spoils of the universe, that, had it not already existed, it would have sprung up there. These doctrines had the

good fortune to be introduced by a great poet, whose
nervous, coloured style in some measure ennobled a
most abject doctrine. Lucretius employed his Epicureanism as an instrument to batter down ancient mythology, against which he expresses himself with indignation and anger. ' Let us trample religion under our
feet, that the victory gained over it may place us on an
equality with heaven.'[1]

Religion appears to him as the climax of immorality.
' What crimes has it not committed?' He would have
it banished earth, in order that, along with its imaginary
gods, should be banished the vain terrors of the soul.
Death is nothing when the soul is found to be mortal.
Thus, by a strange misapprehension, Lucretius ima-
gines man becomes free as soon as he loses his faith in
the Divinity and in immortality, and fails to perceive
that it is the most effectual way of annihilating man's
liberty. The doctrines of Epicurus appeared to him as
a tranquil haven whence he could calmly contemplate
the fluctuations of an ambitious philosophy, not seeing
that this haven contained but slime, which, soon becoming infectious, would prove destructive to the vessel.
Far better the broad ocean, with its tempests, than this
ignoble repose. Imperial Rome but too well demonstrated this lesson to the world.

The poetic inspiration which animated the early
Epicureans, ardent and enthusiastic in Lucretius, graceful and voluptuous in Horace, was altogether wanting
in the followers of this sect under the empire, when
Epicureanism ceased to be anything more than a school
of debauchery, abjuring completely that fine fastidious-
ness which in Greece enjoyed virtue as a seasoning to
pleasure, and temperance as a means of prolonging it.
It now professed and practised gross sensuality. Plutarch truly characterizes it when he makes his Epicurean

[1] Æquat victoria cœlo.—*De natura*, ch. i., v. 80.

philosopher say, 'Let us make all life one agreeable banquet.' The influence of such a doctrine was, of course, perceptible in social as well as in moral life. 'Do not seek,' say its teachers, 'to be brave soldiers, orators, politicians, or magistrates; be satisfied with enjoyment.' 'They enjoin,' Plutarch says again, 'that all political life shall be renounced.' Such a philosophy was no doubt agreeable to despots, but what a falling off it betrayed in that old society which once lived but for the State!

Stoicism was in direct opposition to this odious system, which was a disgrace to rational humanity. In Rome, as in Greece, Stoicism adopted a vague pantheism which deprived morality of all divine sanction. It prudently abstained from all profound speculations, and dignified by the name of principle its own weakness, jocosely sneering at the great philosophers who preceded, and at their metaphysical researches. Were we to believe the Stoics, the man who gives himself up to lofty speculations is like one who makes a complicated knot for the sole pleasure of undoing it: it is a game of chance, that exercises the faculties without a purpose. These sarcasms have a root of bitterness, and gloss over deep discouragement. What deceptions are tacitly implied in the renunciation of all fearless search! When philosophy thus limits itself to the sphere of application, we may liken it to that prince of Syracuse who, from being a king, chose to become a schoolmaster. However, we have already acknowledged the grandeur of Roman Stoicism: slightly theatrical and declamatory as it was, yet it stood out in noble relief from the universal baseness with which it was surrounded. Its doctrine was false and barren, even from the moral point of view. The energy it developed was passive, placing as it did perfection in insensibility. 'We should,' says Seneca, 'dwell on heights above the reach of the arrows of fate.'

A cruel fatalism was at the basis of the system. *Fata nos ducunt*—The Fates lead us! This is the device of the Stoics. Not a very compromising one, or one calculated to render them particularly dangerous to the Cæsars. Besides, they could adapt themselves to human infirmity. In default of attaining to perfect insensibility, they counsel suicide. 'Against the ills of life,' says the Stoic philosopher, 'I have the privilege of death. All times and all places teach us how easy it is to renounce life.' Thus we see that the *final conclusion* of the Stoic school is suicide. Whilst the Epicurean says to the Roman of the decadence, 'Stifle your soul in pleasure,' the Stoic says to him, 'Kill yourself, and die standing, in the consciousness of your egoistical strength.' Both schools were wanting in lofty vital inspiration.

We may take Seneca as the incarnation of Roman Stoicism with all its contradictions. We might suppose we were listening to one of the Fathers of the Church when we hear him eloquently cry out, '*Deo parere libertas.*' (1.) 'To obey God is liberty. I obey no constraint, nor suffer anything contrary to my own will; and not only subject myself to God, but I make His will mine.' (2.) Elsewhere he says, 'God, by affliction, tries, strengthens, and prepares for Himself the soul of the just man.' (3.) He would have us support ingratitude with a serene, compassionate, grand soul, because persistent goodness triumphs over evil. (4.) The image of God should not be fashioned in gold or silver; we should look for it in the heart of the just man who seeks to reunite himself with his original. (5.) There is a friendship, rather, we should say, a resemblance, between the virtuous man and God. (6.) Nevertheless, not one can say of himself, that he is completely innocent, for it would be to speak against the testimony of his conscience. (7.) In other passages of his writings Seneca seems to have a presentiment of some of the great reforms wrought at a later period by Christianity. He pleads the cause of the slave,—pleads for him by virtue of his human nature, 'which we ought always to respect.' He speaks also eloquently of the Great Republic, which is limited by no country, and which contains the whole human race. ' We have the universe for our country.' (8.) He says, speaking of the games at the circus, ' Man, that sacred thing to man, is killed for our pleasure.' (9.) Thus we see that the idea of humanity shone at the decline of the old world, like the rays that announce the dawn of a new day. Cicero had already inculcated what he called the love of mankind. Plutarch invokes that divinity which is neither barbarian nor Greek, but the Supreme Intelligence that, under diverse names, presides over the destiny of nations. Seneca, as well as the younger Pliny and Plutarch, conceived a high notion of marriage. The latter, in his *Conjugal Precept*, requires that the wife's chastity should accompany her even in her husband's arms; that she be gentle, amiable, pure, yet sacrificing to the graces; ornamented, not with diamonds, but with virtue, and seeking the harmony that results from a perfect union, more than we seek the harmony of music. It is strange to find this new ideal presenting itself to the eye of these illustrious pagans, as it were a glimpse of blue sky breaking through thick clouds. But Christianity was in the air, exercising an indirect influence beyond the limits even of its indefatigable missionaries. These noble outbursts, that raised expiring Paganism above itself, were marred by heterogeneous elements. This same Seneca, who seems at moments to utter words that sound like an anticipation of Christianity, incessantly relapses into all the errors of Stoic pantheism. He declares God to be inseparable from Nature, and goes the length of divinizing the sun. He says the soul is but a compound of elements, and virtue but an idea.

He teaches that in the intelligence resides the sovereign good. Thus the wicked man and the man without intelligence are equal in Seneca's eyes. He admits no moral liberty. Philosophy, he says, has no power to reform our natural character. This fine and frequently elevated moralist proposes as highest ideal the absolute indifference of the sage, who from the cold heights of reason casts a look of pity on all creatures, beginning with Jupiter, above whom he does not hesitate to place himself, for 'he admires only himself.' Most certainly a system of philosophy containing such anomalies could exercise no salutary influence; nor do we find it difficult to comprehend how it was that Nero could be the pupil of Seneca.

Epictetus, who lived shortly after him, professed an equally contradictory philosophy, although his life was more in harmony with his doctrine. A vast number of most admirable maxims might be quoted from the *Enchiridion*, a manual edited by his disciples, and containing a summary of his teachings. 'We should only consult the oracles,' says Epictetus, 'when neither reason nor conscience speaks plainly. Conscience demands that we shall be as faithful to our moral character when alone, as when we are in the presence of witnesses. No sophism can absolve us from this fidelity; no pretext that we are labouring for the good of others can justify us in yielding ourselves up to ambition,—it is our morality that is the true good of others.' Epictetus recommends chastity, forgiveness of injuries, the renouncing of all vain-glory, and enjoins a certain humility, not without analogy to Christian humility. Thus he says, 'He who speaks ill of me, would, if he knew me thoroughly, be justified in addressing me in words still stronger. The true sage neither blames nor praises any man, complains of no man; nor does he speak of himself as if he were anything.' It is evident that the spirit of renovation had breathed on Epictetus, and that he also had, in some measure, a foretaste of Christianity. Still, neither does he escape the fatal influence of Stoicism. As long as he speaks of our duties in general, we agree with him; but when he explains what he understands by duty, our agreement ceases. His great principle is, that man should only value what is really his—that is to say, his reason; since neither external goods nor the body are really ours. If we penetrate ourselves with this truth, we shall be secure from suffering; for we shall look on misfortune, sickness, and even death, as not concerning us. Thus we attain to philosophic insensibility. As it is especially important that we should not suffer ourselves to be troubled by what is external, we should not allow ourselves to be moved by the sufferings or wickedness of our neighbours. Epictetus ranks the wife and children of the philosopher amongst things external to him. We can now judge the distance that separates his morality from that of Christianity. It is, in short, a hard, inoperative morality—a morality of abstention. His last word is, Endure and abstain,—'Ανέχου καὶ ἀπέχου. We shall find the same ethical imperfection in Marcus Aurelius, when, in the history of the second century, we come to the study of this virtuous and persecuting Emperor.

If Stoics and Epicureans quietly resigned themselves to the ruin of Greco-Roman Paganism; if this resignation, variously understood, was made the first principle of their philosophy, there were noble hearts who refused to accept this severe sentence pronounced by the ancient world upon itself. They appealed against it, and, like a chosen band who, when others fly, endeavour to rally their comrades round their colours, they reacted with all their might against the general tendency of the age. Finding in none of the cotemporary philosophical schools the elements of religious restoration, they attached themselves to the system which was the highest expression of Hellenism, Platonic idealism, the purest glory of the past. Plutarch is the representative of this class of minds. He left behind him no new doctrine, but contented himself with giving special prominence to certain points of Platonism. In this way he gave a more rigid formula to dualism, and deepened the abyss between the supreme God and creation. Oriental influence is very decided in him, and he partook largely of the syncretism of his time. The religious restoration that he laboured to effect was only apparent, and served but to prepare the way for Neo-Platonism. We find him constantly led away by the current he strove to stem. If he turned towards the past, it was that the actual condition of the world did not satisfy him; and this we may regard as a mode of aspiration towards the future. Besides, he carried with him, in his sympathy with the past, all the preoccupations, all the moral and intellectual complications, of a man of his own time.

Plutarch desired the restoration of antiquity, the memorials of which he strove to perpetuate. He raised to it a grand monument in his *Lives of Illustrious Men*, a work which is his own chief title to glory. Herodotus, who narrated, as Homer sang, without philosophical preoccupation and without calculation, painted in true colours the golden age of Greek polytheism. Plutarch, who at any cost desired the revival of idealism, wrote a treatise for the express purpose of weakening the testimony of the outspoken historian, and entitled it, 'On the Malignity of Herodotus.' At the same time, he combats with a tinge of bitterness both Stoicism and Epicureanism, the natural enemies of idealism, and extols the Pythagorean school, which he very properly regarded as the precursor of Platonism. Dominated by the same preoccupation, he justifies all the religious institutions of ancient Greece, and consecrated a whole treatise to the oracles of the pythonesses, lamenting the refinement of the over-fastidious, enervated Greeks, who rejected them on account of the inelegance of their language. In his *Treatise upon Superstition* he argues against incredulity and fanaticism, the two extremes between which his age oscillated, and endeavours to lead his cotemporaries back to that serene faith which characterized the infancy of mankind. But a feeble, sceptical generation cannot be recast in the mould of infancy. Plutarch is himself a proof of this. In vain he endeavours to glorify the old religion; he feels it is disappearing, and laments it with eloquent sorrow. He himself no longer believes in it,—at least does not admit it under the old form; and maintains that its fundamental creeds are to be found in all religions. In his work on Isis and Osiris he labours to prove the identity of the Egyptian and Greek myths. It would be impossible to ignore more completely the true genius of Hellenism. Sometimes he falls into purely physical explanations,—as, for instance, when, in the treatise just cited, he says that Osiris and Bacchus are the personifications of the humid element in nature; on other occasions he rises to a degree of pure idealism unknown to ancient mythology, as in his admirable work upon the inscription of the temple of Delphi.

If Plutarch failed in his work of restoration, no author of his time surpasses him in keen perception of the new ideal which, by a singular coincidence, the pagan world had foregleams of, at the moment when it was about to be both realized and surpassed. 'Let us beware,' says Plutarch, in his treatise on *Isis* and *Osiris*, 'of confounding the Divinity with His manifestations. This would be to take the anchor and sails of a ship for the pilot who conducts it.' Upon the frontispiece of a temple of Delphi was engraved the word, *El*, Thou art. Plutarch sees in this the real name of God.

'He alone exists: existence does not belong to us, creatures of a day, placed between birth and death. As well try to arrest the running stream as to arrest our fugitive existence. He only really is who is eternal, unengendered, and not subject to change.' The idea of plurality is inconsistent with the Divinity. The Divine Being must be one, alone, inasmuch as He is the essential unity. 'Let us awake,' adds Plutarch; 'we have dreamt enough. Let us no longer confound the work with the workman.' The question of divine justice is treated in a most elevated manner by Plutarch, in a treatise upon 'the Tardy Chastisement of the Gods.' The philosopher almost rises to the Christian notion of probation: punishment, according to him, has almost invariably moral amelioration for its aim. 'If the children of the wicked are punished, if the penalty of a crime weighs upon a whole race, it is that the race is really a moral being, inseparable from its head and principle; not only brought into existence by him, but in a certain sense made of his substance: thus he is punished in his race.' Here we find the great problem of human solidarity handled with singular profundity. In this same treatise Plutarch unfolds, in magnificent imagery, his faith in immortality, alloyed unfortunately by the vagueness and incoherency of his views of the future life. 'God,' he says, 'develops and cultivates immortal souls in frail and mortal bodies, like those women who keep the gardens of Adonis in fragile vases.' Unfortunately, dualism leavens the whole of this noble philosophy, which reads like a distant and sublime echo of Platonism. But there is in it also a deep sense of the interval that separates the present world from the Divinity; and this awakens in Plutarch the corresponding want of mediation. Hence the doctrine of demons, or intermediary divinities, destined to fill the void between men and the Most High God.

Demons, according to Plutarch, are placed between gods and men to establish a certain communion between them. This essentially Oriental idea, at a later period, gave birth to Neo-Platonic emanationism and to Gnosticism. It rested on an erroneous principle, but with it was mixed up a true feeling of the necessity of a mediation to restore harmony between earth and heaven. In fine, Plutarch's system comprehends all the best elements of Hellenism,—all its aspirations, but likewise all its defects.

No philosophy had power to save Antiquity. Philosophy, in its highest representatives, was able to a certain degree to foreshadow the deliverance, and even this in a very incomplete manner; but it was powerless to procure it. Its powerlessness proceeded still more from moral than from intellectual causes. It wanted sincerity. No philosopher had the courage to speak openly his whole thought. They all professed to have some secret doctrine which they only confided to a few initiated disciples; but in public they bowed down before the gods, which in private they denied. 'I believe,' says Cicero, whose real thought we know, 'that we are bound to scrupulously respect religious ceremonies and public worship.' Seneca does not hesitate to declare that the wise man ought to observe the usages of popular religion, 'not in order to render himself agreeable to the gods, but to conform himself to the laws.' Saint Augustine justly stigmatizes this conduct. 'This man,' he says, 'whom philosophy enfranchised, under pretext of being an illustrious senator of Rome, practises what he rejects, does what he condemns, and adores what he believes wrong; acting as an actor, not on the stage, but in the temple of the gods; the more guilty in his duplicity, because the people believed him serious; and whereas upon the stage he would have amused them, at the foot of the altar he led them astray and deceived them.' But what above all was fatal to the philosophers of the time, was the charge made against them by the masses, and which Seneca thus expresses: 'You speak in one sense and you act in another: *Aliter loqueris, aliter vivis.* You do not yourselves act what you prescribe.' Seneca tells us the jests of the people, who ironically asked this eloquent eulogist of poverty what he had done with the tons of gold piled up in his cellars. He condemns himself, and with himself all those theoretical moralists who refuse to touch with their little finger the burden they would impose on others. 'We ought,' he says, 'to choose for our guide one whom we admire more when we see him than when we hear him.' But it was not ancient philosophy, with its want of sincerity and practical inconsistencies, that could be this helpful guide. In the moral world, sincerity alone gives power,—every artifice is a sign of weakness. The philosophers themselves were conscious of their impotence. 'Now that we are alone,' says Cicero, 'we are free to seek truth, without hatred.' The illustrious orator did not understand, like Saint Paul, and even like Socrates, that truth demands witnesses who are ready to suffer all for her; and that humanity also demands them, and will not yield but to heroic conviction. Whilst the Roman philosophers, who met in secret to deliberate at their ease, congratulated themselves upon their solitude, martyrs, who had no other earthly perspective to offer than that of tortures, saw themselves surrounded by ardent disciples. 'There is a charm in those tortures,' says Tertullian. *Est illecebra in illis.* It was precisely this austere charm of a courageous, undaunted faith, that was wanted in the philosophy of the *decadence*. Its powerlessness becomes especially evident when it seeks consolation for the great griefs of mankind. Cicero and Seneca both tried the power of their doctrines to assuage the sorrows of afflicted friends.

They counsel resignation to irreparable evil, the diversion of study, bodily activity,—in other words, oblivion, which is virtually moral death. Seneca goes the length of saying to a friend in affliction, 'You have lost the object of your affection, seek another.' It was in presence of such comforters that the younger Pliny cried out, in the midst of cruel anguish, 'Give me some new, grand, strong consolation, such as I have never heard nor read. All that I have ever read or heard in my life rises to memory; but my grief is too great.'

We believe we are justified in concluding from all these manifestations, that humanity had arrived at that point to which it was God's providence to conduct it. The desire for salvation had become purified and defined, through the evolutions of the different mythologies, and the Greco-Roman world had fearful proofs of its own utter incapacity to satisfy it. Fallen humanity had never for a single day lost its sense of the want of pardon and reparation, as was proved by the multitude of sacrifices, and the smoke of holocausts that rose from all sides towards heaven, carrying thither a confused prayer for mercy. Since the notion of a holy God had dawned on the human conscience, this thirst for pardon and restoration grew more and more urgent— more pure and more profound. But so far was the ancient world from being able to satisfy this want, that it was not even capable of holding for a single moment, in its purity, the notion of one God, which, notwithstanding, it seemed to have definitely mastered—it was incessantly straying back towards dualism. When Plutarch declares that everything here below presents the combination of two opposite causes, he gives in precise terms the result of ancient philosophy.

This fundamental error prevented the complete triumph of spiritualism amongst the more cultivated, and led the masses into the current of materialism. Hence the painful contrast between reality and aspirations; hence those manifold inconsistencies, those abominations of pagan society, and those noble efforts of thought towards heights it could not attain; hence, also, this desire for the unknown God, with which the world was agitated.

This desire was still, no doubt, vague and undefined. Although everywhere diffused, and through all classes of society, yet it smouldered in secret, and only revealed its presence by occasional outbursts. It did not manifest itself with power until after the advent of the religion of Christ; for great religious renovations are not confined to the satisfaction of the higher wants of humanity, —they begin by wakening up the consciousness of them. This explains the rapidity of the first conquests of Christianity in the midst of Paganism. If the opposition which it encountered was equal to the sympathies that hailed it, the reason was that the masses were too profoundly corrupted not to anathematize it. Nevertheless, the frightful corruption of the Greco-Roman world at the moment when the greatest revolution in our history was being accomplished, cannot prevent us recognising that the work of preparation had then precisely reached its maturity.

For of human beings there are two kinds: the one opposes God's plans; the other realizes them, and submits to them, and is such as He would have the entire race to be. The disproportion of numbers is of little importance. The chosen few who walk in God's ways, and who draw from events the lesson intended, often constitute an infinitely small minority. Still, it is most certain that it is on them God reckons for the accomplishment of His designs. But the privilege of the few is here the interest of all: it is in those noble hearts that the hour strikes for great renovations.

In order to know if the world was prepared eighteen centuries ago for the reception of Christianity, we must look elsewhere than at that cruel populace, or at that base aristocracy, which seems to have forgotten everything in the pleasures of the circus. We must ask ourselves what an honest, upright heart, thirsting for truth, must have felt at such a time.

We find in an apocryphal book of the second century a short passage which, distinguished by its simplicity from the general character of the work, paints in colours so true the feelings which must have animated all serious minds, that we do not hesitate to quote it. 'From my earliest youth,' says Clement, the hero of the Clementines, 'I have been disturbed by doubt. I know not how it got possession of my soul. When I shall be dead, I have said to myself, shall I be indeed annihilated, and will all thought of me cease? It were as well never to have been born. When was the world created? What preceded the world? What will become of it in the future? Wherever I went, these thoughts haunted and tormented me. The more I strove to shake them off, the more they pursued me. I felt there was a heavenly guide to lead me to truth, and I sought him from place to place. Harassed from my youth by these thoughts, I went from one school of philosophy to another, and found only opposing principles and contradictions. Here, one proved to me the immortality of the soul; there, another demonstrated that it was mortal. Thus was I driven from doctrine to doctrine, more wretched than ever, as though I had been carried through a vortex of contradictory ideas, and I sighed from the depth of my soul.'

To lead humanity through some of its representatives to breathe forth this sigh, was the great purpose of God in the work of preparation, which we may now consider completed in the pagan world; for, as we have produced abundant proofs, there was a singular correspondence between the general state of minds and the aspirations of those noble spirits.

JUDAISM.

THE desire for a great religious renovation had reached such a degree of clearness in the old pagan world, that its purest organs were enabled to reduce it to a formula. This result of its history was immense, but would not alone have sufficed to open the way for Christianity. Moreover, it is not probable that so notable a progress could have been accomplished in the pagan world, had not elements other than those it could itself supply, entered into the intellectual circulation of that remarkable period. Under the levelling influence of Roman power, all national barriers were struck down, and the various religions of the different peoples allowed free passage, like waves that flow and blend into each other. A purer and higher current of ideas is discernible amidst the vast syncretism of the first century of the Christian era. The source of this was hidden amongst an obscure, despised nation, whose extraordinary destiny must now fix our attention, presenting as it does the directly divine side of the work of preparation. Here, there is not only the remote influence of the Divine Spirit, there is positive revelation. Israel is God's people,— the people whose education was conducted by the hand of God, in order that the salvation destined for the whole human race should first be realized in the land of Judea. 'Salvation is of the Jews.' It now remains for us to examine how the work of preparation was carried on by means of revelation, after having seen how it was realized by means of free experience.

Let us first observe that the history of Judaism proceeds parallel with the history of Paganism—that they both converge to the same end, the two lines eventually meeting at the same point. In Paganism, as in Judaism, we find the human heart tormented by the same wants, sighing after the same deliverance, except that, whilst the one was in a measure left without guidance, in order to bring home to it its powerlessness and misery, the aspirations of the other were purified and informed by a higher intelligence. The various phases of the history of the pagan world we find in the history of Judaism, with this difference, that revelation disengaged from each phase the great lesson it contained, which elsewhere was alloyed by the corruptions of idolatrous nations. The history of Judaism is the divine side of the history of humanity, placed in strong light. Two principal phases are discernible in the work of preparation as it proceeded in the pagan world: the first shows the desire of salvation becoming more defined during the process of mythological evolution; the second, by the utter degradation of ancient society, makes manifest the necessity of supernatural assistance. These two periods have their parallels in the history of God's people, in both of which the religious superiority attaching to the latter is evident. In the first, instead of a mythological evolution, we have a succession of revelations in constant harmony with the moral condition of the people. In the second, we see the eclipse of the national glory of Israel, but not the frightful decomposition that characterized the decline of imperial Rome. The desire of salvation, which grew like a wild olive in pagan soil, sprang up like the true olive in the sacred soil of Judea, cultivated by the hand of God. In this favoured land, which was preserved from idolatry, the Saviour was to be born. But, owing to the parallelism which we have noticed in the histories of Judaism and Paganism, we shall find the general dispositions of humanity, as represented by its finest intellects, in singular unison with the glorious event which is the culminating point of its religious history. We should add, also, that at each important epoch the Jews were brought into contact with those nations that played at the time the most conspicuous part on the theatre of the world. At the patriarchal period, when the race was confined within the limits of a family, its tents were pitched in Mesopotamia. It passed through Egypt before it was definitively constituted under Moses. At a later period it was carried into Babylon, where it witnessed the great revolution that took place in Asia in consequence of the triumph of the Persians. Finally, from the day it became a portion of Alexander's empire, sharing the vicissitudes of his different provinces, its isolation entirely ceased. The fraction of the Jews that emigrated to Alexandria entered into direct communication with the genius of the West. These successive intercommunications between Judaism and Paganism did not enrich the religion of the chosen people; its originality is too marked to allow us to suspect it lived on loans; but they answered the purpose of Divine Providence in maintaining a certain correlation between revealed religion and other religions. The first answers divinely the real wants made manifest by the great mythologies of the ancient world. But this answer was not the less a revelation, for being at each period of history in harmony with the general condition of humanity.

According to a certain school, the Jews had no other revelation than what they carried with them in the blood of their veins as a Semitic race, or than that which they read on the sands of the desert where their fathers had encamped. 'They never would have reached the dogma of divine unity had they not found it in the most imperious instincts of their minds and hearts. The desert is monotheist.'[1] This assertion is, to say the least of it, bold, when we bear in mind how frequently, and often irresistibly, the Jews were tempted into Canaanitish idolatry; let us also remember that the first manifestation of this imperious instinct towards monotheism, was the construction of the golden calf in the desert! For our part, when we compare the moral and religious condition of the Hebrew people with their national temperament, so inferior in many respects to that of other nations; and, above all, when we place their sacred books beside those of India and Persia, we find that no difficulty, in the rational point of view, equals that of its history and development, if we reject the idea of a revelation.

We acknowledge that shade here is singularly blended with light. But a great portion of the objections vanish as soon as we admit the idea of progression in divine revelation,—speaking to man in his infancy the language of infancy, and leading him on gradually and by degrees up to luminous heights.

We cannot sufficiently admire the exact correspondence established by God between the dispositions of those who received revelation and revelation itself. In revelation, as in conversion, grace and liberty are united by a mysterious link. But, as we have already said, this correspondence between God and man was realized upon a grand scale in the general history of religions, as we find it in the relations of Judaism to Paganism. There is nothing in Judaic revelation which does not answer wants made manifest by the ancient mythologies. To complain of the special character it was invested with, is in reality to complain of the aspira-

[1] Renan, Histoire des Langues Sémitiques.

tions of humanity; for, in the Mosaic economy, God confined Himself to doing perfectly what the fallen race vainly attempted in their false religions. Paganism is the religion of the time of preparation altered and disfigured; whilst Judaism is this same religion purified by God. In fact, the problem resolved by the second had been already propounded by the first.

We have sketched the history of ancient religions: it is therefore unnecessary to revert to them, further than to ask ourselves what was their divine base. Let us analyze their last residuum in order to seize what they contained of true and legitimate. All those religions reveal the consciousness man had of his misery, and his sense of the necessity of reparation. This feeling was at its birth falsified by the adoration of Nature. Man attributes his misery to a malevolent power from which he cannot escape; and confounding one of the manifestations of good with absolute good, he demands from the sun and spring, as from benign deities, relief from his misery. But his religious sentiment is not satisfied with this purely naturalistic mythology. He is perpetually tempted by his anthropomorphism to exalt his gods higher than his mythological conceptions permit him. It is a salvation higher and purer than the return of the fine season that he thirsts for, and ills far graver than those of winter and its sterility that he dreads. We always err when we deal with man as with an exclusively logical being, and endeavour to square his many-sided undulating nature with one invariable defined system. All ancient forms of worship are based on four principal institutions, which are, as it were, the four columns of the religious edifice that sheltered humanity up to the advent of Jesus Christ. These four institutions are—Sacrifice; the Priesthood; the Sanctuary, or sacred place for adoration; Religious Festivals, or periods consecrated to adoration. There was no religion without its altars, priests, temples, and holidays. The same idea we trace in all these institutions, and it is the same precisely which God placed at the basis of Judaism.

Sacrifice is an offering to the higher powers. Man recognises the claims of the Divinity upon him, and too frequently has to acknowledge his own shortcomings, which demand reparation on his part. Accordingly, he offers what is most precious to him, what costs him most. When drawing nigh to the altar, he experiences a mixture of fear and hope. He fears Him whom he would appease; but still believes he can appease Him: if not, he would not repeat an attempt he knew to be useless. This same mixture of fear and hope is also discernible in the institution of the priesthood, which was intended as a mediation between man and God. It implies in the former a secret terror, preventing his free access to his Creator, but which does not entirely shut him out from all communication with Him. He accordingly chooses the worthiest of his fellow-men, frequently those of highest rank, rendered venerable by the diadem or crown of white hairs, that they may in his name consult Heaven, report its answer, and present to the gods the homage of earth. The same mixed sentiments he experiences with regard to the world he inhabits. He considers it profaned and sullied, and unworthy of being the habitation of divinity: he therefore seeks an exceptional place—a dwelling worthy of His presence; hence the construction of temples.

He also sets apart certain days, consecrated above the rest, and devoted to worship, for the reason that he considers his ordinary life impure; nevertheless he does not believe he is absolutely rejected by the gods, since he has fixed on times and places when he dares venture to approach them. Thus the religion of the ancient world expressed by significant symbols the situation of humanity since the fall: it felt itself degraded, but not hopelessly lost. This double sentiment is plainly shown by these four great religious institutions, which all rest on the distinction between the profane and sacred; that is to say, upon the setting apart of certain objects, certain localities, certain days, and certain persons in honour of the Divinity. Now this is precisely the fundamental idea of Judaism. What is Judaism, if it does not consist in the setting apart of a certain portion of humanity, to offer, in the holy place at specified periods, sacrifices to the Divinity? Thus we see there is nothing arbitrary or singular in the institutions of the chosen people, since we find their equivalent in all the religions of the ancient world. They were, in short, institutions suited to the religious dispensation intended to complete the work of preparation, and were based on the real wants of the human heart during the time intervening between the fall and the redemption. This mixture of fear and hope, which was expressed by the institution of the priesthood and of sacrifice, as by the erection of sanctuaries and the appointment of religious festivals, was the result of the real situation of a ruined race destined to salvation, and was wrought out by God. We are not, then, to be surprised that He should accept what He Himself produced, and that in the religious constitution of Judaism He should vindicate this universal sentiment. The fundamental analogy between the religion of the Jews and what is really essential in other religions, far from diminishing the importance of its mission, greatly enhances it; for Paganism seriously endangered, and often entirely obscured, this essential and universal religious sentiment. The principle of the religions of Nature radically transformed it; and had it been exclusively committed to them, it would have died out. It was, therefore, of vital importance that it should be disengaged from all those impure elements, and fostered among a people directly under the guidance of God.

Let us consider for a moment what became in the East and West of these four great religious institutions of the old world, under the pernicious influence of Paganism. The worship of Nature, we see, deteriorates the religious sentiment in all its manifestations. The temple becomes gradually the symbolical representation of this multiform divinity, comprehending heaven and earth: it figures the universe. Thus the Egyptian temple, with its azure roof, recalled the star-bespangled sky; its columns, wound round with vegetable ornaments, appeared to bear the edifice of the world. Festivals were appointed to celebrate the principal phases of the life of Nature: the succession of seasons, sterility or fertility, the bursting forth of vegetation, or the mourning of earth. The festivals of Atys and Adonis do not get beyond this materialistic symbolism. Nor is the priesthood less degraded: the priest, mediator between heaven and earth, is degraded to the level of a mere astrologer or magician. Revelation is distorted into a mere manifestation of the hidden laws of Nature: the priest endeavours to surprise the secret of Nature in the motions of the stars, or in the entrails of animals. He tries by magic to master the mysterious forces of earth, and falls into charlatanism, of which he is himself the first dupe. He derives his dignity, not from moral superiority, or from the manifest choice of the divinity, but from a physical connection with it. Thus the caste of Hindoo priests pretended that they issued from the head of Brahma. The character of sacrifice was also altered. It no longer symbolized a moral offering—a painful but salutary return to virtue and to God: it was but an attempt to appease a blind, malevolent power, to obtain his favour by flattering his supposed tastes, in the immolation of animals believed to have a kind of analogy with him.

The degradation of those four great religious institutions was less remarkable in the West than in the East, owing to the predominance of humanism over naturalism. In Greece, temples were considered less as symbols of the universe than as sacred places, the pure abode of the Divinity. Festivals were rather celebrations of the various phases of the lives of the gods than of those of Nature, and bore the human and historic character of the Hellenic religion: they often assumed a thoroughly dramatic character. Sacrifices, especially at Delphi, rose to the height of a moral idea, and were supposed to exercise a purifying action. The priesthood was free from the trammels of caste, and was more free and more human than the Oriental priesthood, and superior to it—attaching more importance to the personal superiority of the individual invested. All the serious errors of Hellenic Paganism are palpable in its religious institutions. The æsthetic passion of the Greeks exercised a fatal influence upon their religion, which became frivolous and external—a spectacle to delight the eyes, rather than a religious rite. The veil of symbols was woven in such dazzling purple, and decked by their great artists with ornaments so attractive, that the people felt no desire to lift it, in order to seek behind for the thing signified. Thus we see that neither the pagan West or East was able to preserve intact the deposit of these holy sentiments of humanity, which constitute its capacity for salvation. It was therefore necessary that God Himself should watch over them, and commit their guardianship to a nation preserved by Himself from all profane contact. Transplanted to a monotheistic soil, these sentiments, and their corresponding institutions, were developed under normal conditions. This hastened the consummation of the work of preparation.

The four great religious institutions which characterized religion during the preparatory dispensation, were closely connected, in Judaism, with a fact which preceded them, and which contained them in germ,—that is to say, the election of the people of Israel.

We find this election sanctions the general fact of the priesthood, and gives to it a more extensive application in the consecration of a whole people to God. But inasmuch as the God of the Old Testament differs from pagan divinities, so the election of Israel had altogether a special character. Most assuredly there is no analogy between this God and that deified Nature before which the East prostrated itself. He is not one of the forces of the organic world, nor, like Brahma, the hidden universal principle of the world, diffused, like a divine lotus, through time and space. He is outside of Nature, and consequently not subject to her power. He produced Nature by an act of free creation. He is the supreme God, the only God. 'I am that I am,' He says. He allows no other God beside Himself. Yet He does not shut Himself up in His solitary majesty. He takes part in the history of humanity, manifests His will and gives laws to His people. He is a Father, and at the same time the Most High God,—a Father combining severity with goodness, never making concessions to evil; with none of that facile indulgence of a divinity whose favour, it was supposed, might be purchased by presents; but neither is He a Moloch, thirsting after tears and blood. With Him we ascend the summits of the moral world. He is the holy God, whose eyes are too pure to see iniquity.[1] This Judaic monotheism is essentially moral. At the first bound it reached heights

---

[1] We should bear in mind the importance of the name of *Jehovah*, which is very different from that of *Elohim*. Whilst the second designates the God whose power is manifested through nature, and which does not carry us much above the general notion of divinity, the first signifies the God who reveals Himself and manifests Himself in the religious history of humanity

which Greece, at the moment of her fullest development, could only catch glimpses of, without being ever able to keep permanently, and without being able to shake off entirely the yoke of polytheism. We cannot conceive how it was possible for such a notion of the Divinity to have been formed by merely natural means in the midst of a small Semitic tribe, of which it has been said, 'compared with the Indo-European race, they represent an inferior combination of human nature.'[1] Of all the miracles contained in the books of the Old Testament, the most amazing appears to us to be the first word of Genesis—'In the beginning God made heaven and earth.' The world of mind is thus mastered at the very outset, and the formidable fascination of dualism overcome. The problem left unsolved in the Vedas and the Avesta, by sacerdotal Egypt and by philosophic Greece, is sovereignly solved for the conscience. Is it possible to doubt that this pure light, appearing thus in the midst of thick darkness, came direct from heaven? God must have unveiled His face to man, who had but impure idols before his eyes, else how could he have reproduced those august features we find in the Old Testament? Without revelation, monotheism was impossible.

Consecration to the holy God implied holiness. Connection with Him does not mean that physical connection which was at the root of the sacerdotal system of the religions of Nature. The chosen people, who were a kind of sacerdotal caste in the midst of humanity, did not owe this privilege to a purely external descent from the Divinity, like the Brahmans of India. It was altogether a moral relation: their exceptional dignity was

by personal intervention. Jehovah is the God of Israel, because He makes Himself known to His people as the God of revelation (Eph. iii. 6). These different names of God in the Pentateuch have given rise to one of the problems of criticism which has excited the greatest division.

[1] Renan.

based upon the exceptional holiness of their ancestors. A great act of faith and obedience explains their election.

Abraham is the father of a privileged race, because he is the father of believers; and the privilege obtained by holiness is preserved by holiness. Israel is the priest of Jehovah, because he is united to Him by the sacred ties of love and submission. In Judaism there is no divorce between devotion and moral life. Devotion, or normal piety, is moral life in all its intensity.

Nevertheless, Judaism was not given as a perfect religion. Whatever may have been its superiority over surrounding forms of worship, it was notwithstanding a provisional form only. The consciousness that it was a preparatory, and not a definitive dispensation, is evident throughout. It points to an end beyond itself, suggests a grander thought than any in itself; its glory precisely consisting in its constant looking forward to a glorious future, which was destined to surpass it. An immense hope permeates its institutions, its sacred books, its history,—a hope not confined to itself, but the universal hope of man. The benediction promised it is no other than the advent of the Divine Restorer, who should build up again the ruins accumulated by the fall,—above all, the most dilapidated of those ruins, human nature, which had become so miserably degraded, and in which there now dimly shone but a few defaced features of the Maker's image. What was elsewhere but a vague expectation, a confused aspiration, was in Judaism a firm hope, disengaging itself more and more from the gross wrappings that environed it. Faith in the most holy God, and the expectation of the Messiah, constitute the whole of the ancient covenant. The idea of the Messiah is as essential a portion of it as is monotheism. Jehovah is not only the God of holiness; He is likewise the God whose will is to save the world by the Messiah, offspring of the seed of Abraham. He not only gives a law, the reflex of His holiness; He gives also a promise. The whole of Judaism is based upon the law and the promise as upon two pillars. The law reveals the One Holy God: prophecy announces and foreshadows the Redeemer. Both revelations unite in concert to develope the desire of salvation. The law, or the revelation of the holy God, renders powerfully prominent the state of sin and corruption, and fosters this disquietude and salutary fear, which make the heart sigh for deliverance. Thus was all combined to produce in the hearts of the people of Israel those precious dispositions which it was the special mission of the preparatory dispensation to develope, and which were adulterated and effaced in Paganism.[1]

PERIOD OF FORMATION.

The vocation of Abraham embodies this alliance of the law and the prophecy, of monotheism and the hope of the Messiah, which traverses the whole history of Judaism. The holy and jealous God revealed Himself to him both by a command and a promise. 'Get thee out of thy country, and from thy kindred;' this is the command. 'In thee shall all families of the earth be blessed;' this was the promise. God is a holy God, who alone should be adored and served. Hence the necessity of the painful separation from pagan humanity as the sole means of preserving monotheism.

[1] M. Bunsen, in his highly interesting work, *Gott in der Geschichte*, p. 138, reduces the mission of the Jews to the proclamation of two truths: the unity of the human race, and the gradual triumph of good in humanity. This second truth he presents in a too general manner. It was inseparable from faith in the Messiah, and was especially connected with the idea of pardon, with the desire for salvation. This aspect of the question has been too much overlooked by the learned author, who knows so well how to sketch with a few quiet, vigorous lines, the grand figures of the theocracy.

But this election God made in the interest of all: the privilege was a ministry and a priesthood in favour of the whole human race destined to be saved. Hence the promise,—that precious inheritance which the descendants of Abraham handed down from generation to generation. The whole law, as well as the prophecy, with all its rich developments, are contained in germ in those two words. Already, under its first form, the law demonstrates the condemnation of fallen man: it proclaims, by the fact of the necessity of the separation, the generality of the corruption, at the same time that it daily brings home their moral impotency to those who receive it in an earnest spirit, and who strive to dedicate themselves unreservedly to God. Already, also, the promise, although limited to terrestrial and inferior blessings, consoles and strengthens the contrite broken heart. Thus the elementary law, as well as the elementary prophecy, speaks of condemnation and pardon. The confused, indistinct hint implied by the ancient sacerdotal institutions is now clearly enunciated, and Judaism at its first stage is presented to us as the divine commentary which gives the profound meaning of the most characteristic institutions of antiquity.

We shall rapidly pass over the patriarchal period, which already foreshadows the destiny of Israel. The humble submission of the patriarchs to God was as a memorial to their descendants that the election of Israel was based on sanctity. Their wandering life, without any fixed dwelling-place, was emblematic of that hope which, in order to live more completely in the future, never folds its wings, and refuses to attach itself to earth. It was fit that these faithful men, dwelling under tents and ever marching towards a 'better country,' should be the ancestors of the race to whom the promise was given. Circumcision, the only positive institution of Judaism, symbolized both the law and the promise, and commemorated the privilege of the chosen family, while at the same time it prefigured the circumcision of the heart. The office of priest belonged by right to the father of the family. Sacrifice was offered on simple altars of stone. Revelation had an external and frequently material character, corresponding to a lower stage of human development. In the history of the patriarchs, Divinity manifests His power in an entirely simple and elementary manner. He reveals Himself immediately by miracle or prophecy, without the intervention of man. The miracle or prophecy proceed directly from God. Later on, it is otherwise; divine power assimilating man, and making use of him as its organ, communicating itself to him as an internal and spiritual gift. But at the patriarchal period it acts externally. The most frequent form revelation then assumed, was that of a vision or dream; sometimes also as a tangible manifestation, such as was the angel of the Eternal, which has been erroneously considered as a kind of intermittent incarnation of the Son of God.

Following the patriarchal period, we distinguish two great epochs in the history of Judaism. In the first, it is definitively constituted, receiving its institutions from God through the medium of Moses. In the second, a cycle of sublime revelations, throwing vivid light upon the future, is unfolded before their eyes. The first period is characterized by the predominance of the legal element; the second, by the predominance of the prophetic element; though neither was ever altogether absent. It was important that they should interpenetrate each other, in order that Judaism should fulfil its vocation by continuing to develope simultaneously in man the consciousness of his condemnation and the hope of his salvation.

The descendants of Abraham had become a numerous

people in Egypt. We know their trials, their painful toil under the lash of the taskmaster, and their marvellous deliverance. It was in the desert, in which the Israelites found refuge against their persecutors, and in which they became consolidated as a nation, that they received the principal revelations which stamped their whole national life. The Decalogue, that contains not only the moral law, as has been asserted, but which, by instituting the Sabbath, likewise consecrates the ceremonial law, embodies the whole Mosaic dispensation. Like the patriarchal economy, it is based upon the revelation of holiness; but this holiness is laid down with far greater clearness in these precise commandments, which define evil and prescribe virtue. This clearness is also more awe-inspiring. From the heights of Sinai issue forth thunders and lightnings. Each commandment is sanctioned by a condemnation; and the Israelite might read in letters of fire upon every page of the book of the law, 'Cursed is he who will not observe to do the things contained herein.' Thus did the law begin by fulfilling that ministration of death, so profoundly understood by St Paul, which consists in pursuing human weakness through all its concealments, in piercing conscience with a sharp-edged dart, and in leading the fallen creature to the avowal of his misery by the excess of his grief and fear.

It behoved that the severity of the law should not at first be too much tempered by the consolations of prophecy. It was necessary to smite the human conscience,—to inflict a wound so deep, that there was no healing for it but at the foot of the cross. This explains the predominance of the legal element during the Mosaic period; which, however, did not prevent prophecy crowning the edifice, and circulating through all its institutions. All the promises, hitherto scattered and preserved as traditions, were collected. The Jews did not comprehend their bearing, but they awoke in them the presentiment of a great destiny. The conquest of the land of Canaan did not exhaust their hopes. Had they not received from their fathers the mysterious promise, that in their seed all the nations of the earth should be blessed? Besides, their institutions contained an effective revelation, the more powerful from its encompassing them about on all sides, following them into all places, and enveloping their whole life by the multiplicity and detail of its precepts and ceremonies, and in which the law and the promise appear closely interwoven.

The four great religious institutions inherent in the preparatory dispensation, and which we have found vestiges of in all the religions of the East and West, receive their full significance in the Mosaic religion. They have both a symbolical and typical value, representing important truths having a present application, and being at the same time 'the shadow of good things to come.' They constitute in their grand features an admirable type of definitive religion. If we require to be on our guard against rabbinical subtleties, seeking to read in the construction of the tabernacle and in sacerdotal ornaments the hidden spirit of the Gospel, we must not less avoid the dry, meagre interpretation of those who see in Judaism but an 'essentially terrestrial monotheism.'

Two institutions, the priesthood and sacrifice, play the chief part in the Mosaic religion, as in all the religions of antiquity. We have already noticed one realization of the idea of the priesthood in the election of the people of Israel. This election, like the special priesthood, was founded on the twofold idea, that humanity in its totality dare not approach God, but might communicate with Him by mediation. Israel, by virtue of being the chosen people and servant of

Jehovah, was the priest-people, dedicated to holiness, and consequently to isolation in the midst of a corrupt and idolatrous humanity. 'Take heed to thyself,' we read in the law, 'lest thou make a covenant with the inhabitants of the land whither thou goest; lest it be for a snare in the midst of thee.' Israel is a people belonging entirely to God,—directly governed by Him. From God they held not only their religious ordinances, but the laws regulating their civil affairs. Everything amongst them bears a religious character. Every offence is against God. The constitution of the nation realized theocracy in its extreme consequences. Even the land belonged to the invisible King. Its first distribution was to be permanent. No landed property could be transferred or curtailed. At the end of fifty years, in the year of the jubilee, all property returned to the family of the first possessors. The Israelites, in recognition of this dependence, offered in the tabernacle the tithes of all the produce of the earth. The first-born of each family was considered as belonging to the Lord, and was redeemed by a special offering.

Such a people were truly a priest-people exclusively dedicated to God's service. A multiplicity of prescriptions were laid down to remind them of this consecration which implied holiness. The distinction between clean and unclean animals, founded doubtless upon a profound symbolism, of which the Zend-Avesta, later on, gives striking examples; the various precepts concerning bodily defilement; the ordinances regulating the purification of the unclean,—all this minute portion of the Mosaic legislation was intended to keep constantly alive the idea of holiness in the hearts of the Israelites, and to teach them that the holy God required internal and external purity on the part of His worshippers. There is nothing puerile in this ritual: it applies to every detail of life the great idea that presided at the election of Israel, and enforces it in the most trifling circumstance; it perpetually recalled the glorious priesthood with which it was formally invested: 'If ye will obey My voice, and keep My covenant, ye shall be unto Me a kingdom of priests and a holy nation.'

This national priesthood was not sufficient for the purposes of the Divine Legislator. He instituted in the midst of the priest-people a special priesthood, which was Judaism in a higher degree; for it was an election within an election, a separation in a nation separated. Aaron's family is set aside for the priest's office, and the tribe of Levi from among the children of Israel to do the service of the tabernacle. But this special priesthood, so far from superseding the general priesthood, was considered as a delegation from the latter. The priests and Levites replaced the first-born of every family, and were maintained by the tithes offered by each Israelite of his possessions. The idea of the priesthood is expressed with as much precision as solemnity in these words,—'To-morrow the Lord will show who are His, and who is holy; and will cause him to come near unto Him: even him whom He hath chosen will He cause to come near unto Him.' Thus the priest has a special relation with God, is chosen by Him, separated from His people by a positive revelation, and whose vocation it is to draw near to the Lord. We here find the principal features which struck us in the election of Israel: direct relation with God, separation from the mass of mankind, and religious consecration.

The priesthood fulfils towards Israel the same part that Israel fulfilled in relation to the rest of humanity —concentrating the privileges and obligations of the chosen people. The high priest, clad in symbolical garments, typifying his consecration to God, and bearing inscribed on the gold plate of his mitre the words, *Holiness to the Lord*, may be considered as the ideal

Jew, the Israelite *par excellence*, the living personification of his nation; while, at the same time, the right possessed by him, alone to enter the holy of holies, served to remind the people of the gravity of their sins, which prevented them freely communicating with God. Though the Israelites felt their transgressions and guilt, they also felt they were not rejected, since through the mediation of their priests they were permitted to approach Jehovah. The function of the priest was chiefly sacrificial: his principal office was to sprinkle the blood of the victims on the altar, to burn the burnt-offerings, and to offer incense on the altar before the Lord. It was they who sounded the sacred trumpets at the time of festivals, and who superintended the observance of the laws of purification. They were established judges over the nation, to whom they interpreted the law. It was required that they should have no bodily infirmity, that they should be of pure life, and should keep themselves from all uncleanness, and purify themselves in a special manner at the time of ministering in the service of the tabernacle. Thus we see that it is the sacrifice that renders the priesthood necessary; for without the co-operation of the priest, sacrifice could not be offered. The man for whose atonement the sacrifice was offered, after having purified himself, brings a victim—'a bullock without blemish; he shall put his hands upon the head of the burnt-offering, and he shall kill the bullock before the Lord: the priests shall bring the blood and sprinkle the blood round about the altar.' There was a distinction between the peace-offerings and sin-offerings, though the ceremonies of both were identical.

The fundamental idea at the basis of the Jewish sacrifices is that of reparation. The holy God cannot tolerate iniquity. The relation between God and man was interrupted by the transgression of His commands.

The sinner, after his offence, could not present himself as he had done before. Some act is necessary, that may lead to a reconciliation. What shall this act be? A sacrifice. A sacrifice is an offering—a gift, the chief feature of which is, that it shall be chosen from what man has, best, purest, and most precious. The second characteristic is, that it implies the suffering and death of the victim. In interpreting the Judaic sacrifice, too much emphasis has been laid on this latter trait, as if the sole object of the Israelite had been to appease the justice of God by means of the blood of bulls and lambs. We do not deny that this point of view was in a measure sanctioned by Mosaism, which, being a revelation of the justice and severity of God, necessarily proclaimed that all disobedience of the law merited death. The immolation of the victim recalled this terrible sanction of the Decalogue. The Jewish sacrifice bore the impress of the dispensation to which it belonged, like it, was incomplete; and, with all the other Mosaic institutions, was at the same time abolished and accomplished by the New Covenant. The sacrifice on Calvary cannot in all points be likened to it; nor have we a right to prejudge the nature of the second by the character of the first. The Gospel brought us new tidings of God; without derogating from His holiness, it reveals His love as well as His justice. Besides, the victim sacrificed on the cross was not identical with the victim offered in the temple. These differences between the two dispensations render a complete assimilation between the two sacrifices impossible. We must, however, remark, that it is unjust to the Jewish sacrifice to view it merely as an expiation by blood. Sufficient importance is not attached to the fact of the offering itself. The sacrifice represented the offering of the heart to God. As the victim was symbolically substituted for the sinner, the latter, in immolating it, expressed his desire to give himself up unreservedly to God—to die to himself. The sacrifice accordingly represented the holiest act possible for man to perform; but the sign evidently exceeded the thing signified. None possessed the symbolic purity of the victim; none consecrated himself entirely to God. Thus did this most important institution develope in man the consciousness of his insufficiency, and at the same time an aspiration towards a higher sacrifice. On one side, by the death of the victim, sacrifice reminded man of the justice of an offended God; on the other, it fostered the hope of pardon. Hope sprung from this death: accepted by God, it became a prophecy of future reconciliation.

We know the importance the Mosaic legislation attached to the erection of a temple. At first portable, as a tent, it became under Solomon, at the time of Israel's greatest glory, a majestic edifice. The holy place was to the Holy Land what the priesthood was to the chosen people. It was there God manifested His presence in a special manner. Sacrifices could only be offered on the altar in the middle of the sanctuary. This one consecrated spot was the sole refuge for the worship of the true God on the earth that had been cursed. The institution of a Sabbath, or day of rest, likewise implies the idea of condemnation. The ordinary occupations of life being profane, it was necessary they should be suspended in order to offer solemn worship to God. But the very possibility of offering this worship implied a promise of reconciliation. The exceptional benediction is the forerunner of the permanent benediction. The time was to come when all men, in all places and at all times, might offer to God their spiritual sacrifice.

Thus we find that the four great institutions of the preparatory dispensation, each penetrated by the fundamental idea that presided at the election of Israel, were completely disengaged by Mosaism from the impure alloy of the religions of Nature. They constantly and energetically proclaimed the fall and the promise of pardon, by recalling the holiness and goodness of God. By their means the law and the promise circulate throughout the whole Mosaic system as blood does through our veins; and the history of Israel, in which divine justice manifests itself by severe chastisements, tempered by miraculous tokens of paternal love, unfolds itself, from Moses to Samuel, like a magnificent commentary upon the national institutions. The solemn feasts, the Passover, the Feast of Tabernacles, and the Pentecost, converge to the same end. The first commemorated the Exodus from Egypt; the second, the remarkable period of the sojourn in the desert; the third celebrated the bounty of God, who fills the earth with abundant harvests.

The great day of atonement, condensing into one great symbolic teaching all the teachings of the Mosaic system, marks with incomparable force the gravity of the fall and the generality of the corruption. Its first rite showed that the sanctuary itself needed to be purified, to hallow it from the uncleanness of the children of Israel; whilst the offering of a goat as a sin-offering for the people, and the sending forth into the wilderness of the scape-goat, bearing all the iniquities and transgressions of the people upon his head, recalled the necessity of a ransom.

The second grand period of the Old Testament is that of the Prophets. Of the two essential elements constituting Judaism, the element of the promise predominates over that of the law, without, however, effacing it. It is a mistake to suppose that the prophet's function was merely limited to prediction of the future. His vocation was to keep alive the fundamental thought underlying the whole of the first covenant; to keep ever before the minds of the people the profound meaning of their election; to save them by solemn warnings from sliding into the paths of idolatry, and to maintain stedfast their faith in their glorious destinies. Prophecy prevented the institutions of the preparatory dispensation from becoming petrified, by constantly seizing and holding before the eyes of the nation their real significance. It reacted against formalism, which threatened to substitute a stupid idolatry of the past, and a mechanical, routine piety, in the place of a living aspiration towards the future. Like the angel of the Apocalypse, who in his golden vial received the prayers of saints, it gathered up into itself the sighs and aspirations of the elect people, at the same time that it announced the future realization of their desires, thus rendering them more clear and more ardent. The prophet was not attached to the sacerdotal order. Inspiration was the source of his office, and not any positive institution. The Spirit of God sought him out sometimes among the shepherds of the desert, as in the case of Hosea; sometimes on the steps of the throne, as in that of Zephaniah, of the royal house of Judah; sometimes among the priests, as with Jeremiah and Ezekiel.

The nature of prophetic inspiration is a subject of constant debate. Some, with Ewald, see in it nothing but a vivid perception of the great laws of the moral world, a profound religious insight, an intuition of the will of Jehovah. According to this hypothesis, the prophet is simply a devout Israelite, whose inspiration is the result of his fervour and moral elevation, and who, by bold deductions, draws conclusions from the general laws which he has seen with more or less distinctness, and thus forecasts the fate of empires. In this way he announces the chastisement of the wicked, however powerful, though seated on the throne of Babylon or Nineveh, and foretells the triumph of the just over their enemies, and the benediction of God. Others, beginning with the Fathers, down to Bossuet, besides many orthodox moderns, assimilate prophetic inspiration to a state of ecstasy, in which the moral life is altogether suspended.

Neither of these points of view can we admit. Although we do not deny the relation subsisting between inspiration and certain religious aptitudes, we cannot look on prophecy as a merely natural process : positive revelations were given which did not spring from the heart of man, but came direct from heaven. Neither, on the other hand, is the prophet a merely passive instrument. By thus considering him, we degrade him to the level of the soothsayer, and assimilate his oracles to those of the Pythoness. The prophet we regard as one penetrated with the truths of which he is the organ, who, while speaking in God's name, yet is it his own voice we hear, preserving all his special idiosyncrasy, through whose heart the word of the Lord had passed before it found an outlet through his lips.

It is precisely this moral harmony, existing between the prophet and the revelation of which he is the bearer, that characterizes the progress accomplished during this period. Revelation has no longer the external character it bore at the time of the patriarchs. God no longer speaks, as it were, outside of man : He speaks not only to man, but by man, who has become His living organ. We are thus drawn closer to the blessed time when humanity and divinity shall be intimately united in the person of the Redeemer.

The symbols used by the prophet are borrowed from the conditions of the time he lived in ; they vary at the various epochs. He represents the future under the colours of the present. There is a profound reason for this method, which naturally imposed itself upon the prophet. For assuredly the present should not be isolated from the future, which it contains in germ and prepares. It contains it as the seed contains the full-grown ear of corn. This truth, which is of universal application, is of special importance in the preparatory dispensation. This dispensation, more than any other, points to an end beyond itself. Each of its periods weighs in importance according to the proportion with which it hastens the accomplishment of the designs of divine love. It is impossible to understand its real significance until we have seized its relation to the future. In order to understand the great law of history, above all, the law of the government of God, we must show the future in the present, as it were, enveloped under cotemporary events. There is, therefore, nothing arbitrary in the method adopted by the prophets. They gradually drew aside the curtain of the present, which hid the glorious prospects of Israel and humanity; but they did it progressively. Each event widened their prophetic horizon, because each event in itself tended effectually to prepare the advent of the Messiah. Thus prophecy kept pace with history, and advanced with each new period.

It is notorious that the sacred books of the Jews contain in their very first pages a promise of salvation extending far beyond the narrow limits of their national prejudices. We read that 'the seed of the woman shall crush the serpent's head.' It is not straining unduly the vague symbolism of these words, to interpret them as the general promise of the future triumph to be gained by humanity over the power of evil. The promise made to Abraham was more defined: from his seed should issue the mysterious Benefactor who was to restore the whole human race. Universalism from the first day hovers over Judaism. Thus the theme, the burden of prophecy, is given. Each new phase of Jewish history enriches it. From generation to gener-

ation the mysterious Benefactor is waited for. Each of
the great religious heroes of Israel contributed his part
in preparing His advent. Prophecy attributed to them
the character of the Messiah. They were His precursors,
and types prefiguring Him. But the type in these instances was far inferior to the reality. No man answers
to the portrait traced of the Messiah. Accordingly,
the hopes fixed for a moment on their persons take new
scope towards the future. The idea of the Saviour
becomes more and more spiritualized, more disengaged
from its national envelope. Royalty, made illustrious
by David, and by him celebrated in his noble Psalms,
in which the great hopes of Israel poured themselves
into sublime songs, long appeared a sufficient type of
the Messiah. It was expected that, as heir of David,
He should ascend the throne of Jerusalem; but none of
his successors, not even Solomon, corresponded to the
great and pure ideal. The moral degradation of the
kings of the chosen people gave new stimulus and a
new field to prophecy. The terrestrial aspect of the
hope becomes more and more effaced. The Deliverer
appears under the image of the servant of the Lord, the
friend of the good, the universal restorer, gathering together all nations on a renovated earth. We are familiar with the great ideal drawn by Isaiah in the second
part of his book. Its exact date signifies little. It,
however, goes back to a period preceding the decline.
The great idea of salvation to be wrought out by sorrow and suffering, is there developed with marvellous
lucidity: we are carried by the prophetic spirit to the
threshold of the Gospel. The sufferings of exile, fore-
seen or actually experienced, paved the way for this important evolution in the hopes of the Messiah. Universalism, which lies at the root of Judaism, blooms out as
its brightest flower at the moment of its highest development. All the nations of the earth are included by the

prophets in the promise of the blessed kingdom of the Messiah. The earlier prophets seem to have connected this reign with the return from exile, which event was paramount to all others in the estimation of their ardent patriotism; but the glorious picture they had traced was not to be realized at that epoch. Hence a new scope to prophecy. A wider and more distant range is opened up, in which all the great promises of the past should be accomplished. Later on we shall see the development of all those precious germs that were deposited under the influence of a salutary humiliation in the hearts of the people. This progress of prophecy, corresponding with the development of the destinies of Israel, should not surprise us, seeing that the Master of revelation is likewise the Master of history: He directs both to the same end, and interpenetrates one with the other, in order that they may each serve as commentary to the other.

We do not overlook the fact that the writings of the prophets contain very positive special predictions. This we firmly believe, though they are far less numerous than is generally supposed. This living organic prophetism, which at each period of history rises, under the inspiration of the Spirit of God, ever higher in its spiritual conceptions of the Saviour, has far more value than could have a simple collection of scattered oracles, whose sole object had been to point out the signs by which the Messiah at His advent might be recognised. Predictions have their value. This we do not contest. But their importance should not be exaggerated to the point of supposing that the principal mission of the prophet was to promulgate them. Judaic prophecy prepared the way for Christianity, not only through the minds it enlightened, but through the hearts which it purified: now severe as the voice that thundered from Sinai against sin, and now gentle and merciful as an

anticipated Gospel, it aroused to its fullest intensity
the desire of salvation,—keeping it alive with vigilant
care, as the Roman priestesses did the sacred fire, and
which it saved from being extinguished beneath the
bushel of external observances. It kept the spirit alive
in the body of Judaism; recalled the true significance of
its institutions; and, when necessary, boldly denounced
sin, though concealed under the most specious piety,
amid the splendid pomp of worship of their solemn
festivals, or in the multiplicity of sacrifices, or in the
affected humility of a hypocritical fast. Armed with the
two-edged sword of the word of God, it pierced through
the impenitent heart; but it was to pour into the bleed-
ing wound the balm of a consoling hope. Under the influence of prophecy, in its great days, Judaism reached
its culminating point of development. The fundamental
thought that lay at the basis of all its religious institutions it amalgamated with itself. Uniting repentance
with hope, it looked to the future, not, as the pagan
world did, with a confused, anxious expectation, based
solely on presentiments, but with a firm faith, built on
positive revelation. The dark days of its degeneracy
reserved to it another severe, and at the same time
precious experience, which was to be added as a last
favour to those with which it had been loaded.

THE DECLINE OF JUDAISM.

The external history of Judaism does not come
within the limits of our plan. We have said nothing
of its glory under David and Solomon; neither shall we
enter into the details of its gradual decline, the signal
for which was given by the disruption of the bond
that had hitherto held together the twelve tribes of
Israel in one organic body. The theocratic people,
heirs of the promise, were henceforth reduced to two
tribes: those of Judah and Benjamin. The ten others,

under kings who were not of the lineage of David, fell more and more into idolatry, in spite of the sublime warnings of their great prophets, through whose voice God's last appeal was heard. Shalmaneser, king of Assyria, gave the final blow to the kingdoms of Israel about the year 720 B.C. He transplanted the majority of the inhabitants into his own country, and replaced them by a numerous colony of Assyrians. Mingled with the residue of the Israelites who had escaped this compulsory emigration, they formed a new nationality, composed of heterogeneous elements, and which joined the worship of idols to the adoration of Jehovah. It appears, however, that the vanquished soon gained a moral ascendency over the conquerors; for the worship of Jehovah finally prevailed over that of false gods, though it never regained its primitive purity. The antipathy between the Jews and Samaritans, so strikingly manifested at the time of the rebuilding of the temple, became more and more envenomed. We shall see in the early days of Christianity that time had not worn down this feeling.

The kingdom of Judah appeared at one moment on the point of sharing the fate of the kingdom of Israel. After having borne the Egyptian yoke for several years, consequent upon their defeat by Pharaoh Necho (609 B.C.), the land was devastated by the armies of Assyria, in punishment of their constant relapses into idolatry, until at last a great portion of the nation was carried away captive by Nebuchadnezzar. Faith in the true God gained strength in a foreign land. The captives hung their harps on the banks of the rivers of Babylon, not only to weep their lost country, but to sing the praises of the God of their fathers. Patriotism, intensified by misfortune, brought them back to monotheism. Accordingly, when, in consequence of the great revolution that took place in Babylon, resulting from its conquest by the Persians, the Jews returned to their own country, under the conduct of Esdras and Nehemiah, they brought back with them an inviolable fidelity to Jehovah (458 to 434 B.C.). However, they never permanently recovered their national independence. Judea, after the conquests of Alexander, passed, like the rest of Asia, of which it formed a part, from one domination to another. From the hands of the Ptolemies it was transferred into those of the Seleucidæ, to return again under the sceptre of Egypt. The cruel yoke of Antiochus Epiphanes weighed heavily upon the people (171 B.C.). His tyranny provoked rebellion. It was then that the heroic sword of the Maccabees won back the national independence, the glorious memory of which cost the nation dear; for in it they found an eternal temptation to rebellion against oppressors too powerful to let go a prey they had once conquered. The Roman eagle, borne by Pompey, swept over the Holy Land. Men unworthy of being the successors of the illustrious champion of national independence, were striving for the possession of power. By one of these parties Roman intervention was solicited (63 B.C.). The family of the Idumean Antipater, which had been mixed up in the intrigues and intestine struggles of the last descendants of the Maccabees, purchased the favour and protection of Rome by their devoted adhesion. Herod the Great, son of Antipater, ascended the throne of Judea, which, by the assistance of his invincible allies, had been considerably aggrandized. He maintained the power thus acquired by baseness and crime,—as clever and successful in his flattery of his protectors as in the terror with which he inspired his subjects, and as in his unscrupulous mode of ridding himself of all rivals (37 B.C.). On his death the kingdom was for a short time divided between his three sons. Archelaus, who reigned at Jerusalem, having provoked his subjects by his cruelties, was dethroned and banished; and Judea, after being incorporated with the province of Syria, received a Roman procurator. Herod Agrippa II., nephew of Herod the Great, succeeded, through the favour of the Emperor Claudius, in uniting once more under his sceptre the entire possessions of the founder of the dynasty (41 A.D.). But on his death, which took place three years after, Judea was again governed by Roman procurators. This subjection kept the nation in a perpetual ferment of rebellion, ever ready to burst out into open insurrection. This constant agitation of men's minds tended to impart a terrestrial and gross character to the national expectations.

We are all familiar with the astute policy of Rome, which, however, was frequently compromised by the venal ambition of its proconsuls. This policy consisted in abstaining as much as possible from interference with the religious beliefs and customs of the conquered peoples. If all that appertained to political administration was confided to the Roman procurators, who virtually held the place of kings, the religious administration was entirely left to the Jews. The Sanhedrim, or great council of the nation, composed of 70 members—priests, elders of the synagogues, and scribes—presided over by the high priest, regulated everything connected with the cultus, and constituted the supreme tribunal, whose office it was to try all grave offences, such as imposture or blasphemy. Since the Roman domination, the right of pronouncing capital punishment, formerly exercised by the Sanhedrim, had become the prerogative of the representative of imperial power. The office of high priest, which had always been immoveable, had become, since the time of the Herods, the disputed prey of parties; it had lost its ancient dignity, and was degraded to the level of a magistracy to be obtained by intrigue and flattery.

To complete the description in broad outlines of the constitution of Judaism at this period, it is necessary to notice an institution which dates from the return from exile, and which filled a conspicuous part in the religious economy of those times—the institution of the synagogues. The synagogues, or houses of assembly and of prayer, were buildings dedicated to worship, or at least to that portion of religious service which did not need the intervention of priests. The dispersion of the people had rendered these places of meeting necessary, which, though they did not replace the temple, served to keep alive piety and the knowledge of the Scriptures amongst Jews in countries remote from Jerusalem. Nothing could be simpler than the arrangement of these edifices, which were merely intended for the reading of the Law and the Prophets, and for prayer. The people assembled in the synagogues on the Sabbath and feast days, when the sacred books were not only read, but commented on in the people's vernacular. The superintendence of the cultus, of discipline, and the care of the poor, was entrusted to a college of elders, who presided over the synagogue. We shall enter more fully into the organization of the synagogue when we come to the examination of the primitive institutions of the Christian Church. It was also this college of elders that received the numerous proselytes who were led by the religious wants of the time to embrace Judaism. These proselytes were divided into two categories: the Proselytes of the Gate, who were subjected to a few general prescriptions sufficient to mark their rupture with idolatry; and the Proselytes of Righteousness, who took upon themselves the obligation of the whole Mosaic law, and were incorporated into the nation. The latter were first circumcised, after which the synagogue, by certain symbolical ablutions, administered a kind of baptism. The celebration of a sacrifice completed the ceremony.

We have seen that the scribes, or doctors of the law, took their seats next the priests in the Sanhedrim. Their influence at this time rapidly increased, to the prejudice of that of the priests, which had so long preponderated. Entrusted with the instruction of youth, the scribes did not confine themselves to the inculcating of a sufficient knowledge of the sacred books into the minds of their pupils, but took upon themselves to fix their meaning by a tradition, which was not only preserved but augmented by themselves. Close by the temple they had schools, which were attended by a crowded audience. In this way sprang up rabbinical science, which, by combining a narrow literalism with the theory of a double meaning, ended in annihilating the spirit of the revelation they professed to guard. The predominance of the rabbis in the Great Synagogue, or Sanhedrim, gave them considerable influence in the nation. Their whole tendency is summed up in this precept: 'Plant (by tradition) a hedge round the law;' but it was a hedge of thorns they planted, which fatally choked the divine plant it should have protected.

This preponderance of the scribes is the characteristic feature of this long period. In place of the prophet speaking directly in the name of God, and adding a new page to revelation, we have grammarians analysing it. In the same way that the great creating period of Hellenic poetry was followed by that of the Alexandrine Aristarchuses, satisfying themselves with the classifying of the treasures of ancient literature, and often burying it beneath their pedantic glossaries, so the period of the Isaiahs and Jeremiahs is succeeded by that of the Gamaliels and the doctors of the law. The worst consequence of this transformation was, that it gave an exclusively intellectual character to religion, reducing it to a system, and in this way cooling the ardour of piety.

The contact of the Jews with other nations, which was frequent since the time of their exile; their numerous voluntary emigrations after their compulsory emigration; the colonies they founded at Babylon, Alexandria, and in all the great cities of the East and West, where they began to manifest their aptitude for commerce,— all these circumstances must be borne in mind in order to form an accurate estimate of their religious condition at the beginning of the Christian era. It appears evident to us that the influence exercised by them was considerably greater than that which was exercised upon them. Proselytes quitting Paganism to embrace Judaism were reckoned by thousands; whereas Paganism made no conquests amongst this despised, vanquished people, who extracted from defeat itself a deeper hatred of the stranger. It cannot, however, be denied that a certain number of Jews endeavoured to amalgamate either the results of Greek philosophy or Oriental philosophy with the teachings of the Old Testament. The farther we go from the religious centre of the nation, the more apparent is this influence; while, on the contrary, the nearer we approach Jerusalem, the more feeble and imperceptible it is.

In the Judaism of the period we are considering, two very different currents are discernible: the one carrying in its troubled waters all the national prejudices, and all errors imported from without. This is the current of degenerate Judaism, straying farther and farther from true religious tradition. The second current is that of normal Judaism, the inheritor of the prophets, which, taught and purified by all the sad experiences of the present, turned towards the future a fixed look of stedfast hope. The existence of the latter is revealed to us as a positive fact by those Israelites who, fearing God

P

and waiting for the Messiah, appear at the threshold of evangelical history. Naturally, the second was less obvious than the first, which drew into itself the leaders of the nation, now that the race of pious kings and prophets had ceased. Normal Judaism remained in the shade; its coming to light at the beginning of evangelical history reveals to us the last link of a long chain. The overlooking this fact has led to the mistake of connecting the Christian Church with official Judaism, which, though popular, was nevertheless an abnormal tendency.

The restoration effected by Esdras and Nehemiah was a revival of the pure religion of their fathers, unadulterated by any foreign influence. It occasioned an energetic reaction, which led the Jews to break off all ties, even the dearest and most tender, formed in the land of exile. Still we cannot overlook the fact, that contact with Persia must, soon or late, have exercised a certain action upon such minds as were more preoccupied about religious speculation than inclined to living piety. It would, however, be an error to attribute the Jewish theology of this period to Parsism; it may have slightly modified the form, but it added no new doctrines, though it may have inspired some modification of the dogma already existing. In this way angels are made to fill a more and more important part, and are sometimes raised to the rank of cosmogonic powers. We have grounds for attributing to the same influence, combined with Alexandrine Platonism, the personification of Wisdom, sketched with such admirable logic, but not realized, by Jesus Sirach, who has been erroneously styled the precursor of Saint John. It was not till a later period that foreign ideas made an inroad into Judaism.

We recognise three dominant tendencies in the Judaism of the decadence. First, the exclusively national and conservative tendency, rigidly keeping guard over tradition, and having Jerusalem for its centre. We have, next, the tendency which largely underwent the influence of Oriental theosophy; and finally, the Alexandrine tendency, related to Platonism, and especially to what we may call the theosophic side of Platonism. These two last tendencies, which have a close analogy, alone claim our attention: the first characterizes itself.

It has been said that the tendency imbued with Oriental theosophy had been reduced to a complete system long before the time of Christ, and that this system was no other than the Kabbala, or secret doctrine, of the rabbis, which had been constantly elaborated and remodelled by them. It is not possible to determine with certainty this historic problem; the nature even of the doctrine, and the veil with which it covers its dogmas, sufficiently explain the obscurity of its origin. It, however, appears to be proved that there did exist a secret doctrine in certain Jewish schools before the Christian era. Probably the fundamental ideas which were subsequently embodied in the Kabbala were already known: these were in all points similar to those dualistic notions which were then so universally diffused, like a vast reservoir enriched by the religions and philosophies of the East, whence all came to drink, in whom the speculative wants of the intellect predominated over the religious nature. One sect of the Jews, which we shall hereafter describe, maintained in Palestine itself this doctrine of dualism, which at one moment appeared destined to overrun the world. If we endeavour to distinguish in the Kabbala the variable form from the groundwork of ideas, bearing the mark of high antiquity, we shall find there a system of emanation, tortured by forced interpretations into an accordance with the letter of the Old Testament. God is the absolute, invisible substance, made manifest by His attributes, not one of which possesses Him exclusively; and from their totality results the Word (Verbe), the prototype of man. All things issue forth from God, and return to Him. Our world is the representation of the world of divine attributes, of which man is the most exalted image. He existed before his terrestrial birth, and is destined to pass through the purifications of the metempsychoses. 'Death is a kiss from God.' This kiss is the union of the soul with the substance whence it derives its origin. Thus the world has no real existence, but is the ever-changing form of the divine thought. Union with the absolute, by losing individuality, is the extreme term of perfection. Who does not see in these theories the traces of that Indian religion whose sole aspiration was absorption into Brahma? Asceticism was the inevitable result of this system. It is probable that it was at an early period associated with magic, then so prevalent in the East; and we may perhaps attribute to it those mysterious books which the Hebrew magicians of Ephesus cast into the flames after they had heard Saint Paul.[1]

If we now quit Asia and turn towards Egypt, we shall find analogous doctrines in Judaism, but developed by a far finer logic, and arrayed in the brilliant mantle of Hellenic philosophy. The Jewish emigration to Alexandria had been considerable; and having been constantly encouraged by the Ptolemies, it eventually formed a nation within a nation. But it was not with impunity that it fixed itself in this sumptuous thoroughfare of the ideas of the time, where the East and West met and amalgamated. Enriched by commerce, respected and cultivated, the Jewish colony removed with its own hands the religious barrier which should have separated it from the pagan world. It renounced

[1] Acts ix. 19.

the language of its fathers, without, however, attaining a complete mastery of the Greek tongue, the plastic, delicate construction of which could little adapt itself to the elementary syntax of the Semitic race. Nevertheless, with new words came new ideas. The Hellenic intellect, already considerably modified by Oriental influence, infiltered itself into the Synagogue of Alexandria, and by means of a perfect system of allegorical interpretation, was enabled to accumulate at its case the advantages of an apostasy according to the spirit, and of a fidelity according to the letter. The most eminent representative of this singular tendency was the Jew Philo, the cotemporary of Jesus Christ, who became illustrious throughout the world, after having obtained from his fellow-citizens the honour of representing them at Rome in an embassy to the court of Caligula. He opened the way to the last philosophy that shed a lustre upon the ruins of Paganism. Philo is evidently the disciple of Plato, but a disciple who makes his selection from amongst the master's doctrines, and assimilates to himself those most accessible. This was the Oriental side, which we have already indicated in Platonism. Philo borrowed from theosophy its mysticism and asceticism, and sought in the sacred books of his nation formulas and religious symbols, in order to justify an attempt which, without such artifice, might have scandalized his countrymen. He sets out from the idea that God is the absolute, immutable Being, —the One eternal and indivisible, alike ineffable and inaccessible to reason. 'This God,' he says, 'better than the good itself, simpler than unity, can be contemplated by none other than Himself. We possess no organ by which to represent Him to our minds. Those who seek Him in creation find but His shadow.' It is from Himself that we must receive the revelation of Himself, as He revealed it to Moses. This absolute ineffable God did not create matter, which existed from all eternity. He gave it order, but not directly; 'for it is not permitted the blessed God to enter into contact with matter.' He organized it by the intermediation of the world of ideas which is personified in the Logos. Philo explains the Logos sometimes as the image of God, sometimes as being multiple and abstract. This reveals the incoherency of his ideas upon a point, on which some have thought they had found in him the inspirer of primitive Christianity. Philo removes all doubt upon this subject, when he declares that 'the Logos is the world of intelligence, and that God is the place filled with incorporeal Logoi.' God creates, rather orders matter in a continuous manner, in the same way that fire necessarily diffuses heat, and snow, cold. This matter, which was not created by God, is the necessary element which we find everywhere. From such a system of metaphysics moral asceticism necessarily flowed. Man cannot, as being a mortal, unite himself with God; 'for it is not permitted for mortal to inhabit with the Immortal.' But if he has by nature the superior illumination that makes the priest and prophet, he may by contemplation attain to losing himself in God. Thus the part allowed liberty is insignificant. Virtue is a gift of Nature; those who have not received it at their birth can only approximate towards it by means of asceticism. The highest ideal, in short, consists in flying from self in order 'to rise from the individual mind into the universal Mind, which is the supreme refuge of the soul.' Without having exactly formalized the doctrine of emanation, Philo developed its ultimate consequences. He went further than Plato in his affinity with the East, and, like India, placed salvation in annihilation and asceticism. It was in vain that he laboured to exalt the religion of his people by proclaiming them a people of prophets and seers, and by making the high priest the universal priest, immolating victims for the whole of creation and humanity. He nevertheless, and notwithstanding his eulogies, sapped the basis of Mosaicism. He annihilated it by transfiguring it; and even in the homage he bestows we can trace his speculative tendencies, which transform profoundly religious institutions into a cosmogonic system.

We have, in the existence of the Therapeutes in Egypt, a striking proof of the influence exercised by Eastern ideas at this period. According to Philo, who on account of his ascetic views must have felt a strong sympathy with them, the Therapeutes professed, as their name indicates, to cure the diseases of the soul. Renouncing their possessions, and seeking solitude, they reserved a hidden sanctuary in their dwellings, where, removed from all eyes, they performed their devotions. Prayer, the meditation of the sacred books, which they interpreted allegorically, and of other writings belonging to their sect, occupied their thoughts. They looked on temperance 'as the bulwark of the soul,' and subjected themselves to lengthened fasts. They assembled on the Sabbath days, and heard an exposition of their doctrine made by one of their elders. Absolute chastity was held in honour among them. Evidently the Therapeutes merely reproduced Indian asceticism : similar theories produce similar practices.

At this period there were three leading sects in Judea : the Essenians, Pharisees, and Sadducees. The first only was a really constituted sect; the other two having been rather parties than sects. The Essenians were the Therapeutes of Judea, equally imbued with Oriental theosophy, but more preoccupied about practice than about speculation, as behoved the Jews of Palestine. They, too, sought solitude and founded convents, without, however, interdicting residence in towns to those amongst them who followed manual arts. Their goods were in common. 'The possession of each,' says Josephus, 'being mixed up with those of the rest, there existed but one property, belonging equally to all as to brothers.' They despised marriage, says the same author, but received the children of others, and trained them to their own mode of life. The Essenians energetically proclaimed the immortality of the soul, declaring the body to be but a prison in which the soul is shut up and held by a charm, which death dissolves. In this we recognise Oriental dualism, as we do also in the practice, followed by the adherents of this sect, of offering prayers to the sun at the moment of its rising. They beheld in it the splendid symbol of the luminous side of the Divinity. Philo leaves no doubt on this point; for he says that the Therapeutes, in all respects the same as the Essenians, prayed, at sunrise, that their minds might be clothed with celestial light. At repasts, which had evidently a religious significance, the Essenians gathered round a table, after having purified themselves by numerous lustrations, and clad themselves in white garments. This repast, which recalled the feast of the Passover, commemorated the Exodus from Egypt, except that in this instance Egypt signified, according to dualistic typology, the body, whose humiliating yoke the soul was called on to shake off. The Essenians thus found means of attaching an ultra-spiritual meaning to practices the most closely connected with the servitude of corporeal life. They celebrated, like the Therapeutes, the Sabbaths and feast days without sacrifices. The cultus consisted in the reading of the sacred books, and the celebration of symbolical rites.

Initiations into this sect were accompanied by solemn ceremonies, and preceded by a severe novitiate. With all these features before us, it is impossible, notwithstanding assertions to the contrary, not to see in them the characteristic signs of Oriental dualism. By its very nature, Essenianism was saved from contact with official Judaism. Having no ambition for power, it did not dispute its possession with those who had. Living in the desert and in obscurity, and holding itself aloof from all strife and intrigues, it excited no uneasiness.

But it was far otherwise with the two great parties that competed for pre-eminence in Jerusalem. The Pharisees, or Separatists, arrogated to themselves the character of Jews *par excellence*. As defenders of the old constitution, they resisted all concessions to the stranger; were ardent patriots and sworn enemies of oppression. They adopted, as a legitimate development of Judaism, the dogma of the resurrection of the body. Unfortunately, in their desire to preserve at all cost the religion of their fathers, they accumulated traditions, and favoured the growth of formalism. Identifying in a great measure politics and religion, they made the latter subordinate to the first. Ambitious of power and authority, they sought to gain the favour of the people by all possible means, especially by an ostentatious piety, that sounded its trumpet when about to perform any of its rare good works. Thus they fell into the error of all who, in religion or in morals, place the letter above the spirit, and invented a subtle casuistry which benumbed the conscience, while it professed to place it in strict harmony with the law.

The Sadducees derive their name either from Tsadoc, the presumed founder of this sect, or from a Hebrew word signifying justice; they assuming to themselves the character of being the just *par excellence*, in opposition to the Pharisees, with whom they present a striking contrast. The Sadducees rejected all tradition, and also rejected, as an absurd prejudice, that inflexible patriotism which refused to treat with the stranger on any terms. They, on the contrary, were always ready for a compromise, provided it secured their repose. Rich and voluptuous, it was for form's sake alone they connected themselves with the national religion; their wish was to enjoy the present life, and not to trouble themselves about the life to come. The Sadducees were the Epicureans of Jerusalem; but they were obliged to act with caution in the presence of the ardent, fanatical people that surrounded them, whose sympathies more inclined to Pharisaism than to Sadduceeism. These two parties—the party of independence and that of the foreigner—are to be found in all states in their decline. In Judea, they appear under the forms appropriate to the nation, which forms, we may say, were the result of its history; but they there reveal the same passions and provoke the same storms which they do in all countries whose subjection is of recent date.

In the midst of this clash of parties, what had become of the hope of the Messiah? It floated above the stormy waves that dashed against each other; but not without undergoing considerable modification from one tendency or another. The dualistic tendency, which strove by contemplation and asceticism to fill up the abyss Judaism created between God and man, had completely changed the nature of the hope of Israel. With Philo and the first propagators of Oriental theosophy, this hope was deprived of its moral import, assuming in their hands a cosmogonic character. Evil was assimilated with matter, and salvation made to depend on the maceration of the body. Still, even this longing to become merged in God, inherent in the Alexandrine doctrine, did not originate in a desire for absolute union with the Divinity, which never seizes the soul but in order to prepare it for salvation. The hope of the Messiah, as entertained by the Pharisees and the people influenced by them, was as ardent as it was gross. We have proofs of the general expectation of the promised deliverance, not only in the frequent insurrections of the Jews, but in some apocryphal writings, in which their highly wrought imaginations endeavoured to paint in vivid colours the future they expected. We shall first cite from among these writings a fragment from those famous Sibylline Books, the mystery of which has been penetrated by cotemporary science. In these the dreams of the ancient world deposited their impress. The Jews of Alexandria were the first who endeavoured to couch their views of the future in this singular form, which had the advantage of being accepted and revered by their cotemporaries. The Sibyl personified in their eyes the earliest of all prophecies,—the prophecy anterior to the oracles contained in the sacred books. They put their own aspirations into her mouth, and sometimes also the expression of their hatred of those powers that had oppressed them. The portion of the Sibylline Books which bears evident tokens of a Jewish hand, begins by announcing the destruction of the different monarchies which had imposed their yoke upon the holy nation, whilst the glory of the elect race is celebrated on every key: from it is to proceed the Saviour. The Messiah shall descend at the destined time, and will bring peace and holiness with Him. The adversaries of theocracy that rise up against Him shall be annihilated in great catastrophes of the physical world. Henceforward the people of God shall dwell in peace and safety round about the temple, and Pagans will unite with them to carry their offerings to Jehovah. Such is the substance of the Sibylline Books, which are, as we see, essentially theocratic. There may be a slight modification in the different oracles, according as the author was preoccupied with such or such enemy of God's people; but in their general character they all bear a close resemblance, and never get beyond temporal dominion.

The Book of Enoch, which was written—at least the essential portion of it—before Christ, is chiefly taken up with the description of the battle of the rebellious angels against God, their pretended relations with the daughters of men, and their fatal influence upon humanity, in order to corrupt it and tempt it to the worship of idols. Enoch, the friend of God, who was translated to heaven, is commissioned to announce to the fallen angels their future condemnation. This singular book enters into minute details of the nature of angels and demons, and of the physical constitution of the earth, connected with a fantastical demonology. In one of his most remarkable visions, the Messiah appears to Enoch in all the glory of heaven. He is pre-eminently the servant of God; and was called into existence before the sun and moon. His mission is to reveal all the secrets of God; then to judge the world. The deluge was the first of His great judgments. The second will take place at the end of time, and will reach not only the living, but the dead, and even the saints in heaven. The kings of the earth shall tremble with fear, and all the enemies of the Messiah shall be overwhelmed by the wrath of God; whilst the society of the saints shall have everlasting life, and shall dwell with the Messiah through all eternity. The Book of Enoch concludes with a general and symbolical sketch of the history of theocracy, divided into ten weeks, or ten periods. The Judaic portion of the apocryphal book known under the title of the 6th Book of Esdras, is animated by the same spirit. The whole of this literature perfectly coincides with what we know of the disposition of the Hebrew people at this period,—with the material character of their hopes; with their exclusive preoccupation about the terrestrial and political side of the work of the Messiah; and finally, with their immoderate predilection for the doctrine of angels and demons. Nevertheless the people lived in expectation—in intense, anxious expectation. They felt themselves drifting on to a great crisis of their history, badly prepared though they were. Another Messiah was reserved for them than that they looked forward to. Like the majority of the Pagans, they misinterpreted their own aspirations. But the universality of the feeling of expectation was not the less an important fact, and one which announced the approaching issue of the period of preparation.

But does this imply that this abnormal Judaism was the sole representative of the people of Abraham and David? Not so. The very first pages of the Gospel initiate us into the life, hopes, and prayers of a few pious Israelites. The hymns of Simeon and of Mary breathe an elevation, a spirituality, a stedfast confidence, —in short, a whole order of sentiments, with which there is nothing in the past comparable. The great religious universalism already contained in the first promise made to Abraham, shines out with admirable clearness through their language, though the latter in form is still Jewish. 'My eyes have seen thy salvation,' says old Simeon, 'which Thou hast prepared before the face of all people, to be a light to lighten the Gentiles.' These upright, humble souls drew out of the very degeneracy of their nation a still more ardent longing for salvation. If we compare these hymns with the apocryphal books of the time, we shall be convinced of the simultaneous existence of two Judaisms, speaking the same language, wearing the same costume, but profoundly separated by their ideas and sentiments. In the eyes of God, humanity is not a question of numbers, but of moral value. Thus this little group of the Simeons and Zachariahs, and others sharing their hopes and expectations, represented true Judaism, in the same way that the Cornelius, the Sergius Paul, and later on the

Justins, represented the Greco-Roman world in its best aspirations.

The time then is ripe at Jerusalem, at Athens, and at Rome. When John the Baptist, the preacher of repentance and of hope, brought with him from the desert the words, 'Repent, for the kingdom of heaven is at hand,' he proclaimed the two great results of the preparatory economy: the salutary contrition of repentance, and the joyful thrill of hope. From the broken heart of the fallen race rises a sigh of sadness and of holy desire. The earth thirsts for the dew of heaven, and heaven is about to open to bestow its most precious gift. The Son of God may descend, for He will now be the Son of man; from East to West suffering and prayers enough invoke Him to permit this earthly name being joined to His heavenly name.

CONCLUSION.

CHRISTIANITY.

ORIGEN, in an allegorical interpretation of the Song of Solomon, the exegetical accuracy of which may be questioned, but not its poetic beauty, has represented the human soul as the mystical bride of the Redeemer. He lets us hear her voice calling to Him out of the midst of Paganism, as out of the midst of Judaism. 'The Church,' he says, 'by which I understand the assembly of the saints, desires her union with Jesus Christ, and thus expresses her desire:—" I have been loaded with blessings. I have received in profusion the pledges and gifts of my divine marriage. During my betrothal with the Son of the King of Heaven, the chief King of all creatures, angels brought me the law as a gift from my Spouse. Prophets, filled with the Holy Spirit, kindled still more my love, and wakened up my desire to behold Him; by speaking to me of His coming, of His countless virtues, of His infinite gifts, they portrayed His noble beauty and His mercy. Therefore I can no longer bear the expectation of such love. Already the present dispensation is drawing to its close, and I still only see His servants ascending and descending the luminous ladder. To Thee I turn, Father of my Spouse. I supplicate Thee to have pity on my love; to send Him to me, that He may speak to me no longer through

His servants and prophets, but that He Himself come, that I may hear Him speaking and teaching." The human soul,' adds Origen, 'even among the Pagan, thirsts for its union with the Word (the Logos); it has received the earnest of its divine marriage. As the law and prophecy were pledges of the future to Israel, in like manner the law of conscience, intelligence, and free will were the nuptial gifts to the human soul, outside of Judaism. In no philosophic doctrine did it find the satisfaction of its desire and of its love: it is the illumination and visitation of the Word that it demands. Neither men nor angels suffice. It seeks the embrace of the Word of God.' The great Alexandrian doctor has in those words admirably painted the state of expectation that prevailed in his day.

He came at last: He, for whose coming all things had been a preparation and an announcement, and towards whom the whole history of the ancient world had gravitated. He came, and with Him was ushered in an entirely new era: definitive religion now superseded all preparatory religions.

This appreciation of Christianity is met at the threshold by two leading objections, which it is necessary to remove. Adversaries, employing as an argument against it the natural analogies existing between definitive religion and those religions which prepared its way, deny to it all originality. Some maintain that Jesus Christ merely carried forward the higher and purer form of Judaism, without adding a single doctrine, and without the consciousness of being the author of a new religion. Others only see in His teachings a happy blending of Jewish and Oriental ideas. Neither hypothesis will stand a careful examination. The first has been developed with vast erudition and considerable ingenuity by a cotemporary school, which would seem to have pledged itself to prove that what has hitherto been held to be primitive Christianity dates from the second century, and to ascribe to Saint Paul all that the Church has attributed to Christ Himself. It would be necessary to recover foot by foot, by a thorough examination of documents, the whole ground of evangelical history. This, however, is not the moment to engage in a discussion devoid of importance so long as it keeps to generalities. In order to refute the essential principles of this school, it will suffice that we establish the authenticity of the fourth Gospel; since it is evident that, if the Gospel of John goes back to its traditional date, there is no possible construction can make out Christ to be merely the most popular rabbi that lived in the time of the Herods.

We shall show that the three first Gospels give us the same Christ that the fourth does, modified, it may be, by certain considerations. It is the aim of our history to overthrow the scaffoldings of this scientific edifice, which, although of imposing proportions, nevertheless stands on a fragile basis. However, even here we shall endeavour to refute the fundamental doctrine of the school of Tubingen. In the work that may be considered the definitive programme of its leader, we are told that Jesus Christ confined Himself to the inculcating of pure morality, and to recommending the development of the inner life. According to Baur, Matthew's Gospel is the only really authentic document that gives the thought of the Founder of Christianity. This thought should be sought for in Christ's own discourses, and especially in the Sermon on the Mount, which bears evident marks of Judaism. If humility, poverty, recourse to grace, renunciation of self and unto God, are therein enforced, these comprise no really new element. The originality of this primitive Christianity consists solely in the predominance of the moral element, and owes, he would say, its good fortune to the coincidence of the over-excited hopes of the Jews of the decadence, and of their feverish expectation of the Messiah, with the remarkable personality of Jesus Christ.[1]

We are justified in asking, By what right does the illustrious scholar, whose views we are combating, single out and isolate certain portions of one Gospel in order to seek therein the whole of the Master's teaching? Evangelical history, taken even from one Gospel, such as Saint Matthew's, suffices to demonstrate the insufficiency of such an explanation of primitive Christianity. No doubt we simplify the process of explanation, if we throw overboard all the embarrassing portions of the document we accept. It is notorious that in the first Gospel, as well as in the others, Jesus Christ represents Himself to be the object of faith. Salvation is identified with this belief. Now this claim is an absolutely new fact in Judaism, and is entirely without precedent. It must have clashed in a special manner with its strict monotheism, so intent on humbling man before God, and on removing every pretext for presumptuous comparisons. To present Himself as the object of faith, was, then, a daring attack upon the narrow circle of ancient ideas, and a wide step beyond the simple moral development we are told of. It is futile to pretend that the national expectation of the Messiah, so general at the time, suggested this form to the teachings of Christ; since, far from responding to the hopes of His time, at least such as circulated among the masses, He carefully discouraged and combated them. The very first words of the Sermon on the Mount are an energetic protest against the deep-rooted prejudices of that multitude, who crowded round to hear the gracious word that carried with it such authority. It taught not only a

---

[1] *Das Christenthum der drei ersten Jahrhunderte*, von Baur. Tubingen, 1853. P. 25 to 37.

pure, humble, fervent Judaism; it preached not only sorrow, repentance, poverty; but it also announced blessing. If, at first, it places this in penitential tears, it is the almost daring proof of its power to pour consolation and salvation into afflicted hearts. The first Gospel, like the others, attributes to Christ pardon of sins; and puts language into His mouth, the terms of which shall be weighed later on, but which, from a purely Judaic point of view, must have been considered as the height of blasphemy, and which was so considered by the sacerdotal tribunal before which Christ was led. It goes the length of placing the name of the Galilean Master on a level with that of the thrice holy name of Jehovah, and of establishing between Christ and God a unique and mysterious relationship implying His divinity, which He Himself tacitly admitted by not repelling the accusation charged against Him in the Sanhedrim, of declaring Himself to be the Son of God. The first Gospel, as well as the others, ascribes such capital significance to His death and resurrection as to confer on them dogmatic importance. It appears to us that, without availing ourselves of the advantages to be derived from a comparative study of the authentic writings of the New Testament, and contenting ourselves for the moment with a rapid glance at the question at issue, we may set aside the assertion of that school which is at present the most powerfully organized against Christianity.

The other hypothesis, which deduces the doctrine of Jesus Christ from the various sources of the ancient world, is it more plausible? Can we give our assent to M. Salvador, when he says that 'the young Galilean Master consummated the union of Judaism and Orientalism without giving originality to His doctrine?' We know what this Orientalism was, which, we are told, formed one of the features of the Gospel. We have traced it through all its transformations; we have seen it oscillate between materialism and extreme asceticism, now glorifying and deifying Nature, now striving to annihilate it, but ever pursued by this element of matter, which it could never shake off, for the reason that it could never explain it. Under its subtlest form, and though invested in hues of a most seductive mysticism, we find, even in the hands of Philo, that it still bears the taint of its original dualism, and in the midst of ecstasy and contemplation is still haunted by this invincible matter. Though it created or revived the term, the Word, yet the meaning it attached to the word expressed the irremediable contradiction of its daring doctrines. It needs great power of self-delusion, or great ignorance, to confound the Word of the Alexandrian Jew with that of Saint John. The West was too destitute of moral ideas, and too rank in corruption and infamy, to permit us for a moment to suppose that the new religion addressed itself to that quarter with a view of borrowing. Assuredly, to create out of nothing is no deep mystery, compared to this creation of a new world out of a decrepit expiring world,—to have recourse to all that was most effete, most impure, most dark, to extract from it this pure, this radiant light! If Christianity be a confused amalgamation, a machine composed of more or less well adjusted pieces, fabricated here and there, how are we to explain the admirable construction of its parts—the life that circulates throughout the whole, and which reveals it to be, not an artificial piece of mechanism, but a perfect organism? What crucible was fervid enough to fuse down these different elements into one glorious metal, and cast it into one single mould? This is a miracle surpassing all those that shock the inventors of the theory we are combating. When they have explained this, it will still remain for them to say why it has never been renewed, and why Neo-Platonism, for example, presents so striking a contrast to the Gospel.

It is supposed that this hypothesis is simplified if we regard Jesus Christ as not having operated the fusion between Judaism and Orientalism, but as being Himself the result of this fusion. We are to regard this incomparable type as being the product of the alembics of philosophical chemistry, thus producing at its pleasure the greatest religious revolution in the annals of humanity. Here again is another prodigy to confound our reason! What! a moral idiosyncrasy so characterized,—a being so perfect, and at the same time so human, at whose feet so many generations have sat to hear His words,— this living personality to be compounded of the empty abstractions of ancient philosophy at its decline! What is there between the Christ of the Gospel, the Friend of Saint John, the Master that sympathized and wept at the tomb of Lazarus, and the Christ of Gnosticism, with those metaphysical phantoms hovering between heaven and earth, intangible and silent, hybrid products of sickly brains, that never detach themselves from the nebulous region of dreams to take definite shape? He who does not feel that we have in the Christ of the Gospel an absolutely different type from these pale creations that never lived, has not the faculty by which we discern the real.

Are they more successful who labour to prove Christ to have been, not the product of the dust of philosophic schools, but of a heated popular imagination, spontaneously weaving out a complex mythology? We admit the learning and talent displayed by Strauss in vindicating this hypothesis. According to him, each event recorded in the Gospels is, as it were, the result of a subtle combination of several myths of the Old Testament. Thus the multitudinous threads that co-operated in working out the wonderful tissue of the Gospel history adjusted themselves, without the aid of a guiding hand to give them method or arrangement. Popular imagination, usually so light and capricious, subordinated itself in this instance to a profoundly conceived plan, which it wrought out consistently and perseveringly, approving itself to be at once spontaneous and ingenious, simple and elaborate,—taking out of all the books of the Old Testament the heterogeneous elements of this mosaic of legends called the Gospel! Still more amazing that it should turn out that this popular mythology, interpreted by a philosopher of the 19th century, should have been in perfect accordance with a system, by which Christ symbolized eighteen centuries ago the inherent existence of the absolute in man. Thus the spontaneous conscience of a fanatical people created unwittingly a transcendental philosophy which has not been fathomed until our day, and the sole mission of the fishermen of the Lake of Gennesareth was to prepare the way for the learned professor of Berlin! It strikes us that the system of Strauss involves even more discrepancies than those he attributes to the Gospel narratives, and that this great adversary of the supernatural demands for his theories a more stalwart faith than is necessary for the admission of the most rare prodigies. Besides, the great question of the authenticity of documents is too often neglected. This is not to be disposed of so easily as we may at first imagine. We shall deal with it in the proper place, when we come to the consideration of the great monuments of apostolic literature. If it be proved, as we believe it is, that all our Gospels date from the first century, then this fact alone will suffice to refute the theories we have been analyzing.

If, then, there be, as we believe, a connection between Christianity and those religions that prepared its way, this connection is not that of effect and cause; for Christianity possessed all the characteristics of an entirely original religion, and inaugurated a new cycle of history. The relation it bore to preceding forms of worship, is the relation existing between the satisfaction of a desire and the desire itself. That there should be certain analogies between the Gospel and the preparatory scheme, ought not to surprise us: they are the analogies existing between the symbol and the thing signified; between the shadow and the body; between the type and the reality; between prophecy and accomplishment. Christianity is, in short, the fulfilment of all that was prefigured, waited for, desired, in the ancient world. Its true nature is evident from this definition. We learn to view it pre-eminently as a fact, an immense fact, whose roots had struck down deep through a past of four thousand years, as they had done in the heart of every man, and whose consequences were to reach as far as the destinies of the immortal soul.

The originality of the Gospel is completely misapprehended when it is viewed simply as an illustration of those moral truths which ancient philosophy embodied, and transmitted through its most distinguished representatives, or when it is considered as the last link of a dogmatic tradition, identical in substance, though varying in form, in all religions. The deistical and traditionalistic schools here coincide in the same error. These great truths, which have been erroneously baptized by the name of Natural Religion—for, since the fall, there is no really natural religion but the religion of the redemption, which is man's restoration to his normal nature—all these moral ideas that play over the surface of Paganism, reveal, in their highest aspects, their own insufficiency. They goad man on to the pursuit of the Good, the True, the Beautiful; they hinder him from being ever consoled at their loss; they haunt him as he kneels before the altars of his false gods.

The idea of the Good calls for its manifestation: even the incomplete perception of the ideal demands its realization. Were Christianity nothing more than the most consummate of systems, it might be reckoned as the best of the preparatory religions, but not as definitive religion. This religion is a living fact: not confined to the perception of the ideal, like Platonism, or to the prophesying of it, like Judaism, this religion realized the ideal. Hence is it the term of the aspirations of the ancient world, and the inauguration of a new era. If Jesus Christ be but the sublimest of teachers, or the greatest of prophets, there is no essential difference between Him and Socrates or Isaiah. What constitutes the grand originality of His work is, that He gives all that His precursors promised or hoped for, and did not merely bear witness to the truth, but was empowered to say, with that calm assurance that carried with it such weight of moral authority, '*I am the truth.*' 'Per me venitur, ad me pervenitur, in me permanetur!'

Humanity, taken as a whole, has never erred in its mode of propounding the religious problem. It has ever held religion to be not a mere communication of ideas concerning the Divinity, but a solemn effort to re-unite the broken bond between heaven and earth, to establish an effectual union between man and God. The religions of the ancient world had all presentiments of this union, and strove to realize it. In the East, it manifested itself under the form of frequent incarnations; in the West, in the apotheoses. In the East, it is the Divinity that stoops to man; in the West, humanity rises to the Divinity; but neither in India nor in Greece was the real union between man and God effected. In India, incarnation was but illusory, and was, to borrow the expression of the *Pouranas*, but a kind of mask with which the friendly divinity invested himself, 'like an actor who puts on a costume to perform a part.' If we consider attentively, we shall find that these repeated incarnations were striking proofs of the contempt which this pantheistic and ascetic religion professed for the human individual, which was, in its eyes, but an evanescent form of the absolute being. Brahma or Vishnou alone possesses real existence. The worshipper seeks to become merged in them, and to utterly annihilate the human element. In Greece, it is the divine element which is compromised. Humanity in its natural state is declared to be divine: if adored in its grandeur, it is so likewise in its passions and in its weaknesses. The Olympian god is but a hero placed on an altar. Thus, we see, the religious problem is far from being solved. Efforts were made to simplify it by reducing it to a factitious unity, alternately ignoring either the divine or the human side. In India, we find all is one vast divinity, devouring the universe which it creates and destroys at the same time. In Greece, we find nothing but one presumptuous humanity trying to cheat, by adoration of itself, its own infinite wants, and hiding its shortcomings under the graceful veil of polytheism. Nevertheless, and in spite of those radical imperfections, the aim and endeavour of those religions of the East and West, even under their grossest myths, was the union of the Divinity with humanity. They impress us like an incoherent dream, which in its incoherency ever dwells upon the same thought, thus revealing the dominant preoccupation of the sufferer.

Besides this persistent yearning to establish an effective union between humanity and the Divinity, there is another element in the aspirations of the ancient world which we cannot omit noticing: its consciousness that this union was only possible by means of a reparation. Notwithstanding its corruption—notwithstanding the falseness of the solutions it gave of the formidable question of the origin of evil—notwithstanding its tendency to see in evil a necessary law of the finite being, the ancient world was still tormented by the want to efface or to expiate it. The errors of its metaphysics, the culpable aberrations of its practices, did not prevent it bearing witness, through the medium of its most characteristic religious institutions, to the immortal truths engraved upon the human conscience. The idea of an inherent impurity, separating man from God, and hindering his free access to the Divinity, without an intermediary, lies at the root of all forms of worship, and which, though altered and alloyed in many ways, bursts forth at times like a flame from amid smouldering ashes. Effectual union with the Divinity, reconciliation with Him by means of reparation,—these form the ultimate groundwork of the creeds and aspirations of the ancient world. We find the same in the Platonic philosophy ennobled and purified, but still blended with heterogeneous elements.

In Judea, this groundwork of creeds and aspirations was entirely sheltered from all corrupting influences; it was fostered by God Himself, and was unfolded in a succession of positive revelations. Judaism was preeminently an energetic reaction against the worship of Nature : its rigid monotheism deepened the abyss between the creature and the Creator. It revealed, above all, the awful sanctity of Jehovah, and by contrast showed man's corruption : this it paints in characters of fire, and shows the impossibility of reconciliation without some great act of reparation. It thus sheds light upon the side which in Paganism was left obscure. We are not, however, to suppose that the idea of union with the Divinity was foreign to it. But, from the Judaic point of view, this union could not be immediate and direct. Mediation was necessary ; and this mediation was to be the work of the Messiah. This hope became progressively clearer and brighter; and though the prophecies, even the most magnificent of them, were surpassed by the event that accomplished them, they nevertheless foreshadowed what was essential in it. A Saviour coming down from heaven, accomplishing through suffering and death the work of reparation,— this was truly the hope of the fallen race under its divine and inspired form. It was this hope that the Divine Redeemer realized. He united in His person humanity and the Divinity, not merely in a moral sense, but in the absolute sense, by His incarnation. The Word became flesh. The only Son of the Father—He who by His word created the world—became like unto us, except sin. He condescended to our low estate, and took our nature upon Him. He was the Son of man and the Son of God—the Man-God, and hence pre-eminently man,—the ideal man; for the destiny of a being created in the image of God, and called to an intimate union with Him, is never really consummated but in God. This glory vouchsafed to humanity, extraordinary as it was, was nevertheless the object of universal aspiration, and we degrade humanity by affirming its incapacity.

We shall not enter here into the metaphysical subtleties which time and the disputations of the schools have gathered round the person of Christ, nor discuss scholastic distinctions concerning the two natures— their relation or penetration. We confine ourselves to the simple, grand declarations of the Scriptures: 'The Word was made flesh.' 'In Him dwells all the fulness of the Godhead bodily.' The humble Christian, who, taking his stand on these promises, and receiving daily the precious earnest of their accomplishment, growing up into Christ as the branch does into the vine, partaking of His substance, receiving His sap, His life, His warmth, carries in his own heart an invincible demonstration of the divinity of Christ. He recognises this divinity under the veil of humiliation which He voluntarily took upon Himself on earth. This humiliation of the Saviour answered to a deep-felt want of reparation by which the human conscience had been tormented. It teaches that Jesus Christ came not only to bring the most signal proof of divine love, but also that He might enter into communion and partake of the sufferings of humanity, to the end that He might represent humanity, and in its name offer the atoning sacrifice. It was not possible that the fallen, guilty race could be restored to its privileges, so long as it continued stiff-necked, proud, and rebellious. God's love, immense though it be, cannot save a being who refuses to respond to it, who even rejects it with disdain. Let us not forget that love is another name for holiness, since it presents the highest form of good. It is at once the supreme benediction and the supreme law. It demands reciprocity: as long as this is refused, it cannot exercise its beneficent influence. The hearts it can neither warm nor fructify, are consumed by it as by a devouring fire. So long as humanity refused to abjure its rebellion, so long as it refused to respond to love by love—by holy, disinterested love; so long is it under the wrath of God, which is another name for the severe aspect of His sanctity. Corrupt to the very core, smitten by fear, the fallen race might desire reconciliation, but was powerless to effect it. To do this, it was necessary it should, in the midst of the condemnation that overwhelmed it, in suffering and death, accomplish such an act of adoration and supreme obedience as should efface the act of rebellion and pride, by which it let loose the power of evil. This act should be a perfect act, without mixture of selfishness,—an act worthy of divine love, a full, complete return to God by a free sacrifice. It is clearly impossible that humanity could do this. He only could do it who, coming down from heaven into the world of the fall, voluntarily took upon Himself the burden of our sorrows and sufferings, and accepted them all. He made a life of suffering, one that was a faithful image of human destiny since the day of its condemnation,—He made it a holy sacrifice to God, and by His obedience restored the race He represented. Condemnation thus borne is no longer condemnation. Christ, by passing through it, transformed it; since with Him extreme suffering was at the same time perfect obedience, and consequently the very condition of reconciliation. A mysterious but real solidarity united Him with humanity. The Desired of nations was indeed the Son of man. It was then the heart of man He brought to God, who only waited this response to His love to pour down upon us all His blessings. Thus was salvation effected by a holy immolation, comprehending the entire life of Christ, and terminating in His bloody death. Justice and love were satisfied; and conscience, bearing God's claims inscribed upon it, was equally so.

The cross was not merely a guarantee of pardon; it not only realized the essential conditions of it, effecting the required reparation, but effecting it in a manner worthy of God. The grandeur of divine love shone out in all its vigour at this supreme moment of our religious history. 'God was in Christ reconciling the world to Himself.' A Father opening His arms to His child returning to Him by a great sacrifice. Above the clouds accumulated by scholastic theology since the time of Anselm, His mercy shines in its pure splendour, and with it His justice. The resurrection of the new Adam—'first fruits of those who sleep'—was the assuring proof that the reparation was judged complete, and that humanity was redeemed from its guilt. His ascension, and the sending forth of the Holy Spirit, demonstrate that His saving action is to be continued through the ages, until the triumph of truth is consummated. Henceforth, whoever by a living, personal faith unites himself to the holy Victim of calvary, whoever accepts His sacrifice, will receive the benefits flowing from it; and all those who die with Him, by crucifying the flesh and its lusts, will rise with Him in holiness and glory. 'He who belives in Him shall not die; he has eternal life.'

It is reluctantly that by distinctions and definitions, which, however, are necessary, we should chill the impression produced on the heart and conscience by the simple view of Christ. The same attraction felt, during His passage through earth, by those whose hearts were not sealed by pride, He still exerts amongst us. It was not after long reasoning on His person, His divine and human nature, that Mary Magdalene the sinner poured her precious box of ointment on His feet—that the afflicted multitudes crowded round Him and followed His footsteps. It sufficed to have seen and heard Him to feel the power of that irresistible attraction. There was in Him such gentleness and purity, in His words such authority and power—a something so consoling and celestial was diffused through His whole person, that all honest hearts felt themselves at once penetrated by sympathy towards Him, blended with tenderness and adoration. A divine virtue surrounded Him like a halo; He was felt to be as powerful as He was compassionate, as able to deliver as He was to console; and amid all His miracles there was the presentiment of a still greater—that which all the others announced and prefigured—the restoration by love of the fallen race. If, at first, the multitude followed Him that their bodily infirmities might be healed, there was another malady, one nobler and deeper, caused by sin, which they looked to Him to heal. They read God's pardon on His countenance before they heard it from His lips.

Infinite love crowned His head as with a glory; and conscience at His contact shuddered with sublime joy, for it felt there was the realization of the perfect ideal. When He spoke those simple words, 'Come to Me, all ye that labour and are heavy laden,' He carried light and peace into hearts by means of the intimate correspondence existing between His person and the wants of the soul. There was not one single noble aspiration of the human heart that did not find its full satisfaction in Him. All seemed to gravitate to Him; hence the prompt obedience to His call on the part of those who were free from infatuation, either about themselves or about their national glory. Christ had no need to prove His right to their confidence; He had but to appear, for them to throw themselves at His feet. And under what august traits does He, oh ideal Christian, appear when on the accursed and bloody cross! The spectacle of this crucified one, crowned with thorns, quenching His thirst with gall, scoffed at by His executioners at the moment He pours out His prayer for their forgiveness, is such an immense, such an unexpected, such an exalted revelation of love, that we must either turn away our eyes or adore.

It suffices to fix one penetrating glance on this cross, to feel constrained to bow down before it, vanquished as well as convinced. And this impression is no mystical ecstasy, the result of the triumph of imagination over enfeebled reason. No; it is a deliberate conviction—a conviction resting on internal reasons, far superior to all logical reasonings, since they imply the accordance of the whole being with truth, and not merely one faculty, the purely intellectual and logical one. If it be true that humanity was made for Christ, there is nothing extraordinary in the fact that, at His appearance, it should prostrate itself at His feet pacified and satisfied, except in those instances when it voluntarily turned away from Him. The cross is the final issue of man's religious history, but an issue long prepared for. Not only was it so for the entire race, but is still in the heart of each individual, whereon the finger of God writes, as it were, an inner Old Testament; where a work of preparation is being slowly elaborated; where, upon the wrecks of many idols, is slowly built up the altar to the unknown God. Accordingly, when this unknown but expected God appears, and is met by no obstinate resistance, He is received with joy; for He responds to all the religious antecedents of the soul, as He answered eighteen centuries ago to the whole religious past of humanity.

Hence the most powerful of all apologies is the simple statement of Christ's life and death. The evangelical narratives resuscitate Him, as it were, anew for us, so perfect is the fidelity and simplicity with which they paint Him. They show Him to us, after His obscure but glorious infancy, manifesting at the very outset of His ministry that elevation and calm which can come alone from absolute devotion. Surrounded for a moment by popular favour, after some striking miracles reflecting His compassionate love, He soon finds Himself reduced to a small number of disciples, recruited from the lowest class of the most despised province of Judea. It is to those He pours out His sublimest teachings: the crowd abandon Him the day He reveals the austere side of His doctrine, and when He refuses to flatter their ambitious nationality. To the chiefs of the nation, who carry on sometimes an underhand, sometimes an open, war against Him, but one always inspired by the worst motives, He opposes an energy the more invincible for its calmness. Once, however, He rose to vehement indignation, denouncing the hypocrisy of the Pharisees; and upon those whited sepulchres writing the sentence for all time of those unscrupulous men who trade upon religion, buyers and sellers of the temple, who make the altar itself the counter for their commerce.

Whether He argues with His adversaries, whether He announces the Gospel to the people, whether He explains His parables to His disciples, or withdraws to the desert or the mountain, He is always pre-eminently the Righteous One, the Saint of Saints, whom sin never even touched; He is Divine Love personified. In the upper chamber, where it seems as if He too wished to pour out before His death His precious box of ointment, in that last discourse into which He discharged His whole heart, at Gethsemane, at the judgment-seat, in the agony of death, He is always true to Himself. What can we say to those who remain unmoved by such a narrative, if not that they are without the sense of the ideal, and the sense of their own infirmities? It is not the moment for reasoning, but for silent, adoring contemplation.[1]

It now remains for us to consider what were the modifications produced by Christ's coming upon the religious institutions of the ancient world. We have shown how closely connected these institutions were with the preparatory scheme. Man makes unavailing efforts by sacrifices to satisfy his desire for reconciliation with God. He builds temples, feeling earth to be sullied and under a curse, but hoping the malediction not irrevocable. He sets aside special days for worship, believing man's nature to be not less sullied than earth, but hoping the evil to be not without remedy. Finally,

---

[1] See the numerous lives of Jesus published in Germany: that by Neander, 1845; by Lange, 5 vols., 1844; *Die Lehre der Person Christi*, by Gess, 1856 (see the analysis given of it by M. Godet in the *Revue Chrétienne*, 1857-1858). We must also mention the admirable work, on the Sinlessness of Jesus Christ, by Ullmann, translated into English by Rev. R. L. Brown (Edinburgh: T. and T. Clark); our articles published in the *Revue Chrétienne* (November and December 1856) on the Divinity of Christ, and our discourse upon the Redeemer.

he appoints priests to represent him in the sanctuary, —imperfect mediators striving to fill up the chasm between the sinning creature and the Divinity, and who seem to predict that this distance should one day disappear. All these institutions were accepted by God, and disengaged from the impure elements with which they were alloyed in Paganism. Jewish theocracy developed these institutions in all their plenitude, the Jews having been isolated from all other people in order to constitute them a national priesthood. It is evident that the accomplishment of the work of redemption must necessarily have introduced a radical change into this order of things, seeing it was impossible that the institutions of the preparatory religion could suit definitive religion, precisely for the reason that they were so admirably adapted to the situation of humanity before Jesus Christ.

First of all, it is evident that redemption once effected, the line of demarcation should disappear, which formerly separated the Jews from all other nations, since there was no other object for the election of the Jews than that one spot of earth should be reserved for monotheism, and that it should be the cradle of the Messiah. Universalism, which had hung like a glorious promise over Judaism, necessarily swept away every barrier, from the day that the salvation of the whole human race was won upon the Cross. Every privilege vanished before the grandeur and universality of the pardon that had been achieved. The Saviour did not merely represent the Jews; He called Himself the Son of Man, the new Adam, and invited to come to Him all the children, without distinction, of the fallen race which He had redeemed.

Since His blood flowed on Calvary, earth, purified, was delivered from the anathema that had weighed upon it. The temple of Jerusalem was no longer to be the sole sanctuary of the holy God. The whole sum of human life was won back to God, rising, for the believer, to the dignity of a permanent worship; thus abolishing the distinction between the profane and the sacred. No other distinction now existed but that between good and evil; which distinction implies that the first should be always practised, and the second always avoided. Finally, the separation between heaven and earth was filled up. One single Mediator had superseded all others. One single offering, one sole sacrifice, was proclaimed acceptable and sufficient. The new people of God were all a people of kings and priests, each called to self-immolation, and by this spiritual, voluntary immolation, to ratify the sacrifice by which redemption was achieved. We should add too, that the severe dispensation of the law was abrogated, and fear replaced by the more fruitful impulses of love. To the complicated system of ordinances, that constituted the preparatory economy, succeeded the ever old and new commandment, that of love, complete self-sacrifice,—a commandment all-powerful in its efficacy, seeing it gives what it orders by the communication of a divine virtue to the heart. The complex ritual was abrogated; the ceremonial law abolished; the Mosaic law, in its highest significance, modified, enlarged, and spiritualized. Redemption opened up to man access to God, rendered communion with Him possible: accordingly, the character of divine authority, though not diminished, was altered; being less external, less legal, and becoming more spiritual, reaching more the inner life, substituting love and persuasion for constraint, and the 'easy yoke' for the iron rod. A formidable sanction was nevertheless attached to this renewed law of liberty and love. The blessings and benefits it involved for the Christian, were reversed for him who neglected so great salvation. His condemnation was measured in proportion to the blessings offered him who had grown up into Christ.

We now see that it was truly a new covenant Christ came to establish. This is sometimes denied, on the pretext that He did not annul the ancient dispensation, and that He Himself submitted to all legal observances; but, in so asserting, we misconceive the nature of the reform He came to effect. He employed means adjusted to the end He had in view. This end was deliverance from the yoke of the law, which deliverance could not itself be invested with a legal character. Hence He did not solemnly proclaim it under the form of a decree; He inspired it rather than instituted it; He prepared hearts—a far more efficacious process than verbal precepts. Besides, before the completion of His work, the abrogation of the old covenant would have been premature. This abrogation flowed necessarily from the redemption, as a consequence flows from its principle. It sufficed that He laid down the principle. The consequence, He knew, was implicitly contained in it, and would in due season be evolved.

He wished the new wine to be poured into new bottles; hence the slow education to which He subjected His disciples—an education destined to be completed by the lessons of experience. He allowed them to foresee, by certain significant expressions, such as those used in His discourse with the woman of Samaria, the transformation to be wrought in the ancient economy; but He imposed nothing on them. He, whose power over souls was so complete, would not do them violence. Acts of authority in the moral world are symptoms of weakness: we only resort to religious despotism when we despair of prevailing by persuasion. This despotism was necessary under the old covenant, but under the new would have been an anachronism. What the latter lost in external and legal authority, it gained in real power, in ascendancy over minds and hearts. It is impossible to overstate the admirable manner in which Christ prepared the transition from one dispensation to the other. He abolished the old covenant, as Neander has well said, by accomplishing it,—that is to say, by fully realizing the desire of salvation manifested by its most characteristic institutions. We are not, however, to suppose that definitive religion, in substituting liberty for constraint, authorized in the least degree either disorder or religious anarchy. Theocracy was abolished. The individual, restored to the possession of all his rights, was put in personal contact with God, but was not left isolated. A new society was founded, under the name of the Church, whose bond of union was love and faith, and which was recruited from among all people and among all ranks. This was the new humanity, the normal society, into which admission was not acquired by right of birth or by any purely external sign, but by the new birth,—that is to say, by adhesion of the heart and conscience. This society was free to constitute itself according to its own will, and to organize its government, provided it did not return to the sacerdotal or hierarchical systems. It was free to appoint days and places for worship, on condition that it did not revive either the Jewish festivals or the sanctuary. The problem to be resolved was the creation of the different institutions necessary to its consolidation, without declining from the spiritualism essential to it, without relapsing from the new covenant to the old, from Christianity back to Judaism. This was just the danger that most menaced the new religion,—the difficulty of escaping, not the hostility, but the fatal attraction, of the religions which preceded it, and which continued to subsist by its side. We are now, at the close of this Introduction, enabled to estimate the extent of this danger. We now understand Paganism and Judaism, which, like Herod and Pilate, became reconciled, in order that they might more effectually put Christ to death, and stifle the Church in its cradle. On both sides, the opposition between God and man was maintained: in Paganism, under the form of dualism, which ultimately prevailed over Greek humanism, when the latter had fulfilled its mission. The human element, matter, the creature as creature, the finite, in a word, is considered as evil in its essence; no redemption being possible but by the annihilation of the finite, which was to be attained by means of ecstasy and exercises of asceticism. Christianity strikes at the root of dualism by the doctrines of creation and of moral evil.

In Judaism the opposition between man and God was not based on this pantheistic theosophy, but on the dogma of the fall. It was therefore grounded in fact, and was perfectly legitimate up to the day redemption was accomplished. Henceforward Christianity effaced it, since the Redeemer removed all opposition between man and God. But neither Paganism nor Judaism was disposed to retire before the religion whose advent they had nevertheless prepared. They opposed it by open violence and by secret perfidy. After the first battle was lost,—that of the Judaic and Gnostic heresies,—they laboured to gain the second by introducing into the Church Oriental asceticism, and the Judaic sacerdotal system, with its sacrifices and hierarchy. This victory was, however, partial; the immortal principles of Christianity could not be stifled. Although more or less compromised by unfortunate alliances, they continued to bear precious fruit for the world, until the time came round when they should be again purified from those foreign and pernicious influences. The history of the first three centuries is the history of the struggle between Christianity and the powers hostile to it. We shall see this struggle pursued from sphere to sphere: from the agitated sphere of the external world, in which, by most sanguinary persecutions, attempts were made to arrest the ardour of the Christian missions, to the apparently more pacific sphere of theology. We shall not overlook the changes introduced into the constitution and forms of worship of the Church, nor the modifications that the Christian life underwent.

Christian missions and persecutions, heresies and the development of dogmas, ecclesiastical organization and the character of piety, during the three first centuries, such is the vast field we have undertaken to explore. Christianity is the religion of the individual as well as that of holiness. We shall accordingly endeavour to place in due light the noble physiognomies of those heroic Christians who have left such luminous tracks in the history of the Church, and who won her victory at the price of their own blood. We shall see how those early times of the Christian community, poor and persecuted as it was, were favourable to the free development of faith and life. We shall find none of that uniform Christianity which has predominated since the era of the great Councils and of their imposed symbols. Nevertheless, even in these days of liberty, fatal tendencies manifested themselves: the servitude of future ages was gradually being prepared. We must have the courage, even when standing by the scaffolds of martyrs, to point out the deviations of the Church, which, however imperceptible at the outset, became serious in their results. We must not suffer our eyes to be dazzled by their pure glory, however painful may be the sacrifice to truth in mixing blame with the homage we pay to men we enthusiastically admire. Nothing, however, can diminish the grandeur of the spectacle presented to the world by the all-powerful weakness of a despised, persecuted Church triumphing over the Roman Colossus, and saving human dignity by dint of sufferings humbly borne. But, before seeing it march on to these incomparable triumphs, we must first see it constituted under the direction of the immediate disciples of its Divine Head. It is not possible to comprehend the Church of the first three centuries without first making the Apostolic Age the object of close study; because, in order to estimate the gravity of the deviations, we must first have contemplated its ideal state.

INDEX.

Æschylus, the Greek tragic poet, 85.
Ahriman—*see* Ormuz.
Alexander and his successors — *see* Greece under Alexander.
Arabian worship of the stars, 23.
Aristophanes, character of his dramatic writings, 87.
Aristotle, the philosophy of, 131-135.
Art—religious in the temples at Tyre, 27—in Babylon and Nineveh, 27, 28—in Egypt, 33-35—in Persia, 43—ancient Greek, 71—its development, 88-93.
Art in Greece, its rise and progress, 88—temple architecture, 89 — great progress in sculpture, 90-93.
Asia, the religions of Western, 21—sun and moon worship by the Asiatics, 21—the gods of the Scythians, 22—the Arabs the first to worship the stars, 23—astrology practised by the Babylonians, 23—sensuality of their worship, 24—the Phœnician religion, 24, 25—the Tyrian Hercules, 26, 27.
Astarte—*see* Tyrian Hercules.
Athens the centre of Hellenic culture, 83.
Atys, festivals of the, 26-28.

Babylonians, the, sensual character of their worship, 23.
Baur on Matthew's Gospel, 241.
Bhagavat-Pouranas, the, bears trace of ancient pantheism, 62.
Brahma, his increase in influence, 48—Nature an emanation from Brahma, 48—Brahminism according to the Laws of Manou, 49—the system of castes, 50 — family relationship as contained in the Laws of Manou, 51—the life of an anchorite the highest perfection in a Brahmin, 52—speculation inherent in the Hindu mind, 53.
Buddha, legend concerning the founder of, 54—its four principles, 55—their passion for death, 56—the true follower of Buddhism is a recluse, 56—their monasteries, 57—rapid spread of Buddhism, 57, 58.

Castes, the system of, according to the Laws of Manou, 50-54.
Christianity, 239—objections to the teaching of the Redeemer, 240—the Gospels and the founder of Christianity, 241-248—union between the humanity and divinity of Christ, 248—Judaism reveals the true God, 251—declarations of Scripture concerning Christ, 251-257 — modifications produced on the religious institution by Christ's appearance on earth, 257.
Christianity—its suitableness to man's wants, 5—the history of religions of human origin a proof of the agreement of revealed religion to the wants of man, 6—importance of the study of ancient history, 6, 7—theories regarding the development of humanity to the time of Christianity, 8—theories regarding the religions of the world, 8-10—the history of religion, what it is, 10—ideas of the Alexandrian fathers, 11—apologetic work of Theodoret, 11—divisions of modern apologists, 12—Schelling's

idea regarding the human conscience, 13—the problem of the fall, 14—Humanity before Jesus, 15–17.
Conservatism a characteristic of the ancient Egyptians, 27.
Covenant, the New, established by Christ's coming, 260.

Decline of Judaism, 219—planting of the Assyrian colony in the land of Israel, 220 — the Babylonish captivity, 220 — the return under Esdras and Nehemiah, 221 — various phases in Jewish history, 221 the Roman policy, 222—institution of the synagogues, 223—preponderating influence of the Scribes, 224— influence exercised by the Jews over the nations amongst which they were scattered, 225—the two currents of Judaism, 225 — revival of religion after the restoration, 226—the influence of Oriental Theosophy, 227— effects of the Jewish emigration to Alexandria, 228—the Therapeutes, 231—the sect of the Pharisees, 233— the Sadducees, 233—hopes regarding the Messiah, 234, 235—the book of Enoch, 236—the representatives of true Judaism, 237, 238.
Divinity of Jesus recognisable by Christians through the veil of His humility, 252, 253.
Dramatic poetry, the advent of, 84.

Egyptian religion, the, 28—character of the people, 29—they worship a multiplicity of gods, 30—gods represented under the forms of sacred animals, 31—the myth of Isis and Osiris, 32, 33—the artistic faculty of the Egyptians highly developed, 33—its aim is to preserve the memory of the past, 34.
Enoch, the Book of, 236.
Epictetus, the philosophy of, 181.
Essenians, the sect of, in Judea, 231-234.

Fusion of the local mythologies of the Egyptians, 30.

Gospel, its originality misapprehended when viewed as an illustration of moral truths which ancient philosophy embodied, 247.
Greco-Roman world, the, 153, 154— luxury of Roman life, 155-157—slavery in Rome, 158, 159—degraded life of women, 160, 161—prevailing licentiousness of men, 162—the aim of luxury, 163, 164—state of literature, 165—state of the fine arts, 166 the complicated religious condition, 167-173—the philosophic spirit, 174 the New Academy, 175—Cicero, 175 —Epicurus, 176, 177—Stoicism, 178 —Seneca the incarnation of Roman Stoicism, 179 — the philosophy of Epictetus, 181—the work of Plutarch, 183-186—shortcomings of philosophy, 186.
Greco-Roman Paganism — see Greece under Alexander and his successors.
Greece, rise of literature in, 74-88—development of art in, 83-93.
Greece under Alexander and his successors, 136—decline of Athens, 136 —Alexandria becomes the centre of Greek civilisation, 137—prevalence of scepticism in religion and philosophy, 138, 140—Epicureanism, 141— Stoicism, 141—the philosophy of the Porch, 143—teaching of Carneades, 143 — decline of Greek literature, 143-145—decline of the plastic arts, 145—development of the mechanical arts, 146, 147.
Greek philosophy to the time of Alexander, 100—the mission of philosophy previous to Christianity, 101—Naturism, 103—the mechanism tendency, 105—the theory of Numbers, 105, 106 —the Idealism of the Eleau school, 107—rise of Sophisism, 107—the mission of Socrates, 108-114—rise of the Platonic philosophy, 115-130—the philosophy of Aristotle, 130-135.

Harmony of the Gospels regarding the character and mission of Jesus, 241.
Hellenic Humanism, its development, 73—the two great events of the heroic age, 73 — Greek literature, 74-88—development of art in Greece, 88-93—Greek mythology, 93-98—
Hellenic life essentially public, 99.
Hercules Sando— see Tyrian Hercules.
History of the three first centuries of Christianity, 262, 263.
Human sacrifices presented to Moloch, 25.
Humanity has not erred in its mode of propounding the religious problem, 248.

Idealism of the Elean school, 107.
Indian religion, the, 44—the Rig Veda, 45, 46—their early form of religion resembled pantheism, 47—priestcraft became the preponderating influence, 48 — Brahminism, 48-54— Buddhism, 54-58—the sect Vischnou, 59-62 — the Bhagavat-Pouranas, 63

INDEX. 267

—legends of the Lapithæ and Centaurs, 71—exploits of Theseus, 72—its historical tendency, 72, 73.
Iran, a land of contrasts, 36.
Isis and Osiris, the myth of, 32, 33.

Joga, the system of, 61.
Judaism, 191—the history of Judaism and Paganism contrasted, 192—intuitive longings of man after salvation, 195—sacrifice and erection of temples dedicated to God, 196—the consecration of the priesthood, 200—Judaism not a perfect religion, 202.
Judaism pre-eminently an energetic reaction against the worship of Nature, 250.
Judaism, the decline of—*see* Decline of Judaism.

Love of Jesus for sinners exemplified in His life and death, 254, 255, 258-262.

Man—Nature the first object of his worship, 18—is brought face to face with the laws of conscience, 19—he yields to sensual enjoyments, 19—the religions of Nature disappear before other creations of conscience, 20.
Manou, the laws of, 49-54.
Melkarth—*see* Tyrian Hercules.
Messiah, the, fallacy of Baur's reasoning concerning, 241—His two natures, 251—modifications produced by His coming on the ancient religions of the world, 257.
Mysteries, the, 96—their dogmas, 98.
Myth of Isis and Osiris, 32.
Mythology of the ancient Egyptians, 30; of the ancient Greeks, 93-96.

Nature—man prostrates himself before, 18—the twofold power manifested in, 19—its worship is voluptuous and barbarous, 19—its religions disappear before other creations of conscience, 20.

Objections to the appreciation of Christianity, 240.
Olympic games, their celebration, 99.
Oriental Paganism—*see* Preparation of Christianity in Paganism.
Origen, his allegorical interpretation of the Song of Solomon, 238.
Ormuz and Ahriman, the gods of Persia, 38-42.
Osiris—*see* Isis and Osiris.

Paganism, preparation of Christianity in, 18.

Pelasgic mythology, 65—community of origin of the first inhabitants of Greece and of the Aryans of Iran, 66—the Hellens divided into four families, 67—the same religion held by the different tribes, 67-70—simplicity of the worship established by the Pelasgians, 71.
Period of formation, 203—God's promise to Abraham, 203—the patriarchal period, 204—the two epochs in the history of Judaism, 205—the Mosaic dispensation embodied in the Decalogue, 206—predominance of the legal element during the Mosaic period, 206—the two institutions of priesthood and sacrifice, 207—the Israelites exclusively dedicated to God, 208—the Mosaic ritual, 208—institution of the priestly office in Aaron's family, 209—the position occupied by the priesthood, 209—reparation the idea of Jewish sacrifices, 210-212—the temple, 212—the four institutions of the preparatory dispensation, 212, 213—the great day of atonement marks the gravity of the fall and the generality of the corruption, 213—the prophetic period, 213—the nature of the prophetic inspiration a subject of constant debate, 214—the promise of salvation, 216—Judaic prophecy prepared the way for Christianity, 218.
Persian religion, the, 35—the prayer of prayers, 38—Ormuz, 38-42—caste distinctions lax, 42—the religious law of the Persians a mixture of material rules and moral ordinances, 44.
Pharisees, the sect of, 233.
Phœnicians, the, inventors of the art of writing, 24—their mytholigical system, 25—voluptuousness and death blended in their rites, 25.
Plato and his philosophy, 115-130.
Plutarch, his work, 183.
Poets, ancient Greek, 82-88.
Prayer of prayers, the Persian, 38.
Preface to the English translation of the Introduction, 1.
Preparation of Christianity in Paganism, 18.
Priest, office of, in the Jewish economy, 209-211.
Prose writing, its advent in Greece, 88.

Ramayana, heroic poetry of, 59-61.
Redemption opened up to man access to God, 258-261.
Religions of Nature, the, 18—the twofold power of the forces of Nature,

19—the worship of Nature is barbarous and voluptuous, 19.
Rig Veda, a collection of sacred hymns, 45.
Rome, its rise and origin, 147—pursuits of the people, 148—their religious ideas, 149—their mythology not only moral but historical, 150—the decline of ancient society owing to the conquest of Greece, 151—its literature, 152.

Sacrifice of the cross, the sinner's salvation, 253.
Sadducees, the, 233.
Scripture testimony to the two natures of the Redeemer, 251, 256, 257.
Sculpture, its rapid progress in Greece, 90-93.
Scythians, their gods Papaios and Tabiti, 22.
Slaves in ancient Rome, 158, 159.
Soma, the symbol of the liquid element, 46.

Song of Solomon, allegorical interpretation of, 238.
Socrates, his mission, 108-114.
Sophocles, his tragic poems, 86.
Stoicism, 178.

Tyrian Hercules, the, his twofold aspect, 26.

Vischnou, the god, 59-61.

Women, degradation of, in pagan worship, 24, 25; in Rome, 160, 161.
Women exalted in a high degree in the Laws of Manou, 51.
World, the ancient, its consciousness that a union between divinity and humanity was only possible by means of a reparation, 249, 250—modifications produced by Christ's coming upon its religious institutions, 257.
Writing, the first elements of, found in Egyptian hieroglyphics, 33.

CLASSIFIED CATALOGUE

OF THE

PUBLICATIONS OF T. AND T. CLARK,

38, GEORGE STREET, EDINBURGH.

HAMILTON, ADAMS, & CO., LONDON.

JOHN ROBERTSON, DUBLIN.

SMITH, ENGLISH, & CO., PHILADELPHIA;

AND ALL BOOKSELLERS IN GREAT BRITAIN AND THE UNITED STATES.

CONTENTS.

		PAGE
I. Foreign Theological Library,		2
II. Calvin's Works and Bengel's Gnomon,		5
III. Dr John Owen's Complete Works,		7
IV. North British Review,		8
V. Herzog's Theological Encyclopædia,		9
VI. Systematic Theology,		9
VII. Introductions,		10
VIII. Biblical Criticism,		10
IX. Commentaries—1. Old Testament. 2. New Testament,		12
X. Church History,		17
XI. Prophecy,		18
XII. Practical Theology,		19
XIII. Philosophy,		21
XIV. Church Law,		22
XV. School Books,		22
XVI. Miscellaneous,		22
„ Forthcoming Works of the late Principal Cunningham,		24

MURRAY AND GIBB, PRINTERS, EDINBURGH.

Works Published by T. and T. Clark, Edinburgh.

FOREIGN THEOLOGICAL LIBRARY.

FOUR LARGE VOLUMES IN DEMY 8vo, FOR ONE GUINEA PER ANNUM.

MESSRS CLARK beg respectfully to invite the attention of the clergy and intelligent laity to their FOREIGN THEOLOGICAL LIBRARY. They trust to receive a continuation of the support hitherto so liberally bestowed on them. The following works comprise the First Series, and Subscribers are still received on remitting EIGHT GUINEAS, which may be paid in instalments.
The Prices to NON-SUBSCRIBERS are placed within parentheses.

Twelve Volumes of this Series (only) will be supplied at the Subscription Price of Three Guineas (or a larger number at same ratio).

Dr E. W. Hengstenberg.—Commentary on the PSALMS. By E. W. HENGSTENBERG, D.D., Professor of Theology in Berlin. In 3 vols. 8vo, (33s.)

Dr K. R. Hagenbach.—Compendium of the History of DOCTRINES. By K. R. HAGENBACH, D.D., Professor of Theology in the University of Basle. In 2 vols. 8vo, (21s.)

Dr J. C. L. Gieseler.—Compendium of Ecclesiastical HISTORY. By J. C. L. GIESELER, D.D., Professor of Theology in Göttingen. 5 vols. 8vo, (L.2, 12s. 6d.)

Dr Hermann Olshausen.—Biblical Commentary on the GOSPELS and ACTS, adapted especially for Preachers and Students. By HERMANN OLSHAUSEN, D.D., Professor of Theology in the University of Erlangen. In 4 vols. demy 8vo, (L.2, 2s.)

Biblical Commentary on the Romans, adapted especially for Preachers and Students. By HERMANN OLSHAUSEN, D.D., Professor of Theology in the University of Erlangen. In 1 vol. 8vo, (10s. 6d.)

Biblical Commentary on St Paul's First and Second EPISTLES to the CORINTHIANS. By HERMANN OLSHAUSEN, D.D., Professor of Theology in the University of Erlangen. In 1 vol. 8vo, (9s.)

Biblical Commentary on St Paul's Epistle to the GALATIANS, EPHESIANS, COLOSSIANS, and THESSALONIANS. By HERMANN OLSHAUSEN, D.D., Professor of Theology in the University of Erlangen. In 1 vol. 8vo, (10s. 6d.)

Biblical Commentary on St Paul's Epistle to the PHILIPPIANS, to TITUS, and the FIRST to TIMOTHY; in Continuation of the Work of Olshausen. By Lic. AUGUST WIESINGER. In 1 vol. 8vo, (10s. 6d.)

Biblical Commentary on the Hebrews. By Dr EBRARD. In continuation of the Work of Olshausen. In one vol. 8vo, (10s. 6d.)

Dr Augustus Neander.—General History of the CHRISTIAN RELIGION and CHURCH. By AUGUSTUS NEANDER, D.D. Translated from the Second and Improved Edition. In 9 vols. 8vo, (L.2, 9s. 6d.)
THIS *is the only Edition in a LIBRARY Size.*

Dr C. J. Nitzsch.—A System of Christian Doctrine. By C. J. NITZSCH, D.D. Translated from the Fifth Revised and Enlarged German Edition. 1 vol. 8vo, (10s. 6d.)

Prof. H. A. Ch. Havernick.—General Introduction TO THE OLD TESTAMENT. By Professor HAVERNICK. 1 vol. 8vo, (10s. 6d.)

Dr Julius Muller.—The Christian Doctrine of Sin. By Dr JULIUS MULLER. 2 vols. 8vo, (21s.)

Works Published by T. and T. Clark.

FOREIGN THEOLOGICAL LIBRARY.

THE SECOND SERIES comprises the following Works. 20 Vols
Subscribers' price, FIVE GUINEAS.

Dr E. W. Hengstenberg.—Christology of the Old
TESTAMENT, and a COMMENTARY ON THE MESSIANIC PREDICTIONS
By E. W. HENGSTENBERG, D.D., Professor of Theology, Berlin. Four vols. (L.2, 2s.)

Dr M. Baumgarten.—The Acts of the Apostles; or,
THE HISTORY OF THE CHURCH IN THE APOSTOLIC AGE. By M.
BAUMGARTEN, Ph.D., and Professor in the University of Rostock. Three vols.
(L.1, 7s.)

Dr Rudolph Stier.—The Words of the Lord Jesus.
By RUDOLPH STIER, D.D., Chief Pastor and Superintendent of Schkeuditz. In Eight
volumes 8vo, (L.4, 4s.)

Dr Carl Ullmann.—Reformers before the Reforma-
TION, Principally in Germany and the Netherlands. Translated by the Rev. R.
MENZIES. Two vols. 8vo, (L.1, 1s.)

Dr K. F. Keil.—Commentary on the Book of Joshua.
By K. F. KEIL, D.D., Ph.D., Professor, Dorpat. 8vo, (10s. 6d.)

Dr K. F. Keil.—Commentary on the Books of Kings.
By Professor KEIL, of Dorpat. Supplemented by Commentary on the BOOKS OF
CHRONICLES. By Professor BERTHEAU of Göttingen. Two vols. 8vo, (L.1, 1s.)

N.B.—A single Year's Books (except in the case of the current Year) cannot be supplied
separately.

The following is the order of Publication of the Second Series :—

1st Year (1854).

Hengstenberg's Christology, Vol. 1.
Baumgarten on the Acts, 3 Vols.

2d Year (1855).

Ullmann's Reformers, 2 Vols.
Stier's Words of Jesus, Vols. 1 and 2.

3d Year (1856).

Hengstenberg's Christology, Vol. 2.
Stier's Words of Jesus, Vols. 3, 4, 5

4th Year (1857).

Stier's Words of Jesus, Vol. 6.
Keil on Joshua.
Keil and Bertheau on Kings and
Chronicles, 2 Vols.

5th Year (1858).

Stier's Words of Jesus, Vols. 7 and 8.
Hengstenberg's Christology, Vols. 3
and 4.

Works Published by T. and T. Clark,

FOREIGN THEOLOGICAL LIBRARY.

The THIRD SERIES comprises the following Works, so far as already published. Subscription 1859–1860–1861–1862, FOUR GUINEAS.

Professor Kurtz.—History of the Old Covenant; or,
OLD TESTAMENT DISPENSATION. By Professor KURTZ of Dorpat. In three volumes. (L.1, 11s. 6d.)

Dr Rudolph Stier.—The Words of the Risen Saviour,
and Commentary on the EPISTLE OF ST JAMES. By RUDOLPH STIER, D.D., Chief Pastor and Superintendent of Schkeuditz. One volume. (10s. 6d.)

Professor Tholuck.—Commentary on the Gospel of
ST JOHN. By Professor THOLUCK, of Halle. Translated from the Sixth Edition of the Original, by CHARLES P. KRAUTH, D.D. In one volume. (9s.)

Professor Tholuck.—Commentary on the Sermon on
THE MOUNT. By Professor THOLUCK, of Halle. Translated from the Fourth Revised and Enlarged Edition, by the Rev. R. LUNDIN BROWN, M.A. In one volume. (10s. 6d.)

Dr E. W. Hengstenberg.—Commentary on the Book
of ECCLESIASTES. To which are appended: Treatises on the Song of Solomon; on the Book of Job; on the Prophet Isaiah; on the Sacrifices of Holy Scripture; and on the Jews and the Christian Church. By E. W. HENGSTENBERG, D.D. Translated by Rev. D. W. SIMON. In one volume, 8vo. (9s.)

Dr John H. A. Ebrard.—Commentary on the Epistles
of ST JOHN. By Dr JOHN H. A. EBRARD, Professor of Theology in the University of Erlangen. Translated by the Rev. W. B. POPE. In one volume. (10s. 6d.)

Dr J. P. Lange.—Theological and Homiletical
COMMENTARY ON THE GOSPEL OF ST MATTHEW. Specially Designed and Adapted for the Use of Ministers and Students. By J. P. LANGE, D.D., Professor of Divinity in the University of Bonn. Translated by the Rev. A. EDERSHEIM, Ph.D. Vols. I., II. (10s. 6d. each.)

Dr J. A. Dorner.—History of the Development of
THE DOCTRINE OF THE PERSON OF CHRIST. By Dr J. A. DORNER, Professor of Theology in the University of Göttingen. Divisions I. and II. Vol. I. Translated by Revs. Dr W. L. ALEXANDER, and D. W. SIMON. (10s. 6d. each.)

N.B.—A single Year's Books (except in the case of the current Year) cannot be supplied separately.

The following is the order of Publication of the THIRD SERIES.

1st Year (1859).
Kurtz on Old Covenant Dispensation, 3 Vols.
Stier on the Risen Saviour, etc., 1 Vol.

2d Year (1860).
Hengstenberg on Ecclesiastes, 1 Vol.
Tholuck on St John, 1 Vol.
Tholuck's Sermon on the Mount, 1 Vol.
Ebrard on Epistles of John, 1 Vol.

3d Year, 1861.
Lange on St Matthew's Gospel, Vols. I. and II.
Dorner on Person of Christ. Div. I., Vol. I.; and Div. II., Vol. I.

The First Issue for 1862, will be Dorner, Div. I., Vol. II., and Lange, Vol. III.

Annual Subscription, ONE GUINEA.
Subscribers' Names received by all Booksellers. (For Non-Subscribers only):
HAMILTON, ADAMS, & Co., London.

38, George Street, Edinburgh.

II.—WORKS OF JOHN CALVIN,
IN 51 VOLUMES, DEMY 8vo.

MESSRS CLARK beg respectfully to announce that the whole STOCK and COPY-RIGHTS of the WORKS OF CALVIN, published by the Calvin Translation Society, are now their property, and that this valuable Series will be issued by them on the following very favourable terms :—

1. Complete Sets in 51 Volumes, Nine Guineas. (Original Subscription price about L.13.) The 'LETTERS,' edited by Dr BONNET, 2 vols., 10s. 6d. additional.
2. Complete Sets of Commentaries, 45 vols., L.7, 17s. 6d.
3. A *Selection* of Six Volumes (or more at the same proportion), for 21s., with the exception of the Institutes, 3 vols.
4. The INSTITUTES, 3 vols., 24s.
5. Any Separate Volume (except INSTITUTES), 6s.

THE CONTENTS OF THE SERIES ARE AS FOLLOW:—

	VOL.		VOL.
Institutes of the Christian Religion,	3	Commentary on Habakkuk, Zephaniah, and Haggai,	1
Tracts on the Reformation,	3	,, Zechariah and Malachi,	1
Commentary on Genesis,	2	Harmony of the Synoptical Evangelists,	3
Harmony of the last Four Books of the Pentateuch,	4	Commentary on John's Gospel,	2
Commentary on Joshua,	1	,, Acts of the Apostles,	2
,, the Psalms,	5	,, Romans,	1
,, Isaiah,	4	,, Corinthians,	2
,, Jeremiah and Lamentations,	5	,, Galatians & Ephesians,	1
,, Ezekiel,	2	,, Philippians, Colossians, and Thessalonians,	1
,, Daniel,	2	,, Timothy, Titus, and Philemon,	1
,, Hosea,	1	,, Hebrews,	1
,, Joel, Amos, and Obadiah,	1	,, Peter, John, James, and Jude,	1
,, Jonah, Micah, and Nahum,	1		

Amongst the Theological Works which were widely circulated in England and Scotland during the latter part of the Sixteenth century, Translations of many of the Writings of JOHN CALVIN had a distinguished place. Of his eminence as a DIVINE and COMMENTATOR ON THE HOLY SCRIPTURES, it is unnecessary here to speak, though few are now fully aware of the very high respect in which his Works were held by all the leading English Reformers and Ecclesiastical Writers from Cranmer to Hooker, and the extensive benefits resulting to the Church of Christ from his literary labours. At that time, doctrines which he never held were not attributed to him; nor were sentiments imputed to him which he never advocated. Bishop Horsley well advised to ascertain what is Calvinism and what is not.

Copious Tables and Indices are appended to each of the Commentaries, etc., to facilitate reference, and to render the whole Series more generally useful and acceptable to every class of readers.

'THE VENERABLE CALVIN.—I hold the memory of Calvin in high veneration; his works have a place in my library; and in the study of the Holy Scriptures he is one of the commentators I most frequently consult.'—*Bishop Horsley.*

'Calvin's Commentaries remain, after three centuries, unparalleled for force of mind, justness of expression, and practical views of Christianity.'—*Bishop of Calcutta (Wilson).*

'The Genevese Reformer (Calvin) surpassed Knox in the extent of his theological learning, and in the unrivalled solidity and clearness of his judgment.'—*M'Crie (Life of Knox).*

'A minister without this, is without one of the best Commentaries on the Scriptures, and a valuable body of divinity.'—*Bickersteth, Christian Student.*

JOHN ALBERT BENGEL'S
GNOMON OF THE NEW TESTAMENT.
Now first Translated into English.
WITH ORIGINAL NOTES, EXPLANATORY AND ILLUSTRATIVE.

The Translation is comprised in Five Large Volumes, Demy 8vo, of (on an average) fully 550 pages each.

SUBSCRIPTION, 31s. 6d., *or free by Post 35s.*

The very large demand for Bengel's Gnomon enables the Publishers still to supply it at the Subscription Price.

The whole work is issued under the Editorship of the Rev. ANDREW R. FAUSSET, M.A., Rector of St Cuthbert's, York, late University and Queen's Scholar, and Senior Classical and Gold Medalist, T.C.D.

For the convenience of such as may wish only a portion of the Commentary, the volumes are sold separately at 8s. 6d. each (except Vol. II. 10s. 6d.).

    Vol. I.—INTRODUCTION, MATTHEW, MARK.
    Vol. II.—LUKE, JOHN, ACTS.
    Vol. III.—ROMANS, CORINTHIANS.
    Vol. IV.—GALATIANS TO HEBREWS.
    Vol. V.—JAMES, TO THE END.

'There are few devout students of the Bible who have not long held Bengel in the highest estimation, nay, revered and loved him. It was not, however, without some apprehension for his reputation with English readers that we saw the announcement of a translation of his work. We feared that his sentences, terse and condensed as they are, would necessarily lose much of their pointedness and force by being clothed in another garb. But we confess, gladly, to a surprise at the success the translators have achieved in preserving so much of the spirit of the original. We are bound to say that it is executed in the most scholarlike and able manner. The translation has the merit of being faithful and perspicuous. Its publication will, we are confident, do much to bring back readers to the *devout* study of the Bible, and at the same time prove one of the most valuable of exegetical aids. The "getting up" of these volumes, combined with their marvellous cheapness, cannot fail, we should hope, to command for them a large sale.'—*Eclectic Review.*

'We are heartily glad that this important work, of an English Translation of Bengel's " Gnomon," has not only been fairly started, but has been successfully completed. Bengel's " Gnomon" has always been held in the highest estimation by all competent judges, as presenting a very remarkable, probably unexampled, combination of learning, sagacity, critical tact, evangelical unction, and terseness and condensation of style. Its growing popularity in Germany is, like the popularity of Calvin's Commentary on the New Testament, as edited by Tholuck, one of the very best signs of the times. . . The enterprising publishers have secured, for this purpose, the services of several accomplished and thoroughly qualified scholars. Mr Fausset, of Trinity College, Dublin, acts as general editor and superintendent, and undertakes the translation of the Commentary upon the Gospels of Mark, Luke, John, and Acts of the Apostles. The Rev. James Bandinel of Wadham College, Oxford, has translated Bengel's General Preface, and his Commentary upon Matthew's Gospel. The Rev. Dr James Bryce, late of Aberdeen, has translated the portion upon the Epistles to the Romans and Corinthians, and has undertaken the rest of Paul's Epistles. The Rev. Dr Fletcher of Wimborne has executed the translation of the remainder of the work on the Catholic Epistles and the Apocalypse.'—*British and Foreign Evangelical Review.*

III.—CHEAP RE-ISSUE OF THE WHOLE WORKS OF
DR JOHN OWEN.
EDITED BY
REV. W. H. GOOLD, D.D., EDINBURGH,
WITH LIFE BY REV. ANDREW THOMSON, D.D.

In 24 Volumes, demy 8vo, handsomely bound in cloth, lettered.
With Two Portraits of Dr Owen.

Several years have now elapsed since the first publication of this Edition of the Works of the greatest of Puritan Divines. Time has tested its merits; and it is now admitted, on all hands, to be the only correct and complete edition.

At the time of publication it was considered—as it really was—a miracle of cheapness, having been issued, by Subscription, for Five Guineas.

In consequence of the abolition of the Paper Duty, the Publishers beg now to issue Proposals for a Re-issue of the Twenty-four Volumes (to Subscribers only) for

FOUR GUINEAS.

As there are above Fourteen Thousand Pages in all, each Volume therefore averages *Five Hundred and Ninety Pages.*

It will be issued on the following conditions:—

1. Six Volumes will be issued annually—in one delivery on 1st March of each year—the Subscription of One Guinea being remitted in advance.
2. A sufficient number having indicated their desire to receive the Twenty-four Volumes in *one* delivery, arrangements are made for this purpose, —the Subscription of Four Guineas being payable in advance.
3. The Publishers greatly prefer that intending Subscribers pay their Subscription through their respective Booksellers; but they beg that, in any case, the names may be forwarded to them *at once.*
4. It is distinctly to be understood, that parties subscribing, subscribe for the whole Twenty-four Volumes.
5. The issue at Four Guineas will be strictly confined to Subscribers; and after the List is complete, the Work will return to its former price.

** *The first issue, Vols. 1 to 6, is now ready, and also the complete set of 24 Volumes.*

Messrs CLARK trust to receive the support of the Clergy and Laity of all Denominations for this undertaking, which, in connection with Mr NICHOL'S Series, and the publication of HOWE by another firm, completes the grand gallery of

PURITAN DIVINES.

'You will find that in John Owen, the learning of Lightfoot, the strength of Charnock, the analysis of Howe, the savour of Leighton, the raciness of Heywood, the glow of Barter, the copiousness of Barrow, the splendour of Bates, are all combined. We should quickly restore the race of great divines if our candidates were disciplined in such lore.'—*The late Dr Hamilton of Leeds.*

IV.—THE NORTH BRITISH REVIEW.
PUBLISHED QUARTERLY.
FEBRUARY—MAY—AUGUST—NOVEMBER.

CONTENTS OF No. LXV.—AUGUST 1860.

1. Romance of the New Planet.
2. Dr John Brown's Life and Works.
3. Scotch Nationality—Social and Intellectual.
4. Colonial Constitutions and Defences.
5. Recent Poetry.
6. Thiers' Last Volume on the Empire.
7. Imaginative Literature.
8. Russia and Serfdom.
9. Recent Rationalism in the Church of England.
10. Severe Winters.
11. Reviews of New Works.

CONTENTS OF No. LXVI.—NOVEMBER 1860.

1. Modern Thought—its Progress and Consummation.
2. The Disturbances in Syria.
3. Leigh Hunt.
4. The Spanish Republics of South America.
5. The Province of Logic and Recent British Logicians—Sir W. Hamilton's Lectures.
6. Lord Macaulay's Place in English Literature.
7. American Humour.
8. Revivals.
9. The Martyrdom of Galileo.
10. The Sicilian Game.

CONTENTS OF No. LXVII.—FEBRUARY 1861.

1. India Convalescent.
2. Shelley and his Recent Biographers.
3. Large Farms and Peasantry of the Scottish Lowlands.
4. Lord Dundonald.
5. Modern Necromancy.
6. Engineering, and Engineers.
7. The Political Press—French, British, and German.
8. Home Ballads and Poems.
9. Hessey's Bampton Lecture.
10. Autobiography of Dr Carlyle.
11. Lord Palmerston and his Foreign Policy.

CONTENTS OF No. LXVIII.—MAY 1861.

1. Present Movement in the Church of England—its Nature, Tendency, and Issue.
2. Alexis de Tocqueville.
3. Poems and Plays of Robert Browning.
4. Bishop Hurd and his Contemporaries.
5. Railway Accidents.
6. Motley's United Netherlands.
7. Berkeley's Idealism.
8. Dr John Brown's Horæ Subsecivæ.
9. The Education Question in Scotland.
10. The Christian Architecture of Europe.
11. The American Secession.

CONTENTS OF No. LXIX.—AUGUST 1861.

1. The British Universities and Academical Polity.
2. Montalembert and Parliamentary Institutions in France.
3. British Columbia and Vancouver Island.
4. Stanley's Eastern Church.
5. Edwin of Deira.
6. Recent Discoveries in Scottish Geology.
7. Freedom of Religious Opinion — Its Conditions and Limits.
8. Marriage and Divorce—The Law of England and Scotland.
9. Du Chaillu's Explorations and Adventures.
10. Mr Buckle on the Civilisation of Scotland.

CONTENTS OF No. LXX.—NOVEMBER 1861.

1. Pascal as a Christian Philosopher.
2. What is Money?
3. Plato and Christianity.
4. Spain.
5. Poets and Poetry of Young Ireland.
6. Edmund Burke, his Life and Genius.
7. Scottish Humour.
8. Comets.
9. Mill on Representative Government.

CONTENTS OF No. LXXI.—FEBRUARY 1862.

1. The Writings of Mr Ruskin.
2. The House of Savoy.
3. Our Single Women.
4. Sir William Lockhart of Lee.
5. Peasants and Poets of Austria and Scotland.
6. Guizot and the Papacy.
7. Sanitary Improvement in the Army—Lord Herbert.
8. Recent Progress of Photographic Art.
9. Mr Martin's Catullus.
10. The American Republic—Resurrection through Dissolution.

38, George Street, Edinburgh.

V.—THEOLOGICAL ENCYCLOPÆDIA.

THE PROTESTANT THEOLOGICAL AND ECCLESIASTICAL ENCYCLOPÆDIA; Being a Condensed Translation of HERZOG's Real Encyclopædia. With Additions from other sources. Edited by Dr J. H. BOMBERGER.

Vols. I. and II. 24s. each, half-bound.

'In its claim to be accepted as the work of reference on a wide range of topics, this elaborate work has certainly no rival.'— *Methodist Magazine.*

'If continued as it has been begun, it will be the only translation of the best Theological and Ecclesiastical Encyclopædia which has yet appeared, or is likely to appear, for a long time to come.'—*News of the Churches.*

VI.—SYSTEMATIC THEOLOGY AND DOGMATICS.

CALVIN'S INSTITUTES OF THE CHRISTIAN RELIGION. Translated by HENRY BEVERIDGE. Three vols. 8vo. 24s.

DORNER (Dr J. A.).—HISTORY OF THE DEVELOPMENT OF THE DOCTRINE OF THE PERSON OF CHRIST. By Dr J. A. DORNER, Professor of Theology in the University of Göttingen. Division 1, Vol. I., and Division 2, Vol. I. 10s. 6d. each. Translated by Rev. Dr LINDSAY ALEXANDER and D. W. SIMON.

The Work is being rapidly completed.

MULLER (Dr Julius).—THE CHRISTIAN DOCTRINE OF SIN. Translated by the Rev. W. PULSFORD. 2 Vols. 8vo. 21s.

'The work before us is undoubtedly to be considered the most weighty and important contribution to the cause of dogmatic theology which Germany has recently produced. It unites in a high degree depth and comprehensiveness with practical earnestness and clearness. It is profound even to the contentment of a German mind, yet rarely obscure or uninstructive. The author evinces his thorough metaphysical training, and his work is pervaded by the presence of a shining and disciplined intellect, and the rare mastery of a large and skilful argumentative grasp.'—*British Quarterly Review.*

NITZSCH'S SYSTEM OF CHRISTIAN DOCTRINE. Translated from the Fifth German Edition. 8vo. 10s. 6d.

'The production of a profoundly learned man, of vast powers of mind—his delineation of the Christian life possesses the rare merit of being more practical and full, more minute and extensive, more clear, accurate, and fresh, than is almost ever heard in the most popular enforcement of the subject from the pulpits of this country.'—*Free Church Magazine.*

OWEN'S (Dr John) WORKS, IN TWENTY-FOUR VOLUMES 8VO. Best and only complete Edition. Edited by Rev. Dr GOOLD. See *Prospectus of Re-issue* at page 7 of this Catalogue.

SCHLEIERMACHER'S BRIEF OUTLINE OF THE STUDY OF THEOLOGY. Drawn up to serve as the basis of Introductory Lectures. With Reminiscences of Schleiermacher by Lücke. Post 8vo. 4s.

ULLMANN (Dr).—THE SINLESSNESS OF JESUS. An Evidence for Christianity. Translated from the Sixth German Edition by Rev. R. L. BROWN. In Crown 8vo. 5s.

'We welcome it in English as one of the most beautiful productions of Germany, as not only readable for an English public, but as possessing, along with not a few defects, many distinguished excellencies. . . We warmly recommend this beautiful work as eminently fitted to diffuse, among those who peruse it, a higher appreciation of the sinlessness and moral eminence of Christ. The work has been blessed already; and may have its use also to an English public. The translation is happy, and a correct rendering of the thought, though occasionally free.'—*British and Foreign Evangelical Review.*

VII.—INTRODUCTIONS.

FAIRBAIRN'S (Professor) HERMENEUTICAL MANUAL; OR, INTRODUCTION TO THE EXEGETICAL STUDY OF THE SCRIPTURES OF THE NEW TESTAMENT. Demy 8vo. 10s. 6d.

'Dr Fairbairn has precisely the training which would enable him to give a fresh and suggestive book on Hermeneutics. Without going into any tedious detail, it presents the points that are important to a student. There is a breadth of view, a clearness and manliness of thought, and a ripeness of learning, which make the work one of peculiar freshness and interest. I consider it a very valuable addition to every student's library.'—*Rev. Dr Moore, Author of the able Commentary on 'The Prophets of the Restoration.'*

GESS ON THE REVELATION OF GOD IN HIS WORD. Fcap. 8vo. 4s.

HAVERNICK'S GENERAL INTRODUCTION TO THE OLD TESTAMENT. Translated by Rev. W. L. ALEXANDER, D.D. Demy 8vo. 10s. 6d.

MACDONALD (Rev. D.).—INTRODUCTION TO THE PENTATEUCH; AN INQUIRY, CRITICAL AND DOCTRINAL, INTO THE GENUINENESS, AUTHORITY, AND DESIGN OF THE MOSAIC WRITINGS. Two Volumes. Demy 8vo. Price 21s.

'The object of this work is very opportune at the present time. It contains a full review of the evidences, external and internal, for the genuineness, authenticity, and Divine character of the Pentateuch. While it gives full space and weight to the purely critical and historical portions of the inquiry, its special attention is devoted to the certainly more profound and more conclusive considerations derived from the connection between the Pentateuch and the great scheme of revelation, of which it forms the basis; and this portion of the work is that upon which the author lays most stress. We entirely agree with him in his view of its importance. Obviously, the entire question of the credibility of the book assumes a totally different aspect, according as it is regarded, either as what it professes to be—the introduction of a gradually developed whole—or as violently dissevered from its professed purpose and relations. Its order, its contents, its omissions, the bearing and purpose of the institutions recorded, the very meaning of large portions of it, fall into their place naturally on the one supposition, are insoluble difficulties on the other. The work is singularly complete also in its view of the literature of the subject, as well as in the outline of its plan.'—*London Guardian.*

'Mr Macdonald's massive volumes form the most important contribution made of late years to biblical criticism by the Scottish press. It is a work of solid architecture, reminding you, in its solemn tone and broad based masonry of induction, of an Egyptian pyramid. The subject was one which could be handled successfully only by a grave, infinitely painstaking, rabbinical mind, exactly such as that of Mr Macdonald; and we ought to be very thankful to him, or to anybody else, who thinks it worth while to analyse the biblical theories of our time in the crucible of a learned intelligence, heated by the fire of a fervent piety. . . We commend his most excellent and laborious treatise to those who are asking for an intelligible digest of the present state of the Mosaic controversy. There can be no doubt that Mr Macdonald will take a very high rank among British theologians.'—*Christian Spectator.*

VIII.—BIBLICAL CRITICISM, ETC., AND EXEGETICAL AUXILIARY SCIENCE.

ERNESTI ON THE INTERPRETATION OF THE NEW TESTAMENT. Two Vols. fcap. 8vo. 12s.

FAIRBAIRN (Professor), ON THE TYPOLOGY OF SCRIPTURE, viewed in connection with the whole series of the Divine Dispensations. Third Edition, greatly enlarged and improved. 2 Vols. 8vo. 18s.

38, George Street, Edinburgh. 11

'I now say, no Biblical Student should be without Professor Fairbairn's Typology.'—*Dr S. Lee, in his 'Events and Times of the Visions of Daniel.'*

'As the product of the labours of an original thinker, and of a sound theologian, who has at the same time scarcely left unexamined one previous writer on the subject, ancient or modern, this work will be a most valuable accession to the library of the theological student. As a whole, we believe it may, with the strictest truth, be pronounced the best work on the subject that has yet been published.'—*Record.*

WINER (Dr G. B.).—A GRAMMAR OF THE NEW TESTAMENT DICTION. Intended as an Introduction to the Critical Study of the Greek New Testament. Translated from the Sixth Enlarged and Improved Edition of the Original. By EDWARD MASSON, M.A. In one thick volume. Third Edition. 12s.

Extract from letter from the late Venerable Archdeacon HARDWICK, *Christian Advocate:*—

'It is a subject of sincere pleasure to all critics of the sacred text that this elaborate and exhaustive treatise is at length in a fair way of becoming familiar to England as it has long been to Germany; I shall have great pleasure in commending it to my divinity class.'

'This is the standard classical work on the Grammar of the New Testament, and it is of course indispensable to every one who would prosecute intelligently the critical study of the most important portion of the inspired record. It is a great service to render such a work accessible to the English reader.'—*British and Foreign Evangelical Review.*

'We gladly welcome the appearance of Winer's great work in an English translation, and most strongly recommend it to all who wish to attain to a sound and accurate knowledge of the language of the New Testament. We need not say it is *the* Grammar of the New Testament. It is not only superior to all others, but *so* superior as to be by common consent the one work of reference on the subject. No other could be mentioned with it.'—*Literary Churchman.*

FORBES (Dr).—THE SYMMETRICAL STRUCTURE OF SCRIPTURE; or, Scripture Parallelism Exemplified in an Analysis of the Decalogue, the Sermon on the Mount, and other Passages of the Sacred Writings. 8vo. 8s. 6d.

'The book is worth study; it is evidently the production of no ordinary man, and is pervaded by a spirit at once scientific and devout.'—*Homilist.*

GLOAG.—THE PRIMEVAL WORLD; A Treatise on the Relations of Geology to Theology. By Rev. PATON J. GLOAG, Author of a 'Treatise on the Assurance of Salvation,' and a 'Treatise on Justification by Faith.' Crown 8vo. 3s. cloth.

'A very able and cautious volume. We can cordially recommend it to those of our readers who take an interest in this class of subjects, and who wish to attain, in a small compass and a very readable form, a fair account of the present state of geological inquiry, in its relations to the interpretation of Scripture.'—*Ecclesiastic.*

HITCHCOCK'S GEOLOGY AND REVELATION. Fcap. 8vo. 6s.

HENGSTENBERG'S EGYPT AND THE BOOKS OF MOSES; or, the Books of Moses Illustrated by the Monuments of Egypt. 8vo. 7s. 6d.

HENGSTENBERG'S DISSERTATIONS ON THE GENUINENESS OF THE PENTATEUCH. 2 vols. 8vo. 21s. (*Only a few Copies remain of this Work.*)

HENGSTENBERG'S DISSERTATIONS ON THE GENUINENESS OF DANIEL AND THE INTEGRITY OF ZECHARIAH. With a Dissertation on the History and Prophecies of Balaam. 8vo. 12s.

PHILOLOGICAL TRACTS, ILLUSTRATIVE OF OLD AND NEW TESTAMENTS. 3 vols. fcap. 8vo. 12s.

PAREAU ON INTERPRETATION OF OLD TESTAMENT. 2 vols. fcap. 8vo. 8s.

ROBINSON AND DUNCAN'S GREEK AND ENGLISH LEXICON OF THE NEW TESTAMENT. By EDWARD ROBINSON, D.D., late Prof. Extraord. of Sac. Lit. in the Theol. Sem., Andover. A new and improved edition, revised by ALEXANDER NEGRIS, Professor of Greek Literature, and by the Rev. JOHN DUNCAN, D.D., Professor of Oriental Languages in the New College, Edinburgh. One thick vol. 8vo. 10s. 6d.

ROHR'S HISTORICO-GEOGRAPHICAL ACCOUNT OF PALESTINE. Fcap. 8vo. 4s.

ROSENMÜLLER'S BIBLICAL GEOGRAPHY. 3 vols. fcap. 8vo. 12s.

ROSENMÜLLER'S BIBLICAL MINERALOGY AND BOTANY. Fcap. 8vo. 4s.

STUART'S GREEK SYNTAX OF NEW TESTAMENT. Fcap. 8vo. 6s.

WEMYSS' CLAVIS SYMBOLICA. Fcap. 8vo. 5s.

IX.—COMMENTARIES.

1. OLD TESTAMENT.

HENGSTENBERG'S CHRISTOLOGY OF THE OLD TESTAMENT, AND A COMMENTARY ON THE MESSIANIC PREDICTIONS. Second Edition. Four Volumes. L.2, 2s.

'We hail with delight a new edition of Dr Hengstenberg's most valuable work in a readable English dress.'—*Churchman's Magazine.*

'A noble specimen of exegetical theology and critical analysis.'—*Clerical Journal.*

'The well-matured production of a great and learned man. It is thoroughly ripe in the spirit of Christian philosophy and true biblical scholarship.'—*Homilist.*

MACDONALD (Rev. D.).—CREATION AND THE FALL: A Defence and Exposition of the First Three Chapters of Genesis. Demy 8vo. 12s.

CALVIN'S COMMENTARY ON GENESIS. Two Vols. 8vo. 12s.

GERLACH (OTTO VON).- COMMENTARY ON THE PENTATEUCH. Demy 8vo. 10s. 6d.

'This work possesses a high character among the Evangelical parties in Germany. It is decidedly orthodox and conservative in its statements; and its spirit and its publication here will confer a great service on sacred literature, especially as writers on the Old Testament are comparatively rare among us. The translation is well executed; and we hope the work will be extensively patronized by the clergy.'—*Clerical Journal.*

CALVIN'S COMMENTARY ON EXODUS, LEVITICUS, NUMBERS, AND DEUTERONOMY. Four Vols. 8vo. 24s.

KURTZ (Professor).—HISTORY OF THE OLD COVENANT: THE PENTATEUCH. By Professor KURTZ of Dorpat. In Three Vols. L.1, 11s. 6d.

'It is intended to form a full and complete History of the Old Covenant, embracing every subject that comes within that range, shirking no difficulty, ignoring no disputed point. The object of the author is to describe the several links in the chain of developments by which God prepared the way, by successive revelations, for the great end of all—the manifestation of Himself in a human form. The work is thus essentially a history. The substance of the Scripture story is given in a series of paragraphs, to which are added copious notes, elucidatory and explanatory, and in them are contained much valuable matter. Not only are there full critical and philological investigations into the meaning of difficult words and phrases—not only are the geographical and historical notices most valuable, as giving a *resumé* of the most recent investigations and conclusions —but the tone and spirit of the narrative is eminently manly and Christian. The work is prefaced with a condensed abstract of the author's "Bible and Astronomy and Geology."'—*Church of England Monthly Review.*

CALVIN'S COMMENTARY ON JOSHUA. 8vo. 6s.

KEIL'S COMMENTARY ON THE BOOK OF JOSHUA. 8vo. 10s. 6d.
 'The spirit of the best old German biblical scholars revives and glows in Keil. His volumes ought to find a place in every clerical library.'—*Christian Times.*

KEIL'S COMMENTARY ON THE BOOK OF KINGS, Supplemented by Bertheau on Chronicles. Two Vols. 8vo. 21s.
 'Keil is clear and sensible in his observations, with the advantage that the portion of Scripture he explains is one for which English students have hitherto enjoyed very scanty assistance.'—*Guardian.*
 'We willingly acknowledge that we should not know where to find so rich a store of valuable materials for the general illustration of the Books of Kings and Chronicles, as in these volumes.'—*Literary Churchman.*

DAVIDSON, Rev. Dr (of Aberdeen).—LECTURES, EXPOSITORY AND PRACTICAL, ON THE BOOK OF ESTHER. Crown 8vo. 5s. 6d.
 'Throughout the volume is marked by sobriety and calm good sense, enlivened by touches of taste and tenderness; it is full of quiet earnestness, without impassioned utterances. It displays great knowledge of human nature, and insight into character, and is rich in counsels of matured Christian wisdom.'—*Witness.*

UMBREIT'S EXPOSITION OF THE BOOK OF JOB. Two Vols. Fcap. 8vo. 8s.

HENGSTENBERG'S COMMENTARY ON THE PSALMS. Three Vols. 8vo. 33s.
 'It strikes us as an important duty to give every encouragement in our power to such courageous pioneers, such devoted, long tried, and successful labourers as Professor Hengstenberg. We notice his Commentary, for the simple purpose of expressing our pleasure at its appearance, and our confident persuasion that it must take a very high place among our standard Commentaries on the Psalms. We have met with no commentator who displays higher powers or sounder qualifications; and we feel persuaded, to quote the words of a very competent judge with reference to his work on the Prophecies of Daniel, that "it will leave nothing to desire."'—*Churchman's Monthly Review.*

CALVIN'S COMMENTARY ON THE PSALMS. Five Vols. 8vo. L.1, 10s.

ROSENMULLER ON THE MESSIANIC PSALMS. Fcap. 8vo. 5s.

HENGSTENBERG (Dr E. W.).—COMMENTARY ON THE BOOK OF ECCLESIASTES. To which are appended—Treatises on the Song of Solomon; on the Book of Job; on the Prophet Isaiah; on the Sacrifices of Holy Scripture; and on the Jews and the Christian Church. By E. W. HENGSTENBERG, D.D. Translated by Rev. D. W. SIMON. In One Vol. 8vo. 9s.
 'The qualifications of Dr Hengstenberg as an eminent expositor, will not be doubted by those familiar with his previous works on the Bible; and a Commentary on this difficult book by one who has so long and so successfully devoted himself to biblical subjects, will awaken new interest in its study. As an exposition of the language and the general current of the writer's views, the work is full and rich.'—*Bibliotheca Sacra.*

CALVIN'S COMMENTARY ON ISAIAH. Four Vols. 8vo. 24s.

CALVIN'S COMMENTARY ON JEREMIAH AND LAMENTATIONS. Five Vols. 8vo. 30s.

CALVIN'S COMMENTARY ON EZEKIEL. Two Vols. 8vo. 12s.

FAIRBAIRN (Professor).—EZEKIEL AND THE BOOK OF HIS PROPHECY. An Exposition. *New Edition preparing.*

CALVIN'S COMMENTARY ON DANIEL. Two Vols. 8vo. 12s.

AUBERLEN (Professor).—THE PROPHECIES OF DANIEL AND THE REVELATION OF ST JOHN, Viewed in their Mutual Relation, with an Exposition of the Principal Passages. Crown 8vo. 7s. 6d.

CALVIN'S COMMENTARY ON HOSEA. One Vol. 8vo. 6s.
CALVIN'S COMMENTARY ON JOEL, AMOS, AND OBADIAH. One Vol. 8vo. 6s.
CALVIN'S COMMENTARY ON JONAH, MICAH, AND NAHUM. One Vol. 8vo. 6s.
CALVIN'S COMMENTARY ON HABAKKUK, ZEPHANIAH, AND HAGGAI. One Vol. 8vo. 6s.
CALVIN'S COMMENTARY ON ZECHARIAH AND MALACHI. One Vol. 8vo. 6s.

2. NEW TESTAMENT.

OLSHAUSEN'S BIBLICAL COMMENTARY ON THE GOSPELS AND ACTS. Four Vols. Demy 8vo. L.2, 2s.

OLSHAUSEN'S BIBLICAL COMMENTARY ON THE GOSPELS AND ACTS. Four Vols. Crown 8vo. 24s. *Cheap Edition.*

' Dr Hermann Olshausen is one of those persons whom the pious hearts of Germany will long remember with affection and veneration. . . On the great and fundamental doctrines of Christianity, Olshausen is as fixed and as stable as the Rock on which the Church is built. The consciousness of sin is, as his translator well remarks, "the pivot in Olshausen's mind which moves all the rest;" deep inward experiences and the pressing need of a Redeemer, make him ever feel and ever avow that we are not following cunningly devised fables, but real, substantial, and vital truths, which breathe and burn through every page of the blessed Gospels. Many passages of real force, eloquence, and piety, have been marked by us in the perusal of these volumes. The translation of Olshausen's work, considering the difficulties inherent in the style of so thoughtful, and often profound writer as Olshausen, is, on the whole, successfully executed.'—*Christian Observer.*

STIER (Dr RUDOLPH).—ON THE WORDS OF THE LORD JESUS. Eight Vols. Demy 8vo. L.4, 4s. Translated by Rev. W. B. POPE.

' We know no work that contains, within anything like the same compass, so many pregnant instances of what true genius under chastened submission to the control of a sound philology, and gratefully accepting the seasonable and suitable helps of a wholesome erudition, is capable of doing in the spiritual exegesis of the sacred volume. Every page is fretted and studded with lines and forms of the most alluring beauty. At every step the reader is constrained to pause and ponder, lest he should overlook one or other of the many precious blossoms that, in the most dazzling profusion, are scattered around his path. We venture to predict that his "Words of Jesus" are destined to produce a great and happy revolution in the interpretation of the New Testament in this country.'—*British and Foreign Evangelical Review.*

' One of the most precious books for the spiritual interpretation of the Gospels.'—*Archdeacon Hare.*

' Dr Stier brings to the exposition of our Lord's discourses sound learning, a vigorous understanding, and a quick discernment; but what is better, he brings also a devout mind, and a habit of thought spiritual and deferential to the truth.'—*Evangelical Christendom.*

STIER (Dr RUDOLPH).—THE WORDS OF THE RISEN SAVIOUR, AND COMMENTARY ON THE EPISTLE OF ST JAMES. By RUDOLPH STIER, D.D., Chief Pastor and Superintendent of Schkeuditz. One Vol. 10s. 6d.

' This volume is in all respects alike remarkable and valuable. It illustrates a principle of which the bulk even of Christian people have little thought, and gives prominence to portions of Scripture which have hitherto been largely overlooked. We are unable to name any exposition so novel, so striking, so instructive, and so edifying. It cannot fail to bring forward those portions of Scripture—portions of infinite moment—which have hitherto, in a great degree, been neglected. The exposition is everywhere most excellent, and adapted to be helpful to the public instructor as well as to the private student. . . The latter half of this volume consists of thirty-two discourses expounding the Epistle of James. By these sermons we set great store. Nothing can be more full, clear, scriptural, and practical. The author has performed an exceeding great service to the Church of God, by whom, we are confident, sooner or later, the work will be highly estimated.'—*Christian Witness.*

THOLUCK'S (Professor) COMMENTARY ON THE SERMON ON THE MOUNT. Translated from the Fourth Revised and Enlarged Edition, by the Rev. R. L. BROWN. 8vo. 10s. 6d.

'Its learning is exhaustive, it avoids no difficulties, and in its exegesis it seizes always the kernel of a passage, and thoroughly and soundly builds up a fair and complete exposition.'—*London Guardian.*

LISCO'S EXPOSITION OF CHRIST'S PARABLES. Fcap. 8vo. 5s.

WITSIUS' EXPOSITION OF THE LORD'S PRAYER. Fcap. 8vo. 4s.

LANGE (Dr J. P.).—THEOLOGICAL AND HOMILETICAL COMMENTARY ON THE GOSPEL OF ST MATTHEW. Specially Designed and Adapted for the use of Ministers and Students. By J. P. LANGE, D.D., Professor of Divinity in the University of Bonn. Translated by the Rev. A. EDERSHEIM, Ph. D. Vols. I. and II. 10s. 6d. each. (Vol. III. *in the press.*)

'The method which Professor Lange pursues in his Commentary, makes it exceedingly valuable both in an exegetical and practical point of view. Having portioned out the original narrative of the Evangelist into sections, according to the contents and connection of the passage, he subjects it to a threefold handling, in order to bring out the meaning and applications of the text. First of all we have a series of *critical notes,* intended to deal with the difficulties in the interpretation of the passage, and bringing all the aids which exegesis supplies to elucidate and exhibit its proper meaning. Next we have a series of *doctrinal reflections,* suggested by the passage interpreted, and intended to exhibit the substance of the scriptural truths which it contains. And lastly, we have a series of *homiletical hints,* founded on the passage elucidated. We must add that the translator, Dr Edersheim, has excellently performed his part.'—*Daily Review.*

CALVIN'S COMMENTARY ON ST MATTHEW, ST MARK, AND ST LUKE. Three Vols. 8vo. 18s.

TITTMAN'S COMMENTARY ON JOHN'S GOSPEL. Two Vols. Fcap. 8vo. 10s.

CALVIN'S COMMENTARY ON ST JOHN. Two Vols. 8vo. 12s.

THOLUCK (Professor).—COMMENTARY ON THE GOSPEL OF ST JOHN. By Professor THOLUCK of Halle. Translated from the Sixth Edition, by CHARLES P. KRAUTH, D.D. In One Vol. 9s.

'Dr Tholuck's volume has been long known and prized in this country in a previous translation, but this new edition, carefully revised and considerably enlarged, contains the result of its author's thought and inquiry for an additional twenty years of a life spent amid such labours. We have no hesitation in placing it, in its present form, at the head of all expositions of the Fourth Gospel, to which the English reader has access.'—*Patriot.*

BESSER (Dr RUDOLPH).—BIBLICAL STUDIES ON ST JOHN'S GOSPEL. Translated from the German by M. G. HUXTABLE. Two Vols. Crown 8vo, handsomely bound in cloth. 12s.

BAUMGARTEN'S APOSTOLIC HISTORY ; Being an Account of the Development of the Early Church, in the Form of a Commentary on the Acts of the Apostles. Three Vols. 8vo. 27s.

'We have felt devoutly thankful to the great Head of the Church, who has raised up a champion able to meet, by an exposition of the Acts at once so profoundly scientific and sublimely Christian as that before us, one of the most pressing wants of our times. We have not the smallest hesitation in expressing our modest conviction, that in no previously uninspired portion of her history has the Church of Christ possessed such means as are here afforded her, of gaining a true insight into the meaning of her own glorious archives.'—*Eclectic Review.*

CALVIN'S COMMENTARY ON THE ACTS OF THE APOSTLES. Two Vols. 8vo. 12s.

OLSHAUSEN'S COMMENTARY ON THE ROMANS. 8vo. 10s. 6d.

THOLUCK'S EXPOSITION OF THE EPISTLE TO THE ROMANS. Two Vols. Fcap. 8vo. 12s.

CALVIN'S COMMENTARY ON THE ROMANS. 8vo. 6s.

OLSHAUSEN'S COMMENTARY ON THE EPISTLE TO THE CORINTHIANS. 8vo. 9s.

BILLROTH'S COMMENTARY ON THE EPISTLE TO THE CORINTHIANS. Two Vols. Fcap. 8vo. 8s.

CALVIN'S COMMENTARY ON THE CORINTHIANS. Two Vols. 8vo. 12s.

OLSHAUSEN'S COMMENTARY ON THE EPISTLES TO THE GALATIANS, EPHESIANS, COLOSSIANS, AND THESSALONIANS. 8vo. 10s. 6d.

CALVIN ON THE EPISTLES TO GALATIANS AND EPHESIANS. Fcap. 8vo. 4s.

CALVIN'S COMMENTARY ON GALATIANS AND EPHESIANS. 8vo. 6s.

OLSHAUSEN'S COMMENTARY ON EPISTLES TO PHILIPPIANS, TITUS, AND FIRST TIMOTHY. 8vo. 10s. 6d.

CALVIN'S COMMENTARY ON PHILIPPIANS, COLOSSIANS, AND THESSALONIANS. 8vo. 6s.

CALVIN AND STORR ON THE EPISTLES TO THE PHILIPPIANS AND COLOSSIANS. Fcap. 8vo. 4s.

PATTERSON'S (Rev. Dr) COMMENTARIES, EXPOSITORY AND PRACTICAL, ON FIRST EPISTLE TO THESSALONIANS, JAMES, AND FIRST JOHN. Fcap. 8vo. 4s. 6d.

'Dr Patterson has endeavoured to give permanence to the more important points in his congregational lectures on the books named in his title-page. Many good people, who want a practical rather than a scholarly Commentary, will read Dr Patterson's book with interest and profit.'—*Eclectic Review.*

NEANDER (Dr).—THE EPISTLE OF PAUL TO THE PHILIPPIANS, AND THE GENERAL EPISTLE OF JAMES, Practically and Historically Explained. Post 8vo. 3s.

'This work consists of a succinct but masterly digest, "historical and practical," of the Epistle to the Philippians and the General Epistle of James—a sort of running commentary, along with which is interwoven a careful explication of the more difficult texts and passages. There is a delightful freshness throughout its pages.'—*Christian Magazine.*

CALVIN'S COMMENTARY ON TIMOTHY, TITUS, AND PHILEMON. 8vo. 6s.

CALVIN'S COMMENTARY ON HEBREWS. 8vo. 6s.

OLSHAUSEN AND EBRARD'S COMMENTARY ON THE EPISTLE TO THE HEBREWS. 8vo. 10s. 6d.

THOLUCK'S COMMENTARY ON THE EPISTLE TO THE HEBREWS. Two Vols. Fcap. 8vo. 12s.

PATTERSON (Rev. Dr A. S.).—COMMENTARY, EXPOSITORY AND PRACTICAL, ON THE EPISTLE TO THE HEBREWS. 8vo. 10s. 6d.

'This is one of these goodly well-proportioned octavos, whose external appearance prepossesses one in their favour; and the author has made a valuable contribution to the department of biblical exegesis. It is precisely the kind of exposition that is required by a large number of intelligent Christians.'—*English Presbyterian Messenger.*

OWEN (Dr JOHN).—EXPOSITION OF THE EPISTLE TO THE HEBREWS. Best Edition. Edited by Dr GOOLD. L.2, 2s.

STEIGER'S EXPOSITION OF FIRST PETER. Two Vols. Fcap. 8vo. 12s.

LUCKE'S EXPOSITION OF THE THREE EPISTLES OF JOHN. Fcap. 8vo. 6s.

CALVIN'S COMMENTARY ON PETER, JOHN, JAMES, AND JUDE. 8vo. 6s.

EBRARD (Dr JOHN).—COMMENTARY ON THE EPISTLES OF ST JOHN. Translated by the Rev. W. B. POPE. Demy 8vo. 10s. 6d.
'Dr Ebrard is one of the finest of German evangelical scholars in the department of philology and criticism. He has comprehensiveness of intellect, and is eminent for spiritual insight and theological depth.'—*Nonconformist.*

AUBERLEN (Professor).—THE PROPHECIES OF DANIEL AND THE REVELATION OF ST JOHN in their Mutual Relation, with an Exposition of the Principal Passages. Crown 8vo. 7s. 6d.
'One of the latest contributions to the study of Apocalyptic prophecy. It is one of a very high order, and which must command attention. The author appears to us to possess, in no ordinary degree, those faculties of head and heart so absolutely necessary for the prosecution of that most difficult branch of sacred exegesis to which he has devoted himself.'—*Ecclesiastic.*

BENGEL'S GNOMON OF THE NEW TESTAMENT: A Commentary on the New Testament. *For full particulars, see page 6 of this Catalogue.*

X.—CHURCH HISTORY.

BAUMGARTEN'S HISTORY OF THE CHURCH DURING THE APOSTOLIC AGE. Three Vols. 8vo. 27s.

COUARD ON THE LIFE OF THE EARLY CHRISTIANS. Fcap. 8vo. 4s.

DORNER (Dr J. A.).—HISTORY OF THE DEVELOPMENT OF THE DOCTRINE OF THE PERSON OF CHRIST. By Dr J. A. DORNER, Professor of Theology, Göttingen. Division 1, Vol. I., and Division 2, Vol. I. 10s. 6d. each. The Work is being rapidly completed.

EDERSHEIM (Rev. Dr).—HISTORY OF THE JEWISH NATION AFTER THE DESTRUCTION OF JERUSALEM UNDER TITUS. Crown 8vo. Second Edition. Price 6s.

GIESELER'S COMPENDIUM OF ECCLESIASTICAL HISTORY. Five Vols. 8vo. L.2, 12s. 6d.

GUERICKE (Professor).—MANUAL OF CHURCH HISTORY: First Six Centuries. Demy 8vo. 10s. 6d.
'The Manual of Professor Guericke, which has just been produced in this country in an English dress, is a valuable attempt to compel the theological student to take something more than a cursory view of the earlier centuries of our religion.'—*Literary Churchman.*

HAGENBACH'S COMPENDIUM OF THE HISTORY OF DOCTRINES. Two Vols. 8vo. 21s.
'It is thoroughly critical; not a phrase nor a fact is suffered to escape its notice; not a document can be found which is not examined and re-examined; step by step it pursues its toilsome course backward into the history of the past, illuminating its records, and making its men to live, and speak, and act again, and giving to all its controversies and speculations an air almost of present reality. It is distinguished for its brevity, its clear statements of the leading points, its great candour, its ample references to the body of a contemporaneous literature.'—*Bibliotheca Sacra.*

HOFFMANN.—CHRISTIANITY IN THE FIRST CENTURY; or, The New Birth of the Social Life of Man through the rising of Christianity. Crown 8vo. 4s. 6d.
'The object of this volume is a noble one. It beautifully exhibits the characteristics of the early Church. The work is, in fact, an attempt to promote Christian union, and it deserves the careful study of all to whom that is dear.'—*Clerical Journal.*

KAHNIS' (Professor) INTERNAL HISTORY OF GERMAN PROTESTANTISM SINCE THE MIDDLE OF THE FIRST CENTURY. Fcap. 8vo. 4s. 6d.
'In no other book could the English reader derive anything like the amount of information and instruction on the subject.'—*Eclectic Review.*

KURTZ.—HANDBOOK OF CHURCH HISTORY TO THE REFORMATION. From the German of Professor KURTZ. With Emendations and Additions, by the Rev. ALFRED EDERSHEIM, Ph.D., Author of 'History of the Jewish Nation.' In One Thick Vol. (of about 520 pp.). 7s. 6d.

'A work executed with great diligence and care, exhibiting an accurate collection of facts, and a succinct though full account of the history and progress of the Church, both external and internal. . . The work is distinguished for the moderation and charity of its expressions, and for a spirit which is truly Christian.'—*English Churchman.*

NEANDER'S GENERAL HISTORY OF THE CHRISTIAN RELIGION AND CHURCH. Nine Vols. 8vo. L.2, 11s. 6d.

This is the only Complete Edition of Neander published in this country.

PRESSENSE.—THE RELIGIONS BEFORE CHRIST; Being an Introduction to the History of the First Three Centuries of the Church. By EDWARD DE PRESSENSE, Pastor of the French Evangelical Church, and Doctor of Divinity of the University of Breslau. Translated by L. CORKRAN. With Preface to this Translation by the Author. Demy 8vo. 7s. 6d. (*Just published.*)

SCHAFF'S (Professor) HISTORY OF the APOSTOLIC CHURCH; with a General Introduction to Church History. Two Vols. 8vo. 10s. 6d.

'Worthy of a German scholar, and of a disciple of Neander, and of a believing and free Christian and Protestant.'—*Bunsen's Hippolytus.*

'Eminently scholarlike and learned, full of matter, not of crude materials, but of various and well-digested knowledge, the result of systematic training and long continued study.' —*Biblical Repertory.*

SCHAFF (Professor).—HISTORY OF THE CHRISTIAN CHURCH FROM THE BIRTH OF CHRIST TO THE REIGN OF CONSTANTINE, A.D. 1-311. Demy 8vo. 12s.

SEMISCH'S LIFE, TIMES, AND WRITINGS OF JUSTIN MARTYR. Two Vols. Fcap. 8vo. 10s.

ULLMANN'S REFORMERS BEFORE THE REFORMATION: Principally in Germany and the Netherlands. Two Vols. 8vo. 21s.

'Beyond doubt one of the finest ornaments of the recent theology of Germany, and a masterpiece of historical research and composition, as profound as it is clear.'—*Dr Schaff.*

WELSH'S (Professor) ELEMENTS OF CHURCH HISTORY. 8vo. 6s.

ZWINGLI; or, The Rise of the Reformation in Switzerland. A Life of the Reformer, with Notices of his Times and Contemporaries. By R. CHRISTOFFEL. Demy 8vo. 6s.

'We hold it in high estimation: shall turn to it as an authority on all points connected with the Reformation in Switzerland, and predict that posterity will consider it not the least interesting account of one of the most eventful periods in the world's history.'—*Wesleyan Times.*

XI.—PROPHECY.

AUBERLEN (Professor).—PROPHECIES OF DANIEL AND THE REVELATION OF ST JOHN, VIEWED IN THEIR MUTUAL RELATION. Crown 8vo. 7s. 6d.

BROWN (Rev. Dr DAVID).—CHRIST'S SECOND COMING; WILL IT BE PREMILLENNIAL? Fifth Edition. Crown 8vo. 7s. 6d.

'This is, in our judgment, one of the most able, comprehensive, and conclusive of the numerous works which the millenarian controversy has called forth. His argument has been very carefully prepared, and is characterized, not only by acuteness in detecting the weak points of the opposing theory, but also by candour in honestly meeting and grappling with the points in which its strength lies. We do not know any single volume which contains so full and satisfactory a digest of the reasonings and interpretations by which the advocates of the side of the question on which Dr Brown has arrayed himself, are accustomed to defend their position.'—*Watchman.*

FAIRBAIRN (Professor).—PROPHECY VIEWED IN ITS DISTINCTIVE NATURE, ITS SPECIAL FUNCTIONS, AND PROPER INTERPRETATION. 8vo. 10s. 6d.

'Its completeness, its clearness, its thorough investigation of the whole subject in a systematic way, will render it, I think, the standard work on prophecy from this time.'—*Rev. Dr Candlish.*

XII.—PRACTICAL THEOLOGY AND EXPOSITION.

AMERICAN PULPIT. Containing Sermons by Barnes, Cheever, Hodge, etc. Royal 12mo. 3s.

'We recommend this volume as furnishing admirable Sabbath reading for our more thoughtful and intelligent Christian families.'—*Guardian.*

BARNES' (Rev. ALBERT) PRACTICAL SERMONS. Fcap. 8vo. 3s.

'These Sermons are stronger in thought and finer in tone than such even of the preacher's own efforts as we have before seen, and are excellently fitted to their purpose.'—*Nonconformist.*

BESSER (Dr RUDOLPH).—CHRIST THE LIGHT OF THE WORLD; Biblical Studies on the First Ten Chapters of St John's Gospel. Translated from the German by M. G. HUXTABLE. Crown 8vo, handsomely bound in cloth. 6s.

BESSER (Dr RUDOLPH).—CHRIST THE LIFE OF THE WORLD; Biblical Studies on the Eleventh Chapter to the End of St John's Gospel. Translated from the German by M. G. HUXTABLE. Crown 8vo, handsomely bound in cloth. 6s. (Just published.)

'This book is full of warm and devout exposition, one peculiarity being the abundance of quotation from Lutheran writers and preachers, ancient and modern. Luther's own rugged words start out, boulder-like, in almost every page.'—*News of the Churches.*

'We now call attention to the great merit of this volume. The character of this commentary is practical and devotional. There are often very exquisite devotional passages, and a vein of earnest piety runs through the whole work. We recommend the book most warmly to all.'—*Literary Churchman.*

'There is a quiet, simple, penetrating good sense in what Dr Besser says, and withal a spirit of truly Christian devoutness, which the reader must feel to be in beautiful accordance with the inspired teachings which seem to awaken it. The multiplication of such preachers must be the multiplication of that simple-hearted power which was so characteristic of primitive Christianity.'—*British Quarterly Review.*

GOTTHOLD'S EMBLEMS; or, Invisible Things understood by Things that are Made. By CHRISTIAN SCRIVER, Minister of Magdeburg, in 1671. Translated from the Twenty-eighth German Edition, by the Rev. ROBERT MENZIES. Cheap Edition. One Vol. Crown 8vo.

'A peculiarly fascinating volume. It is rich in happy and beautiful thoughts, which grow on the root of genuine piety'—*Witness.*

GRIERSON (Rev. Dr).—EARTHLY AND HEAVENLY THINGS; or, The Truths Unfolded by our Lord in His Interview with Nicodemus. By the Rev. JAMES GRIERSON, D.D., Errol. Crown 8vo. 5s.

'It is rich in Christian thought, and will be appreciated by all who know and love evangelical truth.'—*Watchman.*

KRUMMACHER'S SUFFERING SAVIOUR; or, Meditations on the Last Days of the Sufferings of Christ. Fifth Edition. Crown 8vo. 4s. 6d.

'We give it preference to everything hitherto produced by the gifted and devoted author. It is divinity of the most thoroughly evangelical description. Truth and tenderness have seldom been so successfully combined. Its popularity with the people of God, of every evangelical communion, we are confident, will grow with time. A book of the heart, to *that* it appeals in every page, with a force which it will be difficult to resist.'—*Christian Witness.*

KRUMMACHER'S LIFE OF CORNELIUS AND OF ST JOHN THE EVANGELIST. Fcap. 8vo. 4s.

NETTLETON AND HIS LABOURS; Being a Memoir of the Great American Revivalist. Edited by Rev. A. A. BONAR, Author of ' Memoirs of Robert M. M'Cheyne.' Second Edition. Fcap. 8vo. 4s. 6d.
' A very remarkable work. We may safely aver that, so far as the Church is concerned, it is the book of the season, and it will unquestionably exert a very powerful influence upon the ministry of our land. If every minister who has the good of souls at heart would now get it, we might have a summer of awakening throughout the land, and a rich harvest might yet be secured ere the winter, which we fear, set in with its stormy tempests on the Church of God.'—*British Messenger.*

PATTERSON (Rev. J. B.).—ILLUSTRATIONS, EXPOSITORY AND PRACTICAL, OF THE FAREWELL DISCOURSE OF JESUS: Being a Series of Lectures on the Fourteenth, Fifteenth, and Sixteenth Chapters of the Gospel of St John. By the late Rev. JOHN B. PATTERSON, M.A., Minister of Falkirk. Crown 8vo. 6s.
' This is a work worthy of the author's reputation as a preacher. It is well written, quiet in tone, with a high degree of strength and self-possession, as of one who is thoroughly acquainted with his subject, sound in doctrine, and eminently practical.'—*Banffshire Journal.*

PIKE AND HAYWARD'S RELIGIOUS CASES OF CONSCIENCE, Answered in an Evangelical Manner. Fcap. 8vo. 4s.

THOLUCK (Dr).—LIGHT FROM THE CROSS. Sermons on the Passion of our Lord. Translated from the German of A. THOLUCK, D.D. Crown 8vo. Second Edition. 5s.
' With no ordinary confidence and pleasure we commend these most noble, solemnizing, and touching discourses.'—*British and Foreign Evangelical Review.*

THOLUCK'S SERMONS; Life and Character of St Paul; Essay on Nature and Moral Influence of Heathenism. In one vol. fcap. 8vo. 6s.

VINET (Professor).—EVANGELICAL MEDITATIONS. Crown 8vo. 3s. 6d.
' The work before us is one which will be most highly prized by the spiritually-minded and single-hearted Christian.'—*Patriot.*

VINET'S PASTORAL THEOLOGY: the Theory of a Gospel Ministry. Second Edition, Post 8vo. 3s. 6d.
' One or two rapid readings will not suffice to exhaust the treasures of Christian and pastoral experience, of enlightenment, of tenderness, of practical directions, of elevation, and of edification, which fill these pages. We will find it to our profit to read at least once a year this precious volume, if it were only as the means of serving us pastors for the examination of our conscience.'—*Archives du Christianisme.*

VINET'S HOMILETICS; or the Theory of Preaching. Second Edition. Carefully revised and edited, with copious Notes, by the Rev. A. R. FAUSSET, Editor of Translation of Bengel's ' Gnomon.' Demy 8vo. 9s. (Copyright.)
' Vinet, from his previous studies, was especially at home on such a subject, in which he finds scope, not only for his powers of exposition, but also for his rich faculty of criticism, some exquisite gems of which are scattered up and down its pages.'—*North British Review.*

VINET'S VITAL CHRISTIANITY; Essays and Discourses on the Religions of Man and the Religion of God. Post 8vo. 2s.

WILSON.—THE KINGDOM OF OUR LORD JESUS CHRIST: A Practical Exposition of Matthew xvi. 13-28, xvii. xviii.; Mark viii. 27-38, ix.; Luke ix. 18-50. By the Rev. WILLIAM WILSON, Minister of St Paul's Free Church, Dundee. Crown 8vo. 7s. 6d.
' Mr Wilson, by the publication of this volume, has made a valuable contribution to our treasures of modern exposition. . . . . We cordially recommend the volume. From beginning to end it exhibits the incessant action of a keen, sagacious, vigorous intellect, not unfrequently clothing its instructive statements in the eloquence of irrepressible Christian emotion, and the tenderness of a true pastor of souls. Communion, producing conformity, with Christ in His cross, is the predominant thought of the volume; and this fundamental law of the kingdom of Christ is very clearly, impressively, and variously illustrated.'—*British and Foreign Evangelical Review.*

XIII.—PHILOSOPHY.

ACKERMANN (Dr C.).—THE CHRISTIAN ELEMENT IN PLATO, AND THE PLATONIC PHILOSOPHY. Translated from the German, by SAMUEL RALPH ASBURY, B.A. Demy 8vo. Price 7s. 6d.

'Dr Ackermann's valuable treatise on the Platonic Philosophy has been translated from the German by Mr Asbury; and, although we have not been able to compare his version with the original, yet we are inclined to believe it as accurate as, on general grounds, we can discern it to be able and satisfactory. We cannot attempt on the present occasion to show how far we think Dr Ackermann's philosophical views well grounded, or how far we accept his parallel between Platonism and Christianity. In some respects, we profoundly differ from this accomplished thinker and attractive writer; but such divergence of opinion does not prevent us from expressing our sincere admiration of his thoughtful, eloquent, and beautiful treatise, nor from recommending it as an instructive and fascinating exposition.'—*Spectator.*

CHALYBAEUS' HISTORICAL DEVELOPMENT OF SPECULATIVE PHILOSOPHY, from Kant to Hegel. 8vo. 6s.

'An acute speculator, a fair critic, and a lucid writer. These lectures are universally recognised as affording a perspicuous and impartial survey of the various modern systems of German philosophy, at once comprehensive and compendious. I am strongly impressed with the general fidelity and clearness of the translation.'—*Sir William Hamilton.*

COUSIN'S (VICTOR) COURSE OF THE HISTORY OF MODERN PHILOSOPHY. Two Vols. post 8vo. 8s. 6d.

'There is probably nowhere, in any language, an abler critical analysis of the "Essay on the Understanding" than this.'—*Guardian.*

COUSIN'S LECTURES ON THE TRUE, THE BEAUTIFUL, AND THE GOOD. Translated from the *last* French Edition, under the sanction of the Author. Post 8vo. 6s. 6d.

'We cannot too highly recommend this work. It is very long since we had a volume in our hands that has afforded us so much gratification in the perusal.'—*Art Journal.*

COUSIN ON THE DESTINY OF MODERN PHILOSOPHY, AND EXPOSITION OF ECLECTICISM. Fcap. 8vo. 4s. 6d.

FLEMING.—A PLEA FOR THE WAYS OF GOD TO MAN; being an Attempt to vindicate the Moral Government of the World. By WILLIAM FLEMING, D.D., Professor of Moral Philosophy in the University of Glasgow. Crown 8vo. 4s. 6d.

'We have rarely read a metaphysical treatise written with greater richness and beauty of language.'—*Baptist Magazine.*

JOUFFROY'S PHILOSOPHICAL ESSAYS. Fcap. 8vo. 5s.

KANT'S METAPHYSICS OF ETHICS. 8vo. 16s.

KANT'S RELIGION WITHIN THE BOUNDARY OF TRUE REASON. 8vo. 10s.

MURDOCH'S SKETCHES OF MODERN PHILOSOPHY. 2s.

SMITH (Professor).—ON THE RELATIONS OF FAITH AND PHILOSOPHY. Post 8vo. 9d.

STAPFER'S LIFE OF KANT. 1s.

VINET (Professor).—STUDIES ON BLAISE PASCAL. Translated from the French, with an Appendix of Notes, partly taken from the Writings of Lord Bacon and Dr Chalmers. By the Rev. THOMAS SMITH, A.M. Crown 8vo. 5s.

'The "Studies" of Vinet are often as profound as the "Thoughts" of Pascal—and that is the very highest praise. We earnestly request our readers to obtain and study the noble work.'—*Evangelical Magazine.*

'This work of Vinet will materially add to his well-earned renown. He and Pascal were kindred spirits, alike worthy of each other, and here they will go down in company to the remotest posterity.'—*Christian Witness.*

XIV.—CHURCH LAW.

ACTS OF THE GENERAL ASSEMBLY OF THE CHURCH OF SCOTLAND, from 1638 to 1842. Reprinted from the Original Edition under the Superintendence of Church Law Society. Imp. 8vo, 1200 pages. 18s.

SUPPLEMENT TO ABOVE, containing Acts from 1843 to 1850, inclusive. Edited by Dr JOHN COOK. Imp. 8vo. 3s. 6d.

COOK'S (Dr JOHN) STYLES OF WRITS AND FORMS OF PROCEDURE IN CHURCH COURTS OF SCOTLAND. Originally compiled by Church Law Society, and now Revised and Adapted to the Present State of the Law of the Church. Third Edition. 8vo. 12s.

XV.—SCHOOL BOOKS.

HERODOTUS. Edited by NEGRIS, with Notes. Fcap. 8vo. 4s. 6d.

CLIO.* Separately, 1s. 3d. with Wheeler's Notes; 9d. without Notes.

PINDAR.* Edited by NEGRIS. 4s. 6d. With Notes.

STEWART'S ENGLISH GRAMMAR. 18mo. 1s. 3d.

THOMSON'S HISTORY OF SCOTLAND. Royal 12mo. 3s. 6d.

THORNLEY (MARGARET), SKELETON THEMES; intended to assist in Teaching and Acquiring the Art of Composition. Fcap. 8vo. 3s.

THORNLEY (Miss), THE TRUE END OF EDUCATION, and the Means adapted to it, in a Series of Familiar Letters to a Lady entering on the Duties of her Profession as a Private Governess. 12mo. 4s. 6d.

XENOPHON'S ANABASIS.* Edited by NEGRIS. 2s. With Notes.

* The Publishers would invite attention to the above most accurate, as well as cheap, Editions.

XVI.—MISCELLANEOUS.

ANDERSON'S (Rev. JOHN) CHRONICLES OF THE KIRK; or, Scenes and Stories from the History of the Church of Scotland, from the Earliest Period to the Time of the Second Reformation. Fcap. 8vo. 3s. 6d.

BLAIR'S INQUIRY INTO THE STATE OF SLAVERY AMONG THE ROMANS. Fcap. 8vo. 6s.

KRUMMACHER'S LITTLE DOVE. A Story for Children. 6d.

LEWIS (Rev. G.).—THE BIBLE, the MISSAL, AND THE BREVIARY; or, Ritualism Self-Illustrated in the Liturgical Books of Rome, containing the Text of the entire Roman Missal, Rubrics, and Prefaces. Translated from the Latin. With Preliminary Dissertations and Notes from the Breviary, Pontifical, etc. Two vols. 8vo. 10s. 6d.

'The exposition of these matters is conducted by Mr Lewis with great success, in a manner extremely creditable to his talents, judgment, and knowledge of his subject, and well fitted to be useful.'—*Bulwark.*

38, George Street, Edinburgh. 23

MONTGOMERY (Rev. ROBERT).—THE GOSPEL IN ADVANCE OF THE AGE; being a Homily for the Times. 8vo. 6s.

MOWES' MINISTER OF ANDOUSE; a Tale of the Huguenots. 12mo. 2s.

RICHARDS.—LIFE IN ISRAEL; or, Tales Illustrative of Hebrew Character and History at various Epochs. By M. T. RICHARDS. Crown 8vo. 3s. 6d.

'This is a charming volume, and cannot fail to interest the reader. We have been particularly impressed with the happy introduction of Scripture quotations in prose and verse. These passages, in pathos, beauty, and sublimity, far transcend the highest flight of Shakespeare and Milton. The book is true to history. Its type of Christianity is simple, attractive, and evangelic.'—*Christian Times.*

SCHMID'S LITTLE LAMB AND ROBIN REDBREAST, 1s. EASTER EGGS, 1s.

SCHMID'S FLOWER-BASKET; a Story for Children. 12mo. 2s.

THOMSON'S HISTORY OF SCOTLAND. , Royal 12mo. 3s. 6d.

TROLLOPE ON THE GREEK LITURGY OF ST JAMES. Edited, with an English Introduction and Notes, together with a Latin Version of the Syrian Copy, and the Greek Text restored to its Original Purity, and accompanied by a Literal English Translation, by the Rev. W. TROLLOPE, M.A., Pembroke College, Cambridge. 8vo. 3s. 6d. cloth.

VINET'S HISTORY OF FRENCH LITERATURE IN THE EIGHTEENTH CENTURY, including Voltaire, Rousseau, Montesquieu, etc. 8vo. 6s.

'A work of great interest, which abounds in illustrations of the profound views and broad literary sympathies of the author, and is the first attempt to estimate the literary age of Voltaire, etc., from a Christian point of view.'—*North British Review.*

ÆSCHYLI PROMETHEUS VINCTUS. By NEGRIS. 2s. 6d.

BARBACOVIS' LITERARY HISTORY OF ITALY. 2s. 6d.

DOCTRINE OF CHANGES. By the Author of 'The Morning and Evening Sacrifice.' 4s. 6d.

HACKETT'S ILLUSTRATIONS OF SCRIPTURE; with Engravings. American Edition. 3s. 6d.

MACDOUALL ON THE STUDY OF ORIENTAL LANGUAGES. 1s.

MACINTOSH (Sir J.), ON THE LAWS OF NATURE AND NATIONS. 1s. 6d.

M'NAB ON THE CULTIVATION OF EVERGREENS. 1s. 6d.

—— ON THE CULTIVATION OF CAPE HEATHS. 2s. 6d.

ROBERTSON ON INSURANCE POLICIES. 4s.

RUCKERT AND LANGE ON THE RESURRECTION. 1s. 6d.

SPRING'S MERCY SEAT. Meditations on the Lord's Prayer. 2s.

REYNOLD ON PRESERVATION OF THE EYES. 1s.

—— NECESSITY OF PHYSICAL CULTURE TO LITERARY MEN. 6d.

REYNOLDS (Sir JOSHUA).—DISCOURSES TO STUDENTS OF ROYAL ACADEMY. 3s. 6d.

ROBINSON (Professor).—VIEW OF EDUCATION IN GERMAN UNIVERSITIES. 1s. 6d.

RUSSELL, LIFE OF LADY. 1s. 6d.

SAWYER'S ELEMENTS OF BIBLICAL INTERPRETATION. 1s.

STAEL (Madame DE), LIFE OF. 1s. 6d.

STAEUDLIN'S HISTORY OF THEOLOGICAL KNOWLEDGE AND LITERATURE. 6d.
STORY ON THE PROGRESS OF SCIENCE AND LITERATURE. 1s. 6d.
VERPLANCK ON THE RIGHT MORAL INFLUENCE AND USE OF LIBERAL STUDIES. 6d.
WARE ON EXTEMPORANEOUS PREACHING. 1s.
—— ON THE CHARACTER AND DUTIES OF A PHYSICIAN. 6d.
CHANNING ON A NATIONAL LITERATURE. 6d.
——— ON FENELON. 6d.
——— ON NAPOLEON. 1s. 3d.
——— ON SLAVERY. 1s. 6d.
——— ON SELF-CULTURE. 1s. 3d.
EDWARDS ON SLAVERY IN GREECE, AND IN THE EARLY AND MIDDLE AGES. 1s. 3d.
EVERETT ON SCIENTIFIC KNOWLEDGE. 1s. 6d.
NIEBUHR'S LIFE. 1s.
NEGRIS' LITERARY HISTORY OF MODERN GREECE. 6d.
EICHHORN'S (Prof.) ACCOUNT OF THE LIFE AND WRITINGS OF J. D. MICHAELIS. 6d.

FORTHCOMING WORKS OF THE LATE

PRINCIPAL CUNNINGHAM.

The Reformers and the Theology of the Reformation. In One Volume.
[*Shortly will be Published.*]

Theology, Historical and Polemical: A Review of the Principal Discussions in the Christian Church from the Apostolic Age. In Two Volumes.

ESSAYS ON RELIGIOUS PHILOSOPHY.
BY M. EMILE SAISSET.

Translated from the French, with a Preface, Analysis, and Notes, by the Rev. WILLIAM ALEXANDER, M.A., of Brasennose College, Oxford.
[*Shortly will be Published.*]

www.ingramcontent.com/pod-product-compliance
Lightning Source LLC
Chambersburg PA
CBHW032056220426
43664CB00008B/1029